The Business of Sustainable Mobility
From Vision to Reality

THE BUSINESS OF
SUSTAINABLE
MOBILITY

FROM VISION TO REALITY

EDITED BY
**PAUL NIEUWENHUIS, PHILIP VERGRAGT
and PETER WELLS**

Greenleaf
PUBLISHING

2 0 0 6

© 2006 Greenleaf Publishing Ltd

Published by Greenleaf Publishing Limited
Aizlewood's Mill
Nursery Street
Sheffield S3 8GG
UK
www.greenleaf-publishing.com

The paper used for this book is a natural, recyclable product made from wood grown
in sustainable forests; the manufacturing processes conform to the environmental
regulations of the country of origin.
Printed in Great Britain by William Clowes Ltd, Beccles, Suffolk.
Cover by LaliAbril.com.

British Library Cataloguing in Publication Data:
    A catalogue record for this book is available from the British Library.

    ISBN-10: 1-874719-80-2
    ISBN-13: 978-1-874719-80-9

Contents

Boelie Elzen, Centre for Science, Technology and Society, University of Twente,
The Netherlands

Wim Hafkamp, Erasmus University Rotterdam, The NetherlandS

Foreword

One of the characteristics of modern society is its need for and reliance on mobility. People are used to travelling worldwide, and goods may travel long distances. This dramatically increased mobility comes at a high cost, however, and the editors of this book claim no less than the fact that mobility is in crisis. Air pollution, material use, car safety, congestion and climate change are just a few aspects to consider when thinking about the future of mobility. Current problems demand radical change and dramatically new perspectives on mobility—to quote the editors of this book: 'new thinking' on mobility. Systematically improving current systems of mobility with a major role for individual personal vehicles poses difficult questions: What would new systems of mobility look like? How could these be developed and implemented? How would they affect daily lives? Can the actors involved, such as the automotive industry, governments and citizens, combine forces? Who is going to take the lead? These are the very questions the contributors in this volume address.

The book's editors and many of the contributors are long-standing participants of the Greening of Industry Network (GIN). GIN is an international network of professionals from research, education, business, civil-society organisations and government, focusing on issues of industrial development, environment and society, and dedicated to building a sustainable future. With co-ordinating offices in The Netherlands, Thailand and the United States, we engage participants from more than 50 countries to respond to the challenge of sustainable development. Through linked conferences, publications and communications, the Network creates new relationships, visions and practices for sustainability. The GIN conferences, 25 events in 12 countries around the world since 1991, comprise a unique record and experience of bringing people and the issues together for a big perspective on sustainability, forging productive connections among research, policy and practice. The questions raised in the book go to the heart of the debate within the Network.

The book is based on the Sustainable Mobility stream in the 2003 International Greening of Industry Network Conference in San Francisco. This event brought together experts from industry and government, and the book combines some of the papers presented there, developed and updated into full chapters, with a number of additional chapters to capture some of the themes that emerged from the conference.

Much of the debate within GIN goes to the question of how to envision sustainable societies. As mobility is central and will play a major role in future societies, this book addresses crucial issues in creating sustainable societies. We welcome its contribution to the debate and hope the reader will find inspiration in it.

The Network Co-ordinators

Theo de Bruijn
Somporn Kamolsiripichaiporn
Kurt Fischer

www.greeningofindustry.org

1
The business of sustainable mobility

Paul Nieuwenhuis and Peter Wells
ESRC Centre for Business Relationships, Accountability, Sustainability and Society, Cardiff University, UK

Philip J. Vergragt
Tellus Institute, Boston, USA

The international Greening of Industry Network (GIN) has, for more than ten years, been working to bring together experts and thinkers from business, industry, academia, government and non-governmental organisations (NGOs). Its main aim is to deal with issues of how to build a more sustainable industrial culture by combining the conceptual with the practical. The Network's 2003 conference, held that year in San Francisco, saw **sustainable mobility** designated as a key theme: this book is based on that conference. It develops and updates some of the papers presented at San Francisco and includes a number of additional chapters to capture many of the themes to emerge from the 2003 conference. We hope this publication makes a significant contribution to the ongoing sustainable mobility debate.

Crisis, what crisis?

In many parts of the world, there is a crisis of mobility. The choices we have made over the past 200 years about modes and technologies of transportation have brought us unprecedented global interaction and, in many respects, increased personal freedom. However, this enhanced mobility has come at a high cost—to society, to the economy and to the environment—but few seem aware of the full extent of the mobility crisis. Though most people are aware of issues such as congestion, accidents (although this aspect is often overlooked), parking restrictions and fuel prices, few will have considered the implications of the dramatic increase in personal mobility anticipated in China, India and elsewhere. Nor do many people consider the contribution of cars to climate change or the impact of climate change on the environment.

It is often thought that technology alone can solve this problem. For some observers, salvation could be achieved by means of hydrogen fuel cells, hybrid cars, increased fuel efficiency or even by telematics to reduce congestion. This book shows that 'technology' may well not be enough in itself and that for a genuinely sustainable transport future far more radical change, affecting many aspects of society, is needed. It is likely that, as well as users and consumers adopting new forms of behaviour, **new business models** will be needed. Technological innovation may well contribute, but it will need to be induced by a combination of market forces and government regulation.

Few cultural artefacts of the modern era reflect the dilemma of sustainability as well as the car. At the social level, many people have been excluded from the advances offered by the car, and many have become its victims—in many of the poorest countries more people are killed or injured by cars and trucks than by war or famine. At the economic level, congestion, resource depletion and pollution bring significant, though largely uncertain, costs. At the environmental level, although some areas of concern, notably toxic emissions, are relatively well understood, the impact of others, such as carbon dioxide emissions on climate change, are not. As other causes of climate change begin to be addressed in the near future, car transportation will stand out as the single most intractable issue.

Even for those of us who benefit from the advances in personal and collective mobility, the costs are undeniable. In the US, more citizens have been killed on roads than in all the wars the US has ever been involved in, including terrorist acts (Williams 1991). Road building has reconfigured urban and suburban areas, creating social exclusion for many while enhancing the means of social interaction for others. Urban centres around the world have become congested with barely moving metal, while air quality has deteriorated. Urban sprawl, spreading suburbs far out into the countryside, is entirely due to individual car ownership; sprawl also makes it difficult to conceptualise a transportation alternative without the individually owned car, thus creating a situation of **technological lock-in**. Indeed, the environmental and social impacts of car ownership are extremely diverse, pervasive and complex (Nielsen *et al.* 1996; Sydbom *et al.* 2001).

Addressing the challenges

The recognition that we need to do something about these interconnected problems came initially with the realisation that deteriorating urban air quality, particularly in southern California, was car-related (Brilliant 1989; Mondt 2000), prompting a wave of legislation aimed at controlling automobile emissions. This has now extended into other areas, including car production and use. Regulation now applies to safety, noise, end-of-life vehicles and fuel efficiency, while in the future it is likely to take an increasingly holistic or life-cycle perspective.

The roll-out of such legislation is very much a cat-and-mouse game whereby legislators acting on the basis of political imperatives try to tighten regulation, industry claims dire consequences if the regulation goes ahead, and some kind of compromise position is reached. Not all of this regulation has been concerned with 'control' in the traditional sense; indeed, it was in recognition of the limitations of such regulation that initiatives such as the US Partnership for a New Generation of Vehicles were originally conceived (Wells 1996; Nieuwenhuis and Wells 1997: 54-62). Nevertheless, the regulatory approach, with successive generations of emissions standards, has created vehicles that are much improved in many respects. A modern car, driven under the right conditions, can be up to 95–99% 'cleaner' in terms of toxic emissions than its equivalent of 40 years ago (Mondt 2000: 213). By 2008, EU truck emissions will have improved tenfold compared with those of a truck built in the late 1980s (ACEA 2000).

So, have we solved the problem of sustainability for the automotive industry and its products? It would appear not. While individual vehicles have become cleaner, quieter, more durable, more recyclable and, in some respects, more efficient, various factors have combined to undermine these achievements. First, there is the fact that vehicle numbers have increased, distances driven have increased and growing congestion has resulted in longer periods where stationary cars continue to consume fuel and emit toxic exhaust gases. In addition, cars themselves have become heavier and more complex, with many more comfort and safety features. At the same time, there has been a move—led by the US—to generally heavier sports utility vehicles (SUVs), pick-up trucks and minivans or 'people carriers' for personal transport. Just as importantly, the newly motorising economies of China, India, Indonesia, Russia and Brazil are potentially markets of such magnitude that, collectively, they could easily outgrow the established 'triad' markets of Europe, North America and Japan within the next 20 or 30 years, thus doubling the global burden imposed by motorisation in many respects. Clearly, we need to think of more radical solutions than have been implemented so far. It was the **factor x debate** that first highlighted the need to improve resource efficiency by an order of magnitude if people in the emerging economies are to enjoy an equivalent standard of material welfare to those in the established economies (Vergragt and van Grootveld 1994; Ryan 1998; von Weizsäcker *et al.* 1997). As the single largest manufacturing sector in the world, the automotive industry is strongly implicated in this debate.

The industry has largely ignored the challenges described above and has continued to produce heavier and less efficient cars and SUVs in order to benefit financially from the high profit margins on these vehicles. Nevertheless, the large car companies have also engaged in R&D on alternative fuels and powertrains, recognising the challenges and seeing the profitable opportunities that environmentalism can offer the sector. Consequently, radical alternative technologies are under development by many of the world's largest car- and truck-making concerns and their suppliers. However, moving these from the R&D arena to the commercial market is a bigger step than is often appreciated, especially for an essentially conservative industrial culture. The industry appears almost paralysed by its own structural condition, characterised by high capital intensity alongside low returns on capital (Nieuwenhuis and Wells 1997, 2003; Maxton and Wormald 2004). More profoundly, it is simply not possible for there to be a magic-bullet solution in the form of a new car technology that can render the industry entirely sustainable. Although theoretically imaginable, the practical barriers are such as to make it impossible from the current perspective. The best that can be achieved is that the industry will become relatively more sustainable than it is today, with products that are less polluting and more resource-efficient.

Beyond the technofix

Much of the effort reflected in the chapters in this book is concerned with going beyond the **technofix** of designing new, more environmentally friendly cars, to confront the more difficult challenges of institutional, cultural and social change within and beyond the industry that must be resolved in the transition towards sustainability. We therefore seek to break through the conventional boundary between engineering and the social sciences, with contributors from both sides of this traditional albeit unnecessary divide, including economists, engineers, geographers and designers.

About this book

The focus of this book is on motorised land-based mobility. We consider it obvious that a world of pedestrians and cyclists would be much more sustainable, and have therefore not covered these. Air transport has also been excluded. Although we recognise that this is a growing and significant issue, research on its impact is still in progress and thinking about possible solutions is in its infancy. For these reasons we therefore focus on land transport.

The central problem is the private car—how to power it; how to build it; and how to deliver it to customers in a more sustainable way. We start with ideas of radical innovation in the propulsion system of the car, notably the hydrogen fuel cell. In this context, Chapter 3 by Renato Orsato explores why the battery electric vehicle (BEV) has once again failed to make its long-awaited breakthrough. The competition for credibility between fuel-cell cars and hybrid electric cars is explored by Marko Hekkert and Robert van den Hoed in Chapter 4, while Chapter 5, by Robert van den Hoed and Philip Vergragt, examines the gradual rise of fuel-cell technology to a more institutionalised status. Many of the chapters thus deal with particular aspects of these broader changes. Chapters 2–5 therefore have the broad theme of **transition to a hydrogen economy** with a focus on one of the more promising alternative powertrain technologies, the fuel cell. The issue of transition has been given considerable theoretical and empirical treatment by those concerned with sustainability, particularly academics and policy-makers. Techniques and approaches have been developed. **Backcasting** (Quist and Vergragt 2004), for example, sets a final target or state, and then looks backwards from that point to ask what steps have to be taken in order to reach that point from the position we are in today. An alternative approach, much favoured by those charged with disbursing public R&D funds as well as with companies, is the **technology road map**. This is somewhat akin to **critical path analysis** (and is therefore popular with those from an engineering and science tradition), as it seeks to identify the necessary features or steps that need to be in place in order for some future scenario to come to pass. Chapter 3, however, sounds a warning over the difficulties inherent in this kind of forecasting by wondering whatever happened to the BEV: just ten years ago this technology was hailed as a possible saviour. Why, then, did it fail to gain market acceptance?

We are nevertheless aware that powertrain improvements alone cannot solve the problem of sustainable mobility. The section on **sustainable business and industry models** (Chapters 6–7) considers the possible business models that could be used to deliver **automobility** in a more sustainable manner. In line with our assertion that we cannot change one element of the system without considering the impact of such change on the whole, the section looks at how the car is made and used, and at how these aspects affect the quest for sustainable mobility. So embedded are notions of status and aesthetic pleasure with car ownership, changing the culture of automobility is by no means easy. Nevertheless, it must be seriously doubted whether automobility will ever be sustainable under the current philosophy of **fire-and-forget production**. New business models are needed that not only allow product-service system (PSS) concepts to become reality, but that also offer an escape from relentless over-production as well as a means of realising the potential of **product stewardship** while enhancing customer care in the process. Chapter 5 begins to address this issue and can be seen as providing a link to Chapters 6 and 7. In Chapter 6, Andrew Williams explores the opportunities offered by the PSS concept in introducing new business models to the automotive sector. It also introduces the concept of **micro-factory retailing** as a possible alternative business model for delivering automobility in a more sustainable world. Chapter 7 by Peter Wells and Paul Nieuwenhuis presents this concept in more detail and highlights some of its social and economic advantages, particularly within the context of a relocalisation of economic activity, thus linking in with a debate rarely addressed in the context of the automotive manufacturing sector.

The theme of **vehicle alternatives and their introduction trajectories** is explored in Chapters 8–10 which consider a number of recently introduced vehicles and alternative vehicle concepts and how these might be introduced within the context of a dominant existing paradigm. The history of the automotive industry shows how extremely difficult it has been to introduce alternative technology concepts, particularly when associated with new-entrant companies with no brand identity in the market. The alternative concepts discussed vary from a powertrain exchange concept that could breathe new life into the electric vehicle (Chapter 8) to minimalist single-seater commuter vehicles (Chapters 9 and 10). Again, important lessons can be learned even where such new concepts fail to achieve market success, not least by seeking to identify the reasons for such a failure, be they 'internal' to the technology itself, associated with the company that sought to introduce the alternative or embedded in the operating context by virtue of existing regulations, etc. In Chapter 8, Gordon Dower presents a concept that addresses one of the key concerns of electric vehicles—battery range—but broadens this into a more universally applicable vehicle concept which could be of particular interest for certain transport niches. This is followed, in Chapter 9, by Halina Szejnwald Brown and Catherine Carbone who report on their investigation into the modest success of two personal electric vehicles in the US, and by Tom van der Horst and Philip Vergragt in Chapter 10 with his report on the development of a hybrid electric–human-powered vehicle. Chapter 10 pulls together a number of stakeholders in a novel experiment in system innovation, so providing a link to the next section.

The section, **current trends and cases in greening mobility**, reports on current practice and experience in the initial moves towards sustainable automobility. Chapters 11–15 give a more near-term perspective on how we can start this process. Again, this is important because there is clearly a need to resolve issues in the 'here and now' as much as to construct elegant long-term trajectories to a sustainable future. This section is intended to show the sceptics (who may have raised questions during their reading of the previous sections) that it is possible to initiate change towards greater sustainability today and that people are actually doing so. We recognise that there is an underlying tension here between ameliorative reformism and radical systemic change, but the approach taken is one of inclusiveness. This book reveals the broad range of work being undertaken within the general theme of sustainable (automotive) mobility.

Thus, Charles White in Chapter 11 reports on efforts in the US towards greener cars, particularly the role of new combinations of stakeholders in this process. In Chapter 12, Carla Smink, Eskild Holm Nielsen and Tine Herreborg Jørgensen provide their analysis of the extent to which multinational car-makers have been able to transfer their environmental policies to developing countries, particularly South Africa.

Public transport is often presented as a greener alternative to private or personal modes, although the delivery of public transport via large 10–15 tonne diesel-powered commercial vehicles (buses) in urban areas is often not ideal, as such vehicles do not tend to mix well with more benign modes, such as walking or cycling, while most are significant polluters in their own right. Cleaning up existing buses may well be a first step towards more optimised urban public transport delivery and some initiatives are currently under way to do this, from compressed natural gas (CNG) and liquefied petroleum gas (LPG) buses to fuel-cell experiments. In Chapter 13, Mahesh Patankar and Anand Patwardhan describe and analyse the very rapid adoption of CNG as a cleaner fuel for public transport vehicles in Delhi and Mumbai—a transition possible thanks only to the involvement of a number of key stakeholders. In Chapter 14, Merih Kunur draws on his background in product design, offering a more radical solution to the problem of mixing heavy public transport vehicles with more benign modes, by presenting a concept of a more sustainable system for delivering public transport in urban and suburban areas.

This issue is also relevant for goods transport and, here too, considerable improvement is possible. Thus, Chapter 15, by Adeline Maijala, Lassi Linnanen and Tuula Pohjola, describes a simple management tool aimed at transport operators, particularly smaller businesses, which enables them to analyse their own environmental performance. Many players currently involved in the transport business do not recognise the problem; this tool offers a first step towards change.

The final section, comprising Chapters 16–18, presents some more visionary views. Chris Borroni-Bird's explanation in Chapter 16 of the thinking behind, and implications of, some of General Motors' more radical concept vehicles shows that even the existing players recognise the need for radical change and that some are actively working to meet that need. At the same time, more sceptical voices are raised over the roar of a more exciting automotive future: given social, economic, regulatory and market constraints, what can we realistically achieve, how soon and by what means? This final section also considers what conclusions can be drawn from the chapters outlined above and incorporates some of the outcomes of the workshops at GIN 2003 in San Francisco. Chapter 17 draws these strands together and suggests possible future scenarios. Finally, in Chapter 18, Wim Hafkamp and Boelie Elzen present a vision of a future mobility lifestyle.

We must accept that personal and, in particular, private motorised transport—the car—is one of the greatest obstacles slowing our progress towards sustainable mobility. Un-inventing the car or returning to human and animal power alone is not a viable option if we want to retain the complex economies and flexible lifestyles we have created. For this reason, much of the book is focused on ways of improving the automobility system in terms of sustainability. Tackling 'the car' in isolation may seem easier to many commentators; however, it is important to recognise the car as part of a system we have created over the past 100 years or so. This system, which we have called the **automobility paradigm** (Nieuwenhuis and Wells 1997, 2003), includes the car, truck and bus production system and its complete supply chain from mineral extraction onwards. It includes the car itself, how it is used and the social and cultural changes it has brought with it. It also includes the infrastructures created for it and the fuels that power these vehicles and their supply chains.

It is often not appreciated to what extent our modern culture is integrated with the car and its systems: we have built our world around the car and this inevitably shapes the scope for constructing sustainable mobility. We therefore need to tackle any change to the current automobility paradigm on a very broad front, and we need to be prepared for the possibly dramatic social and economic impacts we may bring about by changing just a few of these elements.

References

ACEA (Association des Constructeurs Européens d'Automobiles) (2000) *On the Road for You: The Truth about Trucks* (Brussels: ACEA).

Brilliant, A. (1989) *The Great Car Craze: How Southern California Collided with the Automobile in the 1920s* (Santa Barbara, CA: Woodbridge Press).

Maxton, G., and J. Wormald (2004) *Time for a Model Change: Re-engineering the Global Automotive Industry* (Cambridge, UK: Cambridge: University Press).

Mondt, R. (2000) *Cleaner Cars: The History and Technology of Emission Control Since the 1960s* (Warrendale, PA: Society of Automotive Engineers).

Nielsen, T., H.E. Jørgensen, J.C. Larsen and M. Poulsen (1996) 'City air pollution of polycyclic aromatic hydrocarbons and other mutagens: occurrence, sources and health effects', *Science of the Total Environment* 189/190: 41-49.

Nieuwenhuis, P., and P. Wells (2003) *The Automotive Industry and the Environment: A Technical, Business and Social Future* (Cambridge, UK: Woodhead).

—— and —— (1997) *The Death of Motoring? Car Making and Automobility in the 21st Century* (Chichester, UK: John Wiley).

Quist, J., and P.J. Vergragt (2004) 'Backcasting for industrial transformations and system innovations towards sustainability: relevance for governance?', in K. Jacob, M. Binder and A. Wieczorek (eds.), *Governance for Industrial Transformation: Proceedings of the 2003 Berlin Conference on the Human Dimensions of Global Environmental Change FFU rep 04-03,* www.fu-berlin.de/ffu/ffu_e/Publications/bc2003proceedings.htm.

Ryan, C. (1998) 'Designing for factor 20 improvements', *Journal of Industrial Ecology* 2.2: 3-5.

Sydbom, A.A., S. Blomberg, N. Parnia, T. Stenfors, T. Sandstrom and S.-E. Dahlen (2001) 'Health effects of diesel exhaust emissions', *European Respiratory Journal* 17.4: 733-46.

Vergragt, P.J., and G. van Grootveld (1994) 'Sustainable technology development in the Netherlands: the first phase of the Dutch STD program', *Journal of Cleaner Production* 2.3/4: 133-39.

Von Weizsäcker, E., A.B. Lovins and L.H. Lovins (1997) *Factor Four: Doubling Wealth: Halving Resource Use* (London: Earthscan).

Wells, P. (1996) 'Competitive and collaborative R&D: a comparison of policies for the technological transformation of the automotive industry in the European Union and North America', paper presented at the *Fifth International Conference of the Greening of Industry Network on 'Global Restructuring: A Place for Ecology?'*, Heidelberg, Germany, 24–27 November 1996.

Williams, H. (1991) *Autogeddon* (London: Jonathan Cape).

2
Transition management for sustainable personal mobility
THE CASE OF HYDROGEN FUEL CELLS

Philip J. Vergragt
Tellus Institute, Boston, USA

This chapter addresses one of the most persistent environmental and social problems in our society: the ecological effects of personal mobility. The dominant form of personal transportation is the car. As well as the obvious benefits of door-to-door transportation, freedom to move, satisfaction in driving and perceived social status, there are many disadvantages: local air pollution, mainly in cities; greenhouse gas emissions; road congestion; noise; accidents; use of space; and urban sprawl. On a personal level, many people are aware of the disadvantages but feel unable to act differently, especially as there are also many disadvantages to alternative forms of transportation (see, for example, Hardin 1968). Many people, however, also feel that the social effects of the car system are becoming unbearable. In the US the discussion of urban sprawl is often on the agenda (Gillham 2002). High levels of vehicle-related air pollution urged the state of California to develop its mandate for zero-emission vehicles (ZEV). Both in the US and in Europe local emissions are increasingly regulated (although until recently sports utility vehicles [SUVs] in the US escaped such regulatory control). Greenhouse gas emissions are high on the agenda, not only in Europe but also in many US states, municipalities and civil institutions.

Increasingly, attention is being directed at urban mobility problems, not just in developed countries but in developing ones too. For example, a recent Indian court order has ensured that many buses and taxis operating in New Delhi are now fuelled by liquefied natural gas (LNG), a cleaner alternative to petrol (Beella *et al.* 2002). In some cities, such as Curitiba and Bogotá in Colombia, daring experiments with alternative mobility systems are being tried,[1] while Brazil has had its 'gasohol' (alcohol from biomass for car propulsion) programme for many years now. If the world population eventually reaches nine to ten billion, and if the current direction of personal mobility continues to develop without some form of action to reduce its adverse effects, there will be a global ecological disaster, with countries such as India and China in the front line.

In the 1990s, the Dutch sustainable technological development (STD) programme argued that increasing population growth and increasing production and consumption could be met in a sustainable way only by developing so-called **factor 20 solutions** (Vergragt and van Grootveld 1994; Weaver *et al.* 2000). These solutions are not about redesigning the car, but about rethinking the system of personal mobility over the long term. Factor 20 is derived from a 50-year perspective in which the global population will have doubled and the standard of living will, on average, have increased fivefold, while the environmental burden should be at least halved. For greenhouse gas emissions, especially carbon dioxide, reductions of factor 20 per unit of need fulfilment are now generally accepted as global aims for the long term and as a necessary condition for increasing wealth in developing countries without unacceptable consequences for the climate.

Redesigning the car, or even just its propulsion system, will not be enough to achieve 95% reduction of emissions over the entire life-cycle. In the long term, personal mobility needs must be fulfilled in other ways than by the car. The most radical solution is to reduce transportation needs. There are two ways of achieving this. One is by increasing use of communications technologies (ICT) for teleworking, teleshopping, e-conferencing, e-tourism and e-leisure. The other is by radically rethinking and re-envisioning nations' infrastructure in order to locate the main functions (i.e. living, working, recreation) within close (e.g. cycling) proximity. Projects and experiments are under way to pilot these solutions, but they are not covered in this chapter.

A somewhat less radical approach is to shift personal mobility to other modes: walking, cycling and public transport. This approach has received a lot of attention in recent years. For instance, the Mitka project developed a three-wheeled bicycle that affords better protection from wind and rain, with an electric motor providing additional power (Brown *et al.* 2003; see Chapter 10). Public transport can be, and is being, transformed and upgraded; however, some fundamental issues need to be addressed, notably personal comfort, time consumption and privacy.

A third potential approach lies in the realm of **sustainable mobility services**. One of these is **car sharing**, which results in a slight reduction of the environmental burden (Meijkamp 2000; Truffer 2003). Another is **chain mobility solutions**, in which the consumer is presented with door-to-door mobility solutions that use both personal and mass transportation. A further dimension is sustainable mobility solutions offered by employers to employees, or by service providers to employers. These solutions may use an appropriate mix of sustainable vehicles ranging from personal to mass, and from two to four wheels, including forms of sharing.

So far, each of these solutions has captured only a very small fraction of the market, with the car (including SUVs and vans) continuing to be the preferred solution for personal mobility. This is no surprise if we take into account the entrenchment of the car system, and with it the petrol system, in Western industrialised societies (Knot *et al.*

---

1   See www.transmilenio.gov.co/Transmilenio.htm.

2001). The inertia in such a system is enormous, not just for economic, scientific and technological infrastructure reasons, but also because of the vested interests of powerful key actors such as vehicle manufacturers and oil companies, mining companies, petrol stations, dealers and repair shops. Moreover, many authors have noted the powerful position of the car as a modern cultural icon (Grin *et al.* 2003).

Governments do not escape societal preferences; on the contrary, government policies are expressions of such preferences. Furthermore, governments can do what societal interest groups cannot: for instance, regulate emissions to air. However, governments in democratic industrialised societies do not regulate personal car use or choice of car. Hence, government regulation has, until recently, concentrated on controlling the negative impacts of car use (such as exhaust emissions), through technologies such as the catalytic converter, and by providing fiscal incentives to change consumers' behaviour: for example, by reducing fuel duty on unleaded petrol. Further, governments can increase tax on unleaded petrol (as has been done in Europe but much less so in the US) and they can regulate access to inner cities by permits, parking fees and congestion charges.

Recently, an interesting change in US state government rhetoric has been observed. First, the state of California adopted the ZEV regulation which mandates that a certain percentage of cars should be zero-emission.[2] With the present technologies this means either electric cars or fuel-cell cars. Although over the years the ZEV regulation has been watered down, it has certainly given an incentive to R&D into alternatives such as fuel-cell propulsion systems. The other interesting shift is that the Dutch government has adopted **transition management** as part of its policy repertoire (Dutch Ministry of Housing 2001). The Dutch *National Environmental Policy Plan 4* recognises that persistent environmental problems (such as climate change caused by greenhouse gases) cannot be solved by traditional policy instruments or by technological innovation alone. Transitions are necessary and have been defined as long-term, continuous processes in which a society or a subsystem changes fundamentally: these are interconnected changes which reinforce each other through technology, the economy, institutions, ecology, culture, behaviour and belief systems. One of the examples where transitions are necessary is in the realm of mobility.

Grin *et al.* (2003) call this **third-generation environmental policy**, in which the government facilitates transition processes by setting long-term goals and bringing stakeholders together. Transition management has been derived from **system dynamics** in combination with **evolutionary economics** (Rotmans *et al.* 2001). It presupposes that there will be a transition from an **initial state** towards a **final state**, which may take as long as 50 years. Examples of these types of transition are the transition from coal to gas heating in the Netherlands in the 1960s and the transition from sailing ships to steam ships (Geels 2002).

Another aspect of transitions is that they are **multi-level**. They encompass regime shifts at the **meso level** (sociotechnical regimes) which can be reinforced by changes at the **macro** (the 'landscape') and **micro levels** ('experimentation in niches'). They are multi-phased in the sense that in each of the four phases (pre-development, take-off, acceleration, stabilisation) different mechanisms are at work and different gov-

2 California Air Resources Board (CARB), www.arb.ca.gov/msprog/zevprog/factsheets/factsheets. htm.

ernment policies should be applied. They are multi-stakeholder in the sense that many stakeholders (business, non-governmental organisations [NGOs], civil society, consumers and governments) can be part of a transition process.

One of the problems with transition management is that it is not at all clear whether there will be a stable final state or, if there is, what it will look like. In part, this can be handled by constructing scenarios describing possible final states or different pathways (Vergragt and Green 2001; Green and Vergragt 2002; Ashford *et al.* 2001, 2002).[3] **Sociotechnical** scenarios have been proposed in order to describe possible paths to a possible future state (Elzen *et al.* 2004; Suurs *et al.* 2003). In the case of car transportation and personal mobility it is clear that there is no consensus at all about a possible final state. We simply do not know whether the car will continue its dominant position in the long term or whether one of the other solutions—other modes, new services, e-solutions, infrastructural changes—will become dominant. We also do not know whether future solutions for individual personal mobility will be in the form of oversized cars, as at present, or small electric vehicles.

In this context, it is interesting to note that the Tellus Institute has developed a number of scenarios including the so-called **great transition scenario** (Raskin 2002). The interesting difference between the Tellus approach and that taken by Rotmans *et al.* (2001) is that it does not assume a final state; rather, the transition takes place in a time-frame of 50–100 years.

Transition management thus amounts to a lot of experimentation and learning about solutions and their acceptability before any move towards a macro-scale solution can take place. The problem with the government as transition manager is that it often has a dual role: it sets the rules for emissions and taxes (and subsidies) while also managing a multi-stakeholder, multi-level transition process in which **social learning** is central. The paradox is that the government is supposed to learn about its own role as transition manager, but bureaucratic divisions between agencies often act as barriers for experimentation and higher-order learning. The same applies to divisions between local, national and federal governments (including EU member states). Despite this paradox, transition management is an interesting new idea that should be endorsed and monitored carefully. However, it remains to be seen how successful it can be in the context of sustainable mobility.

In this chapter I focus on one aspect of a possible transition to sustainable personal mobility: that of hydrogen fuel cells as the propulsion system for cars and buses. Hydrogen fuel cells have been in the limelight over the past few years. There are basically two aspects to this: the introduction of fuel cells as a source of electrical energy, mainly for propulsion, and the use of hydrogen as a fuel. As we shall see, although these are connected they are also quite different as fuel cells are possible without hydrogen and hydrogen for propulsion can be used without fuel cells. The question is: 'What are the possible and optimal solutions for car and bus propulsion, taking into consideration the possibilities and restrictions of both fuel cells and hydrogen?'

---

3   See also www.shell.com/static/royal-en/downloads/scenarios/global_scenarios.zip *or* www. shell.com → About Shell → Our strategy → Looking ahead: Scenarios

The hydrogen fuel cell and its potentialities

Hydrogen fuel cells are electrochemical devices that convert hydrogen with oxygen into water, creating an electrical current in the process. This is the reversal of the electrolysis of water, in which an electric current splits water into hydrogen and oxygen. The fuel-cell reaction requires a catalyst (often platinum) in order to function at low temperatures with enough speed and yield. Fuel cells have been known for a long time; they obtained practical application in the Apollo space programme in the 1960s.

There are many different types of fuel cells, using different electrolytes and fuels, operating at different temperatures. Presently, the most widespread fuel cell for transportation is the proton exchange membrane (PEM) which uses a special plastic membrane separating the cathode and the anode (Vergragt and van Noort 1996). The most common fuel is hydrogen, although mixtures of hydrogen and methane are also used, and a methanol fuel cell is under development. Fuel cells are used in stacks in order to obtain the required voltage and current density; in addition, provisions have to be made to add hydrogen and oxygen, to remove water and heat, and to handle the electrical current.

In the past few years, fuel cells have undergone a tremendous decrease in weight and volume, in conjunction with an increase in efficiency and reliability. This has enabled vehicle manufacturers to mount them in prototype vehicles and even in experimental city buses. Also, fuel cell costs have gone down, although they remain much more expensive than the internal combustion engine (ICE).

The advantages of fuel cells for car transportation lie in their high efficiency and their potential for zero emissions in use, which makes them especially suited for city traffic (like other electric cars). Furthermore, the absence of moving parts removes the need for lubrication and reduces maintenance costs. Their primary disadvantages are high investment costs, high costs of infrastructure changes and, more generally, the costs associated with a large system shift.

It is feasible that fuel cells will break through in other sectors earlier than in the transportation sector. One sector where there is considerable progress is in the stationary generation of electricity, where large-scale fuel-cell systems are used. Another promising area is the market for portable electrical appliances, such as mobile phones and laptop computers, where conventional batteries have too limited a lifespan. It is quite feasible that these sectors will eventually lead the breakthrough to the mass market that is necessary to achieve the economies of scale needed for drastic price reductions.

One of the potential bottlenecks in the transition to fuel-cell vehicles (FCVs) is the provision of the fuel. For a long time, hydrogen was considered unsuitable for storage in a car. Its energy density is too low, making it impossible to transport enough hydrogen to travel an acceptable distance. Now it appears that, by storing hydrogen under high pressure, sufficient density can be achieved.

Neither hydrogen nor methanol are currently available at commercial fuelling stations, except in Reykjavik.[4] The building of a fuelling infrastructure is extremely expensive (US$5,000/car, according to Keith and Ferrell 2003) and the problem is that hardly any FCVs will be sold until a fuel delivery infrastructure is in place. This problem is par-

---

4   Since April 2003; see www.newenergy.is.

tially being tackled by experimenting with bus and taxi fleets which have a limited range and need only one central fuelling station.

A complication is that there does not seem to be a consensus about what should be the preferred fuel of the future (van den Hoed and Vergragt 2004). From the outset, Mercedes (post-merger, DaimlerChrysler) has lobbied for the use of methanol which can be converted 'under the hood' into hydrogen, although this still produces emissions. However, DaimlerChrysler has also built prototypes of cars and buses with hydrogen storage, especially for fleet use. On the other hand, General Motors and Toyota, followed by PSA, Renault and Nissan, have switched their position on **petrol-reforming** under the hood. Petrol-reforming means the production of hydrogen from petrol by a chemical reaction (a so-called **reformer**) in the car. However, such a reaction generates emissions and reduces the overall efficiency of this method of propulsion. General Motors also uses hydrogen for testing vehicles. BMW uses hydrogen in an ICE: the reaction does not produce hydrocarbon emissions but, because the temperature is high, it generates nitrous oxides. BMW also uses hydrogen in fuel cells, not for propulsion but mainly for enhancing the provision of electricity for other functions in the car (such as air conditioning).

Because there is no consensus about the long-term commercial future of fuel cells in vehicles, governments are unwilling to make the infrastructure changes needed to support fuel-cell transportation technology. As a complicating factor, there is a number of other solutions for propulsion, for example hybrid vehicles and bio-diesel (see Chapter 4), that may be equally sustainable from an environmental point of view. To complicate matters further, there is no consensus about the overall environmental gains (the so-called **well-to-wheel** efficiency) of the hydrogen fuel cell as compared to other solutions. Before we look into that, let us first take a closer look at hydrogen.

Hydrogen and its problems

For many years hydrogen has been lauded as the fuel of the future, with talk of the **hydrogen economy** (Hoffman 2000). Although hydrogen is abundantly available, turning it into transportation fuel costs energy and generates pollution. There are generally two routes available to generate hydrogen: **electrolysis** and **steam-reforming**. To produce hydrogen by electrolysis sustainably requires green electricity produced from renewable sources. In most places, renewable energy sources are not widely available: moreover, electrolytic production of hydrogen must compete with other consumers of green electricity, such as households. One report, looking at the situation in England (Eyre *et al.* 2002), argues that, for at least the next 30 years, there will not be enough renewable energy available to produce hydrogen sustainably. Except for Iceland, with its abundance of geothermal and hydroelectric power, this is also likely to be the situation in most other countries.

To produce hydrogen by steam-reforming, natural gas is needed as a feedstock. Although natural gas reserves are large, they are by no means infinite. Moreover, steam-reforming generates carbon dioxide, a greenhouse gas. While it is possible for carbon to be stored (known as **sequestration**), the technology involved is not yet proven and itself requires energy, so reducing the life-cycle efficiency of steam-reformed hydrogen.

Instead of talking about the hydrogen economy and looking at hydrogen as 'the fuel of the future', it may be more realistic to view hydrogen as a medium for transporting and storing energy that has been generated elsewhere (preferably from renewable resources) and which might be used for fuelling mobility. The question then is: 'What is the most sustainable and cost-effective way to store and transport energy, and to make it available for cars and buses?' It may be that, in the end, hydrogen is not the solution: for instance, because electrical solutions or bio-fuels are more cost-effective and sustainable.

Thus, it appears to be better to be agnostic about the use of hydrogen as a solution in the final state after the transition to sustainable mobility. As we have seen before, we do not even know whether personal vehicles will be part of such a final state (or, indeed, whether a stable final state will ever emerge). On the one hand, there will be no hydrogen option if there is no R&D to develop and test the associated technology. On the other, opting for hydrogen now seems somewhat premature (Keith and Ferrell 2003).

Moreover, we need to be careful about the hype surrounding hydrogen. In his 2003 State of the Union address, President Bush allocated US$1.2 billion for research on hydrogen as a transportation fuel. There are doubts, however, about how the hydrogen is to be produced: for example, there are fears that nuclear energy may be used to generate hydrogen on a large scale.

Future scenarios and their assessments

Recently, many papers have appeared with scenarios and expectations about the potentialities of hydrogen fuel cells for personal vehicle propulsion. Ogden *et al.* (2001) have developed what they call an **optimistic scenario** under a number of assumptions, including aggressive ZEV mandates (50%), a quickly developing infrastructure and the continuation of falling prices with cumulative FCV production (see Table 2.1).

Ogden *et al.* conclude that, even under the most favourable conditions, FCVs will not contribute to the solution of environmental problems much before 2025 at the earliest.

A UK report *Fuelling Road Transport* (Eyre *et al.* 2002) details three demand-side scenarios: baseline, world markets (high demand scenario) and global sustainability (low demand scenario). In addition, five technical vehicle scenarios are outlined, among them rapid progress (hybrids and fuel cells), biomass (methanol) and a combination of the two. In the energy system, four scenarios are sketched, business as usual (BAU), high renewables, electrolytic hydrogen and high bio-fuels. Some of the most salient combinations of these scenarios are elaborated. Vehicle innovations (hybrid and hydrogen fuel cells) could lead to significant reductions in greenhouse gases in 2050, with greater reductions achieved through a combination of renewables and biomass hydrogen. The most promising in terms of greenhouse gas reductions in 2050 are in the high-biomass scenarios. Moreover, the report argues that in the UK there are no carbon benefits in producing hydrogen for use in transport from renewable energy, at least not

Year	Production of FCVs per year	As a percentage of total cars on the road
2000–2004	10	
2005–2008	10,000	Pilot manufacturing facility
2010	300,000	First commercial factory
2015–2019	900,000 extra each year	0.7%
2020	Cost-competitive	3.3%
2020–2025	10 new factories/year	9.7%

TABLE 2.1 Production of fuel cell vehicles

Source: Ogden et al. 2001

before 2030. Instead, using it for power generation yields a larger reduction in carbon dioxide emissions. Only in cases where there is excess capacity of renewable energy (such as in Iceland) or an additional effective market demand for renewable energy or potential for the production of renewable hydrogen off-grid, could there be a net carbon benefit.

In 2000, a team at the Massachusetts Institute of Technology (MIT) published an influential report which concluded that hybrid ICE vehicles have advantages over hybrid (and non-hybrid) FCVs with respect to life-cycle greenhouse gas emissions, energy efficiency and vehicle cost (Weiss *et al.* 2000: 5-30):

> vehicles with hybrid propulsion systems using either ICE or fuel cell power plants are the most efficient and lowest emitting technologies assessed. In general, ICE hybrids appear to have advantages over fuel cell hybrids with respect to life cycle GHG emissions, energy efficiency, and vehicles costs, but the differences are within the uncertainties of our results and depend on the source of fuel energy . . . if automobile systems with drastically lower GHG emissions are required in the very long run future (perhaps 30–50 years or more) hydrogen and electrical energy are the only identified option for 'fuels', but only if both are produced from non-fossil fuels of primary energy (such as nuclear or solar) or from fossil primary energy with carbon sequestration.

In 2003, a further report appeared in which these conclusions were refined (Weiss *et al.* 2003: 11):

> there is no current basis for preferring either fuel cell or ICE hybrid power plants for mid-sized automobiles over the next 20 years or so. Hybrid vehicles are superior to their non-hybrid counterparts and their advantages are greater for ICE than for FC designs. Hybrids can reduce both life-cycle energy use and greenhouse gas emissions to about 37% to 47% of current comparable vehicles and to about 52% to 65% of what might be expected in 2020 as a result of normal evolution of conventional technology.

On the other hand, a General Motors study (General Motors 2001) reports that hybrid hydrogen–FCVs give a 47% reduction in greenhouse gas emissions, as compared to the present benchmark vehicle. This is consistent with General Motors' current interest in developing hydrogen FCVs for the market, albeit with a petrol infrastructure and with petrol-reforming under the hood.

An Feng *et al.* (2003) have made a comparative analysis between these two conflicting forecasts and two other studies in order to identify the reasons for the difference in outcomes. They clearly show that these can be largely explained by differences in methodology, time-frames, vehicle sizes and assumptions about the baseline. Taking all these into account, they calculate that in all studies the hybrid hydrogen fuel cell car has the greatest fuel efficiency (and lowest greenhouse gas emissions), ranging from 92% miles per gallon equivalent gains in the MIT study, 138% in the General Motors study to 173% in one of the other studies. It needs to be taken into account that, according to An Feng *et al.* (2003): 'MIT results imply greater gains from 2010 to 2020 for conventional drivetrain technology than for FCV'. However, the analysis does not discuss how much of the fuel efficiency increase comes from hybridisation and how much from the fuel-cell component.

Ogden *et al.* (2001) take the life-cycle costing (LCC) of fuels as their yardstick. They calculate that for hybrid vehicles the LCC is about 50% that of conventional ICE vehicles and for compressed natural gas (CNG) vehicles it is 33%. The hydrogen FCV would give one-eighth of the LCC if the hydrogen was derived from natural gas without carbon sequestration and one-fifteenth with carbon sequestration. If the hydrogen was derived from on-board fuel processors the LCC reductions would be much lower. These figures would mean that greenhouse gas emissions over the entire life-cycle of a hydrogen FCV would be much lower than other studies have shown.

Erdmann and Grahl (2000) calculate that, in Germany by 2010, the hydrogen FCV may be cost-competitive for the user in the long run because the higher price of the vehicle will be offset by the lower price of fuel. In a situation in 2010 where 2.5% of all cars are driving on compressed hydrogen and 10% of all fuel stations provide compressed hydrogen, a higher price of $4,000 on top of the price of an equivalent ICE vehicle based on 1997 prices may be acceptable to German consumers. Such hydrogen FCVs would be attractive to customers who travel long distances. According to Erdmann and Grahl, neither hybrid cars nor methanol fuel cells will outperform hydrogen fuel cells. The most likely entry point for such vehicles would be the upper-middle segment of the market. The macroeconomic cost–benefit analysis shows that the net outcome of hydrogen FCVs and infrastructure for the economy could be positive, despite the costs associated with developing the fuel-cell infrastructure and a drop in tax-take (as duty on alternative fuels is lower than on petrol and diesel).

Concluding thus far, we can state that the environmental gains from hydrogen FCVs are widely disputed. One dispute is about the relative environmental gains of hydrogen fuel cells relative to hybrid vehicles. One gets the impression that the environmental gains of hybrid vehicles as compared to ICE vehicles is much larger than the environmental gain of hybrid FCVs as compared to hybrid ICE vehicles. Of course, a lot depends on how the hydrogen is produced (known as **well-to-tank**). The actual differences between vehicles show up in **tank-to-wheel** comparisons.

Transition towards hydrogen fuel cell mobility?

A future transition to a car system fuelled by hydrogen fuel cells requires that hydrogen is available on a large scale and at highly dispersed fuelling stations. Moreover, the hydrogen will need to be produced in a sustainable manner. There are two possible options, both of which can be carried out centrally or decentrally: steam-reforming with carbon sequestration; and electrolysis of water. Both have disadvantages. Central steam-reforming makes carbon sequestration viable but the technology is not yet proven and its risks are largely unknown; moreover, it requires natural gas as a feedstock. Sustainable electrolysis of water requires large amounts of green electricity which will not be available for at least another 30 years in the UK, according to Eyre *et al.* (2002). Thus, in the shorter term, the electrolysis approach may actually increase rather than decrease carbon dioxide emissions.

Acceptance by users is crucial for a successful transition. Adamson (2003) suggests that a hydrogen FCV will have to address three different adopter groups each with different requirements. The first, the primary niche market, will require that the FCV provides a new function with a high economic value to the customer. The secondary niche market will require that the subjective usefulness of the FCV is greater than of the current vehicle. And, finally, in order to enter the mass market, a market pull will have to be developed and costs brought down.

It is wise to try out the elements of a future system transformation *before* attempting to change the entire system. In evolutionary economics this is called strategic niche management (SNM) (see Hoogma *et al.* 2002) and in the social learning literature it is called bounded sociotechnical experiments (BSTE) (see Brown *et al.* 2003). In SNM the government creates a **technological niche**, a protected space in which stakeholders can experiment with a new technology. We can see many of these niches arising. For instance, in the EU Clean Urban Transport for Europe (CUTE) project,[5] stakeholders collaborated in setting up an experimental trial for hydrogen fuel cell buses in ten European cities.[6] The niche consists mainly of government funding; the buses have to comply with all safety standards and need to fulfil all other regulations for passenger transportation. However, the project does not aim to change urban public transport to a hydrogen fuel-cell system.

It is probably more appropriate in this case to use the conceptual analytic scheme of BSTE. BSTE is an experiment that is:

● Bounded in space and time

● Undertaken by heterogeneous stakeholders

● Driven by a shared long-term vision

● Aimed at higher-order learning about the technology, stakeholders' needs and interests, conditions for success and failure, and consumer acceptance

---

5   See www.fuel-cell-bus-club.com.
6   Amsterdam, Barcelona, Hamburg, London, Luxembourg, Madrid, Perth, Porto, Reykjavik, Stockholm, Stuttgart.

Iceland, with its abundance of renewable energy resources, is an interesting case as lack of green electricity is not an obstacle, at least not in the short term. Furthermore, the Icelandic experiment is driven by a shared common vision of a hydrogen economy, with private vehicles, public transport and even fishing vessels powered by green hydrogen. Moreover, this vision embraces independence from oil and gas imports, and thus appeals to the traditional Icelandic value of self-reliance. It also creates potential export markets of sustainable hydrogen to Europe.

In other European cities, such as Amsterdam, the CUTE project is driven by a heterogeneous group of stakeholders seeking to learn more about the application of hydrogen in specific applications, such as passenger buses. Research by Suzanne van den Bosch (2003) revealed that, although the various participants in the project shared a common vision, they had quite different short-term objectives and interests. Thus, for DaimlerChrysler the CUTE experiment provided an opportunity to test the reliability of fuel-cell systems in buses under real-life conditions. For Shell Hydrogen it helped explore the market for hydrogen and the potentialities for investment in hydrogen fuelling stations. For the Amsterdam transit authority CUTE chimed with the authority's aim to be the front-runner in environmentally friendly mass transit. For NUON, the energy company, the main issue was how to generate hydrogen from renewable sources.

The CUTE project is in its infancy and should not be seen as a sign of any fundamental shift towards hydrogen fuel-cell bus transportation. However, it is helping to raise interest in the provision of green electricity for generating sustainable hydrogen. Thus, Hoek Loos, a producer of hydrogen for industry, sees the generation of sustainable hydrogen for the transportation market as a promising new business opportunity. NOVEM (Nederlandse Organisatie voor Energie en Milieu [Dutch Organisation for Energy and Environment], a government funding agency) is co-funding the project because it fits with its policy of supporting pre-market pilots aimed at overcoming barriers and communicating new sustainable technology options.

It is interesting that this kind of radical innovation has been introduced by a coalition of heterogeneous stakeholders who share a common vision but have quite different short-term interests, as reflected in their success criteria. For instance, Daimler-Chrysler sees the project as successful when there are 30 buses in operation in 11 European cities generating a lot of data on performance in real-life situations. For the transit authority and the municipality of Amsterdam the most important success criterion is lack of complaints from transit passengers. For Shell Hydrogen the project is important as a worldwide communication tool and for developing new markets, while Hoek Loos hopes to be a partner in future hydrogen fuel-cell projects. Most stakeholders see the development of reliable and efficient technology as the clearest measure of success. NOVEM, however, also counts the project as successful when learning takes place from failure.

Some partners, especially Shell Hydrogen and the transit authority, are very interested in consumer acceptance of hydrogen fuel-cell buses, as they realise that adverse publicity could kill the project in an early stage. The provision of high-quality consumer information is therefore considered crucial for the success of the project.

Case study: consumer acceptance of hydrogen fuel-cell buses in Amsterdam[7]

Consumer acceptance can be defined as 'a positive attitude of individuals towards an innovation and the intention to consume the product or service' (van den Bosch 2003: 1). Note that we are talking of an intention because the innovation may not yet be commercially available and the actual behaviour of consumers may not yet have been tested. This situation is similar to that of the SusHouse project where a methodology for consumer assessment of long-term scenarios has been developed (Bode 2000; Vergragt and Green 2001).

Behavioural intention is derived from consumer attitudes and social norms (Raaij *et al.* 1999). From earlier consumer acceptance research on hydrogen fuel cells carried out by the California Fuel Cell Partnership,[8] J.D. Power and Associates[9] and others (Pembina Institute 2002; Altmann and Gräsel 1998; Gruber and Wurster 2002), it appears that consumer acceptance is determined by the following key issues:

- **Basic requirements:** affordability, comfort, range, storage capacity, acceleration, reliability, safety

- **Extra benefits:** faster acceleration, reduced noise level, more electric power available for other functions

- **External benefits:** fuel prices, supply security, tax incentives, environment

- **Barriers:** shorter driving range, lack of performance, lack of information

- **Price:** consumers are willing to pay slightly more for the benefits

- **Perception of safety:** consumers expect the technology to be safe; however, communication about safety aspects may raise concerns

- **Awareness/knowledge:** level of knowledge is very low; demonstration projects may help, but additional measures may be needed

- **Positive attitude:** although consumers have a positive attitude, this is not based on level of knowledge or perception of safety

- **High level of acceptance:** environmental aspects play hardly any role

- **Direct experience:** significant positive effect on acceptance (and attitude)

In order to test these assumptions, and to obtain a measure of consumer acceptance of hydrogen fuel-cell buses before their introduction (zero measurement), qualitative research was carried out among bus passengers in the Amsterdam region. The aim of the research was to investigate the knowledge, attitude and behavioural intentions of Amsterdam bus passengers.

In order to assess knowledge, passengers were asked about associations with the words 'fuel cells' and 'hydrogen', and were also asked what they knew about the

---

7   This section is mainly based on the work of Suzanne van den Bosch (2003).
8   See www.fuelcellpartnership.org/releases/2000-10-1_media_update.htm.
9   See www.jdpa.com/news/releases/pressrelease.asp?ID=2002016.

planned introduction of the hydrogen fuel-cell buses. In order to assess attitudes, questions were asked about advantages and disadvantages, about environmental aspects, safety, noise and smell, as well as about general attitude. In order to assess behavioural intention, passengers were asked if they intended to make use of a hydrogen fuel-cell bus. The research was carried out on 22 bus passengers on a working day.

Knowledge of both fuel cells and hydrogen on the basis of associations was found to be low; most of the associations were either absent or incorrect. After a short explanation, most passengers were able to make a correct assessment of advantages and disadvantages. Attitudes towards fuel cells and hydrogen were predominantly positive, with only a very small number negative towards hydrogen. The overall attitude towards the introduction of hydrogen fuel-cell buses ranged from neutral to positive. Attitudes towards the environment were predominantly positive, but mixed for other aspects such as sound, smell and safety. The importance given to the (positive) environmental aspects of hydrogen fuel-cell buses was high. The behavioural intention to use the hydrogen fuel cell bus was 100%.

The overall results of this investigation suggest that general attitudes and behavioural intentions tend to be positive, but level of knowledge is generally low. It is expected that the level of knowledge will rise either as a result of the communications strategy or from direct experience with the hydrogen fuel-cell bus. It is remarkable that the safety of the bus is regarded as obvious; the passengers had confidence that the buses comply with current safety standards.

The results of this qualitative research are in accordance with the published literature. However, because they are not firmly rooted in knowledge, the stability over time of the attitudes reported here is likely to be low. Negative incidents and press reports tend to influence attitudes and thus behavioural intentions. On the other hand, greater knowledge may reinforce existing attitudes which are a good starting point for general consumer acceptance of the new technology.

However, it was surprising that the stakeholders (and in particular the transit authority) were quite satisfied with the findings of this study and were not interested in carrying out any follow-up research. Indeed, the transit authority plans to use the findings to inform its public communications strategy on hydrogen fuel-cell buses.

Conclusions

In this chapter I first argued that a transition towards a future sustainable personal mobility system is hard to envisage because there are so many options available and so many uncertainties about their potential for implementation. I then argued that hydrogen FCVs offer a promising option for a future sustainable personal mobility system. However, due to the large number of uncertainties identified in this chapter, it is highly improbable that a fundamental shift to a hydrogen FCV system will take place in the foreseeable future.

First, hydrogen FCVs are, at present, very expensive. In order to obtain economies of scale large quantities need to be produced and sold. However, due to uncertainties about the necessary infrastructure, and the high costs involved, it will take a long time before commercial production is considered possible. In the meantime, there are other options such as biomass fuels or hybrid vehicles that may be more environmentally friendly and that may better fit the present infrastructure.

Second, even if these barriers are overcome, there are uncertainties over whether sufficient sustainable hydrogen can be produced and distributed. Ideally, hydrogen should be produced by electrolysis using green electricity generated from renewable energy sources. However, it is highly unlikely that there will be enough renewable energy sources available in the long term to achieve this. Another option, steam-reforming of natural gas, is not sustainable because gas is a fossil fuel; moreover, it presupposes that carbon can be sequestered safely in the long term. Nevertheless, if carbon sequestration is possible and there are enough natural gas reserves, this option could be an attractive intermediate stage on the route towards sustainable hydrogen.

For the short and medium term, it is more probable that hydrogen fuel cells will be applied in niches such as city buses with central fuelling depots, thus making an extensive hydrogen delivery infrastructure system unnecessary. Reduction of local air pollution and noise may be important drivers for local authorities to promote these systems for in-city use. An additional advantage of this strategy is that learning can take place both about the technology and the motivations and desired outcomes of the heterogeneous stakeholders (businesses, governments, transit authorities, civil society, passengers and others). Monitoring of these (possibly higher-order) learning processes is highly advisable using conceptual frameworks such as the BSTE approach.

It is possible that hydrogen fuel cells will take off earlier in other sectors: for instance, on ships or in portable laptops and mobile phones. With regard to ships, for example, there are significant environmental problems associated with the use of crude oil for transportation. By contrast, there are likely to be far fewer environmental problems associated with storing and transporting large amounts of cooled or pressurised hydrogen. In mobile phones and laptops there is another driver: the demand for long-use batteries that are easy to replace. Fuel cells could fill this gap, provided that hydrogen storage problems can be solved.

Another possible route for transition is via stationary fuel cells. It is possible that in the future the provision of electricity to households comes from fuel cells, either in the form of large or micro units. Either way, electricity may be used for transportation or for charging batteries for electric vehicles.

Thus, the role for governments in transition management should be to foster learning experiments with alternative fuels, vehicles and infrastructures, without opting prematurely for a solution that may or may not be sustainable and cost-effective. These experiments should be carried out in conjunction with heterogeneous stakeholders (from business, local government and transport agencies, civil society and users/consumers). Monitoring these experiments in order to analyse learning processes is extremely important and is often neglected; moreover, making the results available to other projects is essential in order to create a broader understanding of the sociocultural aspects of the new technology. Governments can play an important role in connecting dispersed sociotechnical experiments and in monitoring learning processes and follow-up activities. Many experiments end when the project is terminated, with no clear follow-up stage.

It will be a long time before we are able to reach a consensus on what the final system will look like. Visioning exercises can help create a common understanding among stakeholders about possible future scenarios and to exchange what has been learned from experiments (Vergragt and Green 2001; Brown *et al.* 2003). Ongoing learning about different aspects, including consumer acceptance, cost-effectiveness and long-term sustainability, will remain necessary for a long time. Furthermore, because the options are rapidly changing, investments in new infrastructure will remain low. Nevertheless, limited investment in experimental schemes is worthwhile as without this there can be no alternative to the present ICE trajectory.

References

Adamson, K.-A. (2003) 'An examination of consumer demand in the secondary niche market for fuel cell vehicles in Europe', *International Journal of Hydrogen Energy* 28.7: 771-80.

Altmann, M., and C. Gräsel (1998) 'The acceptance of hydrogen technology', www.HyWeb.de/accepth2.

An Feng (2003) *Assessing Tank-to-Wheel Efficiencies of Advanced Technology Vehicles* (Argonne, IL: Argonne National Laboratory): 2003-01-0412.

Ashford, N., W. Hafkamp, F. Prakke and P.J. Vergragt (with contributions from A. Bakker, R. Kemp, H.W. Kua, J. Quist, B. ter Weel and G. Zwetsloot) (2001) *Pathways to Sustainable Industrial Transformations: Co-optimising Competitiveness, Employment and Environment* (final report; The Hague: VROM, 30 June 2001).

—— (2002) 'Pathways to sustainable industrial transformations: co-optimising competitiveness, employment and environment', paper presented at the EESD (*Engineering Education in Science*) *Conference*, TU Delft, 24–25 October 2002.

Beella, S.K., J.C. Diehl and P.J. Vergragt (2002) 'Sustainable transport scenarios for New Delhi', paper presented at the *Tenth Greening of Industry Conference*, *'Corporate Social Responsibility: Governance for Sustainability'*, Goteborg, Sweden, 23–26 June 2002.

Bode, M. (2000) *Consumers' Acceptance Analysis of Scenarios: Summary Report* (SusHouse Project, Hanover University, Germany: Lehrstuhl Markt und Konsum).

Brown, H.S., P.J. Vergragt, K. Green and L. Berchicci (2003) 'Learning for sustainability transition through bounded sociotechnical experiments in personal mobility', *Technology Analysis and Strategic Management* 13.3: 298-315.

Dutch Ministry of Housing (2001) *National Environmental Policy Plan 4* (The Hague: VROM).

Elzen, B., F.W. Geels, P. Hoffman and K. Green (2004) 'Sociotechnical scenarios as a tool for transition policy: an example from the traffic and transport domain', in B. Elzen, F.W. Geels and K. Green (eds.), *System Innovation and the Transition to Sustainability: Theory, Evidence and Policy* (Cheltenham, UK: Edward Elgar): 251.

Erdmann, G., and M. Grahl (2000) 'Competitiveness and economic impacts of fuel cell electric vehicles on future German markets', paper presented at the *Hyforum Conference*, Munich, Germany, 11–15 September 2000.

Eyre, N., M. Fergusson and R. Mills (2002) *Fuelling Road Transport: Implications for Energy Policy* (London: Department of Transport).

Geels, F.W. (2002) *Understanding the Dynamics of Technological Transitions: A Co-evolutionary and Sociotechnical Analysis* (PhD thesis; Enschede, Netherlands: Twente University Press).

General Motors (2001) *Well-to-Wheel Energy Use and Greenhouse Gas Emissions of Advanced Fuel/Vehicles Systems: North American Analysis: Executive Summary* (Argonne, IL: Argonne National Laboratory).

Gillham, O. (2002) *The Limitless City: A Primer on the Urban Sprawl Debate* (Washington, DC: Island Press).

Green, K., and P.J. Vergragt (2002) 'Towards sustainable households: a methodology for developing sustainable technological and social innovations', *Futures* 34.5: 381-400.

Grin, J., H. van der Graaf and P. Vergragt (2003) 'Een derde generatie milieubeleid: een sociologisch perspectief en een beleidswetenschappelijk programma' ['A third-generation environmental policy: a sociological perspective and a policy scientific programme'], *Beleidswetenschap* 1: 51-72.

Gruber, C., and R. Wurster (2002) 'Hydrogen fuelled buses: the Bavarian fuel cell bus project', www.ieahia.org/pdfs/bavarian_proj.pdf.

Hardin, G. (1968) 'The tragedy of the commons', *Science* 162: 1,243-48.

Hoffman, P. (2000) *Tomorrow's Energy: Hydrogen Fuel Cells and the Prospects for a Cleaner Planet* (Cambridge, MA: MIT Press).

Hoogma, R., R. Kemp, J. Schot and B. Truffer (2002) *Experimenting for Sustainable Transport: The Approach of Strategic Niche Management* (London: E&F Spon).

Keith, D.W., and A.E. Ferrell (2003) 'Rethinking hydrogen cars', *Science* 301 (18 July 2003): 315-16.

Knot J., C. Marjolijn, J.C.M. van den Ende and P.J. Vergragt (2001) 'Flexibility strategies for sustainable technology development', *Technovation* 21.6: 335-43.

Meijkamp, R.G. (2000) 'Changing consumer behaviour through eco-efficient services: an empirical study on car-sharing in the Netherlands', PhD thesis Delft University of Technology, Netherlands.

Ogden, J.M., R.H. Williams and E.L. Larson (2001) *Toward a Hydrogen-Based Transportation System* (Princeton, NJ: Princeton University Press).

Pembina Institute (2002) 'Life-cycle value assessment (LCVA) of fuel supply options for fuel cell vehicles in Canada', www.pembina.org/publications_search_newsitem.asp?id=131&section=.

Raaij, W.F., G. van Antonides, V. van Oppedijk and J.P.L. Schoormans (1999) *Product en Consument* [*Product and Consumer*] (Utrecht, Netherlands: LEMMA Publishers).

Raskin, P. (2002) *Great Transition: The Promise and Lure of the Time Ahead* (Boston, MA: Tellus Institute).

Rotmans, J., R. Kemp and M. van Asselt (2001) 'More Evolution than Revolution: Transition Management in Public Policy', *Foresight* 3: 15-31.

Suurs, R., M. Hekkert, M. Meeus and E. Nieuwlaar (2003) 'An actor-oriented approach for assessing transition trajectories towards a sustainable energy system', paper presented at *Advances in the Economic and Social Analysis of Technology' (ASEAT) Conference, 'Knowledge and Economic and Social Change: New Challenges to Innovation Studies'*, organised by ASEAT and the Institute of Innovation Research, Manchester, UK, 7–9 April 2003, les1.man.ac.uk/cric/2003conf/programme.htm.

Truffer, B. (2003) 'User led innovation processes: the development of professional car-sharing by environmentally concerned citizens', *Innovation: The European Journal of Social Science Research* 16.2: 139-54.

Van den Bosch, S. (2003) *Consumer Acceptance of a Hydrogen Fuel Cell System: A Case Study on the Introduction of Hydrogen Fuel Cell Buses in Amsterdam* (Delft, Netherlands: Delft University of Technology, Industrial Design Engineering, April 2003, unpublished).

Van den Hoed, R., and P.J. Vergragt (2004) 'Technological shifts and industry reaction: shifts in fuel preference for the fuel cell vehicle in the automotive industry', in K. Green, M. Miozzo and P. Dewick (eds.), *Technology, Knowledge and the Firm: Implications for Strategy and Industrial Change* (Cheltenham, UK: Edward Elgar): 126-51.

Vergragt, P.J., and G. van Grootveld (1994) 'Sustainable technology development in the Netherlands: the first phase of the Dutch STD program', *Journal of Cleaner Production* 2.3–4: 13,339.

—— and D. van Noort (1996) 'Sustainable technology development: the mobile hydrogen fuel cell', *Business Strategy and the Environment* 5: 16,877.

—— and K. Green (2001) 'The SusHouse methodology: design orienting scenarios for sustainable solutions', *Journal of Design Research* 1.2.

Weaver, P., L. Jansen, G. van Grootveld, E. van Spiegel and P. Vergragt (2000) *Sustainable Technology Development* (Sheffield, UK: Greenleaf Publishing).

Weiss, M.A., J.B. Heywood, A. Schaefer, E. Drake and F.F. Au Yeung (2000) *On the Road in 2020: A Life-Cycle Analysis of New Automobile Technologies* (Cambridge, MA: MIT Press).

——, J.B. Heywood, A. Schaefer and V. Natarajan (2003) *Comparative Assessment of Fuel Cell Cars* (Cambridge, MA: MIT Press).

3
Future imperfect
THE ENDURING STRUGGLE FOR ELECTRIC VEHICLES

Renato Orsato

INSEAD, Fontainebleau, France

During the last quarter of the 20th century, developments in engine technology and cleaner fuels have significantly reduced emissions of pollutants from cars powered by the internal combustion engine (ICE) (Nieuwenhuis and Wells 2003). Such advances have not, however, reduced the pressure on vehicle manufacturers to design progressively cleaner cars. As petrol is expected to cost substantially more in coming years, vehicle manufacturers are likely to be under continuous pressure as overall world oil production decreases. In other words, no matter what level of air emission reductions vehicle manufacturers have achieved, they will always be under pressure to reach zero emissions (Peake 1997).

Interestingly, an alternative to the ICE has been known since the very invention of the automobile, more than a 100 years ago. The electric car, which lost its battle against gasoline-powered vehicles at the beginning of the 20th century (Yergin 1992), has long been considered a viable solution for urban personal transportation (Cronk 1995; Renner 1988). The lowest level of vehicle air emissions is achieved with electric powertrains using electricity generated from hydroelectric or other renewable sources of energy.[1] Hence, by commercialising electric vehicles (EVs)[2] vehicle manufacturers would satisfy

---

1   For instance, in the US, gasoline engines generate a total of 222–282 g/km carbon dioxide equivalent of greenhouse gas emissions, while the range of a compressed natural gas (CNG) engine is 164–253. An electric motor using a hydro/renewable source of electricity will emit only 44–48 g/km carbon dioxide equivalent.

2   The concept of EV used in this chapter is that of 'pure' or 'battery' vehicles (BEVs). Unlike hybrid vehicles, these do not use inboard engines such as small ICEs or fuel cells to supply electricity to the electric motors or the batteries.

the strictest regulatory requirements on air emissions while simultaneously fulfilling consumers' needs for private transport in urban areas.

Indeed, several experts (see, for example, Elzen *et al.*; Sperling 1995; Cronk 1995) erroneously predicted that by the year 2000 a substantial number of EVs would be on the roads. Why, then, do EVs continue to be 'marginal' products in the portfolio of traditional car manufacturers? Why have new entrants not succeeded in commercialising EVs (that is, to produce them in high volumes)? What explains the marginal market presence of this type of vehicle on our roads?

An unsophisticated answer to such questions would anchor its arguments in the technical performance of EVs, which currently are the only commercially available zero-emission vehicles (ZEVs). Automotive experts and autoindustrialists have time and again claimed that EV technology is not yet sufficiently developed and, therefore, is not an economically viable alternative to the petrol-powered car (see Atkin and Storey 1998). More sophisticated answers can be found in studies based on evolutionary and quasi-evolutionary economics, and in constructivist sociology.[3] According to these perspectives, the relative absence of EVs on the roads relates to the 'lock-in' situation created around ICE technology (Kemp 1994; Schot *et al.* 1994). A self-reinforcing system of rules and beliefs embedded in design and engineering practices has been created around the sociotechnical context of the modern automobile, characterising what Nelson and Winter (1977) called a *technological regime*. Generically, these two set of answers—the intrinsic technological advantage of ICE cars and the degree to which they are embedded in a broad technological regime—represent the scope of possible explanations for the (relative) market failure of EVs.

This chapter explores answers that are neither too technical nor too theoretical. It focuses on the rationale for and against EVs, as well as the 'subtleties' of the discussion. In other words, it uncovers some 'myths and realities' that foster and/or hinder the mass commercialisation of EVs.[4]

Myth and reality about battery electric vehicles

If EVs are technologically inferior to vehicles powered by the ICE, why has there been an enduring interest in developing markets for them? To pose this question is to challenge those who use essentially technical (or 'technocentric') arguments to justify the dominance of cars powered by petrol engines. Technological dominance by the ICE should, in theory, retard interest in electric powertrains. But historical evidence shows that, although interest in EVs has always been subject to cycles, it has never faded away totally (Cronk 1995). Today, interest seems to be on the rise once more but some autoindustrialists and experts believe that this is a cycle similar to the previous ones, and the technological superiority of the ICE car will once again prevail, as has always been the case. Considering this an ongoing debate, the following sections will briefly

---

3   An overview and comparison of these fields can be found in Schot 1992; see also Schot *et al.* 1994.
4   The chapter is based on an extensive study of BEV trials in France and Norway, developed by the author (see Orsato 2001).

uncover the main reasons for both the enduring interest in, and discredit attributed to, EVs.

Technological superiority of the ICE

One explanation for the enduring interest in EVs addresses a fundamental flaw in the argument that justifies the technological superiority of ICE cars. Basically, the high energy content of hydrocarbon-based fuels, rather than the overall efficiency of the ICE car, is responsible for its advantage when compared with EVs (Lovins and Lovins 1995). In other words, the technological advantage of petrol-powered cars is located in the qualities of the fuel, rather than in the technology embedded in the vehicle per se. Indeed, the energy content and qualities of hydrocarbons are so remarkable that it is almost impossible to imagine modern technological development without fossil fuels (Fleay 1995). The keyboard used to type these words represents just one among hundreds of thousands of products which have petrochemicals as constituents. Given that hydrocarbons are so important to modern industrial society the justification for burning them may become increasingly difficult, not on the basis of the environmental impacts of combustion processes but because burning hydrocarbons may not make economic sense (Campbell and Laherrère 1998).

The energy content of petrol allowed the automobile industry to produce car bodies weighing 20 or more times the driver's weight (a significantly low ratio when compared with a bicycle, for example) and yet remain economically viable (Hawken *et al.* 1999). Although the vast majority of the fuel burned by ICE cars serves to transport the vehicle's mass rather than the driver's mass, the high energy content of fossil fuels nevertheless allowed a relatively energy-inefficient product to dominate the market. Hence, while the automobile industry is a mature economic sector, current ICE cars are certainly not ecologically mature products. In terms of environmental performance, a lightweight EV, for instance, outperforms a conventional automobile in almost every regard, from production of waste during manufacture through to energy demand during production and use, as well as having better durability, lower maintenance and higher rates of recycling of car parts (Whitelegg 1993).

The motoring myth

Lightweight EVs may present environmental advantages but motorists simply do not seem to be interested in them. Among the multitude of benefits attributed to cars, (high) speed and fuel autonomy appear to be the more important motoring variables for car users. Freund and Martin (1993) link such preferences with 'the ideology of the automobile', in which individual freedom has been associated with the speed and mobility that cars provide. Indeed, the glamour and challenge presented by motor racing certainly encompasses the importance of such variables for automobile enthusiasts. Environmentally sound vehicles, such as lightweight EVs, tend to be slow to drive and to recharge. The relative low energy storage capacity of commercially available batteries means that, if ranges greater than 100 km are to be achieved without recharging, cumbersome quantities of batteries need to be carried. Hence, these two sets of automobile performance—environmental and motoring—have been in opposition throughout the history of the automobile and thus, possibly, justify the reluctance of vehicle manufacturers to commit to EV technology.

Traditionally, sports cars have been the only area of market success for two-seater cars. Roadsters, such as the BMW Z3, Mercedes-Benz SLK 230 and Porsche Boxster suggest that preferences for two-seater cars have little to do with environmental concerns, even if some vehicles present low emissions, as is the case with the Lotus Elise.[5] These market successes represent a specialised niche preference associated with velocity and freedom. The case of the Smart car, a two-seater launched by Mercedes in 1997, demonstrates that consumers have not responded so well to cars whose appeal is premised on their environmental friendliness (Ostle 1999a). In the case of Smart, it was only when the marketing strategy refocused on its appeal as 'fun-to-drive' and its high-technology equipment, such as racing-car-style soft-tip gearshifts and the design of interior parts, that consumers started to respond. In fact, the continued survival of the Smart car seems to depend on a 'traditional' roadster, launched in 2003, which competes with other sports cars (Ostle 1999b). In this case, the Smart brand slowly moved its competitive focus from environmental prerogatives to the motoring appeal of fun-to-drive.

The dominance of MPVs

The basic characteristics of the modern automobile—the all-steel car body and ICE-based powertrain—influenced the definition of a feature of car design that is certainly detrimental to the mass commercialisation of EVs. Today, three market segments (denominated core segments) account for approximately 70% of total sales of automobiles in Europe. Although the other 30% comprise niche-market vehicles, such as four-wheel drive, luxury and sports vehicles, most of these cars can be classified as multi-purpose vehicles (MPVs).[6] Basically, these cars can carry one to five passengers, reach speeds of more than 220 km/h and have sufficient fuel capacity for approximately 400 km. This technical possibility contrasts with a less permissive traffic reality. With rare exceptions (such as Germany), the legal limit in most countries is never greater than 130 km/h and the average traffic speed is approximately 70 km/h.

Most trips do not demand such performance but the vast majority of cars currently available in the market present these characteristics. The average drive in cities (the place where most cars spend the largest part of their time) requires less than 20% of such performance, and the average occupancy is also much lower than the capacity of these cars to comfortably accommodate five people (Gibbs 1997). Thus, one could question the reasons for consumers to keep buying over-dimensioned and over-specified cars. Simply, what could explain the success of the MPV? If a smaller (electric or otherwise) car with substantially reduced performance (presumably costing less than a MPV) could potentially satisfy the needs of most motorists, why do they continue paying relatively more for larger cars?

---

5   163 g/km of carbon dioxide.
6   The concept used here differs from the one referring to MPV eventually used in classifications of market segmentation to denominate a specific market niche.

From the consumers' perspective, the answer is quite simple: cost and convenience. After all, who wants to pay twice as much for a car that takes eight hours to refuel? In simple terms, contemporary battery technology is responsible for a high price with a compromised performance. Faced with the choice, one should not be surprised that consumers opt for conventional cars.

From the manufacturers' perspective, the preference for MPVs, and the consequent (and relative) market failure of EVs, is based on clear techno-economic rationale. Technological options in systems of production impose high break-even points for car manufacturing and, consequently, denote that there are large economies of scale to be achieved in the automotive industry in general. Having cars with similar dimensions increases the chances of auto-makers achieving economies of scale. For instance, manufacturing cars to fit only two people, although apparently simple, requires a substantially new approach to car design and material use. Lightweight vehicles entail a shift from the all-steel car body to materials that may require a new set of safety technologies; such a move would inevitably incur additional costs for car-makers. Significantly smaller ICE engines, or other sources of propulsion, could power smaller cars. Developing such powertrains, besides representing increased costs, may constitute a risky strategy for the industry as the consumer must be willing to buy such cars. Hence, for most car-makers, manufacturing MPVs simply makes better business sense than ecologically preferable alternatives.

The structure of the after-sales market also influences people's choices in buying MPVs. For most consumers, the relatively high economic value of vehicles transforms them into major sources of investment. Generically, average cars are easier to commercialise than those designed for specific market niches. In these circumstances, a second-hand two-seater could expect to attract only a very select number of buyers. By contrast, a car such as the Volkswagen Beetle has a high commercial value in many countries, mainly because of its potential to be traded further.

A niche for neighbourhood EVs?

The inferior motoring performance of EVs may not satisfy a great number of consumers, but EV enthusiasts believe that this should not hinder the development of markets for this type of vehicle. One of the reasons for the continuing effort to transform EVs into a commercial reality is based on the assumption that drivers do not always require the equivalent performance of petrol-powered cars for every journey they make, and that current levels of performance of EVs make them suitable for specialised applications. Small lightweight EVs, described by Sperling (1995), among others, as neighbourhood electric vehicles (NEVs), could be used to perform short local trips. In such applications, the majority of potential users are expected to use the EV for journeys that do not require equivalent performance to ICE cars (Orsato 2001). In addition to those consumers willing to buy NEVs, fleets of these EVs could be bought by municipalities and offered as individual–public commuting vehicles.

Although market niches for EVs may motivate some (small) new entrants in the automotive industry, it is possible that the uncertain potential of these niches contributes to the reluctance of high-volume manufacturers to invest in EV technology. After all, during the greater part of their history vehicle manufacturers have been busy commercialising high volumes of petrol-powered cars that (apparently) satisfied consumer preferences. It was only in the last quarter of the 20th century that vehicle manufacturers started to face pressure to reduce the environmental impacts of their products. However, these pressures have increased to such an extent in the past few decades that the environmental advantages associated with EV technology have started to be reconsidered by the industry. During the past three decades some vehicle manufacturers have invested considerable resources to make EVs a commercial reality.

Fuel independence: everybody's dream

One rationale for investing in EVs relates to the expectation that an eventual breakthrough in battery technology will not only solve the problem of automobile emissions but will also help the sector reduce its dependency on oil—a recognised weakness for the long-term survival of the business. Moreover, R&D efforts that eventually result in a significant improvement in the overall performance of batteries could represent a 'first-mover advantage' for the companies involved in such projects. Improved performance of batteries could reduce the cost per unit, facilitate manufacturers to explore economies of scale and make batteries more competitive in relation to ICE technology. In other words, a self-reinforcing system could be created around EV technology, similar to the one that has historically favoured ICE.

Will hybrid vehicles make the EV enterprise obsolete?

Some experts assert that it is unrealistic to expect that hybrid vehicles will make EVs obsolete. Sperling (1995) argues that the cost reductions resulting from improved performance of batteries and their mass production will never bring the price of 'pure' or 'battery' electric vehicles (BEVs) down to that of petrol-powered cars. Nonetheless, the author of this chapter believes that the higher initial purchase price of EVs can be mitigated throughout the full life-cycle of the vehicle. Hawken *et al.* (1999) and Atkin and Storey (1998), on the other hand, have a more pessimistic view for the future of BEVs. In their opinion, the intrinsic weaknesses of pure EVs (mainly resulting from limitations in battery storage capacity) are extremely difficult to overcome, with the only viable solution being the mass production of environmentally sound vehicles based on hybrid technology.

Amory Lovins, the main proponent of this technological option, believes that the fate of the automotive industry will be determined by those manufacturers capable of offering vehicles based on the concept of the *hypercar*—lightweight vehicles with bodies made of advanced polymers and powered by fuel-cell electric powertrains (Baukus Mello 2000). Whether the defenders of the hybrid technology are right or not—and what kind of technology will power automobiles in the first decades of the new millennium—constitutes the debate around the solutions for automotive emissions in the long term: in this case, 2030 onwards. The future of powertrain technology is open to speculation. But if it is impossible to forecast the 'winner' of this technology race, there are already clear indications of what will constitute its core elements.

EVs as a learning technology

BEVs may deserve some of the criticisms attributed to them, such as low speed and limited range, but the technology they encompass has been recognised as central to the direction the automotive industry will need to take in the coming decades. As Nieuwenhuis (1998) has signalled, all long-term alternatives for the ICE car currently under consideration—BEVs and vehicles combining ICEs or fuel cells with electric powertrains (hybrid EVs)—involve electric traction. The debate centres on where and how the electricity that will power electric motors will be generated and stored, rather than whether electric motors will be used in powertrains of future cars. Viewed from this perspective, developments in the field of EVs assume strategic importance.

According to Nieuwenhuis and Wells (1997: 97), with today's technology, EVs not only represent the cleanest available technology for automobile powertains, they also constitute the means by which the current industry paradigm could undergo radical changes:

> A wholesale move towards electric traction would render existing engine production systems obsolete. In addition, it would have the strongest impact on the future of car body and chassis design; in particular, a switch to electric traction exposes the problems of overall vehicle weight, which are currently obscured by the power delivered by internal combustion engines . . . Any move to increase the number of electric vehicles is likely to have a greater impact on the basic design of the motorcar than most of the other alternatives that are likely to be available over the next few decades. A significant move towards electric vehicles . . . has serious implications for our existing transport infrastructure as well as for the design of cars themselves.

The above identifies an underlying rationale for auto-makers to invest in EV technology. Rather than a market niche of small cars that take many hours to refuel, EV knowledge is central to all longer-term alternatives under consideration by existing auto-makers and new entrants (i.e. BEVs or hybrid powertrains combining ICE or fuel cells with electric motors) (Nieuwenhuis 1998).

Do new entrants have a chance?

The final question that needs to be addressed here relates to the role of potential new entrants in the automobile industry. If car manufactures were unable to succeed with their converted vehicles why, then, have new entrants to the sector not fulfilled such a market niche? Besides the general conditions necessary for the use of such vehicles, the main problem they face is the high purchase price of EVs. While traditional car-makers have been unwilling to adopt a completely new concept of the car body, new entrants face significant technological, economic and political limitations to develop, manufacture and commercialise their products. The overall conditions within the industry require resources that are not so easy to acquire or maintain. As a result, the niche market for EVs remains dormant.

Final considerations

This chapter has addressed questions that are often treated as having 'obvious' answers:

- Why do EVs continue to be marginal products in the portfolio of traditional vehicle manufacturers?

- Why has the opportunity to commercialise EVs (that is, to produce them in high volumes) not been explored by new entrants?

- What explains the marginal market presence of this type of vehicle on roads worldwide?

Fundamentally, the chapter intended to answer these questions by uncovering problem areas associated with the EV technology, as well as socioeconomic obstacles. Such problem areas may not be new to experts in the field or, indeed, to a substantial number of interested lay persons. Factors limiting the use of EVs have long been identified (see, for example, Schot et al. 1994), and a significant number of non-experts have a fairly good idea about these limitations, such as the lack of infrastructure for recharging and the relatively high price of EVs. Nonetheless, many of the points addressed here are not often spelled out during debates (academic or otherwise) about the enduring failure to achieve the mass commercialisation of EVs. By exploring these rather marginalised rationales, the chapter aims to contribute to a better understanding of the problem, as well as help those interested in overcoming the barriers for the mass commercialisation of these types of vehicles.

Overall, the arguments emphasise that existing battery technology makes it extremely difficult for EVs to compete with conventional cars in similar applications. Quite simply, battery technology limits EVs to niche market applications. The mass commercialisation of EVs will therefore require an extensive range of factors to come together in favour of the technology. For instance, in 1970, the revival of EVs emerged as a consequence of the scarcity and increase in the price of petrol. Some may see today's resurgence of interest in EV technology as another 'wave of despair', and one that will certainly fade away once again. Fluctuations in the price of petrol caused by changes in the production targets of the Organisation of Petroleum Exporting Countries (OPEC) in the year 2000 recalled the oil shortages of 1973 and 1979–80 (Yergin 1992). Prices of oil during the last quarter of the 20th century behaved similarly to other commodities.[7] New technologies increased productivity and resulted in a steady fall in prices over the years. In trying to raise prices, OPEC reduced oil production and, as a result, prices jumped from €10 per barrel in March 1999 to €30 in September 2000. In the following years, the political turmoil caused by oil prices intensified with the invasion of Iraq in May 2002 (Economist 2003; Time 2000). By May 2006, the price of oil climbed to more than US$70 per barrel.

There is no doubt that such 'shocks' agitate politicians to reduce dependency on oil, but the current wave of environmentalism differs substantially from that of the 1970s.

---

7   After the second oil shock, during 1979–80, the price of oil fell from around US$68 to US$13 a barrel (Economist 2003).

Ironically, the risk of scarcity of oil is not seen as the main factor influencing the development of more eco-efficient vehicles (Wells 1998). Rather, traffic-related problems have become a more important issue in promoting the use of low- and zero-emissions vehicles, mainly in urban municipalities in Europe. Public authorities have been under increasing pressure to reduce the dominance of the ICE automobile as a means of urban transport in city centres (Newman and Kenworthy 1999). Although the difficulties associated with the introduction of EVs are very much still in place, public opinion is apparently shifting in favour of policies encouraging the exclusive use of EVs in congested urban centres.

Finally, it should be clear that this chapter does not intend to 'defend' EVs, but rather to explain why their presence in the marketplace has, so far, been marginal. The convergence of interest on the part of the energy utilities to sell dormant electric capacity, the demand for new jobs in EV-related businesses and increasing demands for more environmentally sound automobiles appear to be giving EV technologies a new competitive edge (Atkin and Storey 1998). Even if it is not possible to foresee their future significance, the identification and analysis of such technologies should help to pinpoint the most probable sources of innovation and resistance that are likely to occur.

References

Atkin, G., and J. Storey (1998) *Electric Vehicles: Prospects for Battery, Fuel Cell and Hybrid Powered Vehicles* (London: Financial Times Business Ltd).

Baukus Mello, T. (2000) 'Turning inside out', *Automotive World*, July/August 2000: 39-41.

Campbell, C.J., and J.H. Laherrère (1998) 'The end of cheap oil', *Scientific American* 278.3: 60-65.

Cronk, S.A. (1995) *Building the E-Motive Industry: Essays and Conversations about Strategies for Creating an Electric Vehicle Industry* (Washington, DC: Society of Automotive Engineers Inc.).

Economist (2003) 'Still holding customers over a barrel', *The Economist*, 25 October 2003: 71-73.

Elzen, B., R. Hoogma and J. Schot (1995) 'Optimising development and use of electric vehicles from an environmental perspective', paper presented at *EVT '95 Conference*, Paris, November 1995.

Fleay, B.J. (1995) *The Decline of the Age of Oil* (Sydney: Pluto Press).

Freund, P., and G. Martin (1993) *The Ecology of the Automobile* (Toronto: Black Rose Books).

Gibbs, W.W. (1997) 'Transportation's perennial problems', *Scientific American* 277.4: 32-35.

Hawken, P., A.B. Lovins and L.H. Lovins (1999) *Natural Capitalism: The Next Industrial Revolution* (London: Earthscan).

Kemp, R. (1994) 'Technology and the transition to environmental sustainability', *Futures* 26.10: 1,023-46.

Lovins, A.B., and L.H. Lovins (1995) 'Reinventing the wheels', in S.A. Cronk, (ed.), *Building the E-Motive Industry: Essays and Conversations about Strategies for Creating an Electric Vehicle Industry* (Washington, DC: Society of Automotive Engineers Inc.): 16-29.

Nelson, R.R., and S.G. Winter (1977) 'In search of useful theory of innovation', *Research Policy* 6: 36-76.

Newman, P., and K. Kenworthy (1999) *Sustainability and Cities: Overcoming Automobile Dependence* (Washington, DC: Island Press).

Nieuwenhuis, P. (1998) 'Developments in alternative powertrains', in P. Wells (ed.), *Automotive Materials: The Challenge of Globalisation and Technological Change* (London: Financial Times Automotive): ch. 9.

—— and P. Wells (1997) *The Death of Motoring? Car Making and Automobility in the 21st Century* (Chichester, UK: John Wiley).

—— and —— (2003) *The Automotive Industry and the Environment: A Technical, Business and Social Future* (Cambridge, UK: Woodhead).

Orsato, R.J. (2001) 'The ecological modernisation of industry: developing multi-disciplinary research on organisation and environment', PhD thesis, University of Technology Sydney, Australia.

Ostle, D. (1999a) 'How Smart is fighting back', *Automotive News Europe*, 12 April 1999: 3-18.

—— (1999b) 'Smart set for remarkable recovery with roadster and PSA platform deal', *Automotive News Europe*, 16 August 1999: 1.

Peake, S. (1997) *Vehicle and Fuel Challenges beyond 2000: Market Impacts of the EU's Auto Oil Programme* (London: Financial Times Automotive Publishing).

Renner, M. (1988) 'Rethinking the role of the automobile', *Worldwatch Paper 84* (Washington, DC: Worldwatch Institute).

Schot, J.W. (1992) 'Constructive technology assessment and technology dynamics: the case of the clean technologies', *Science, Technology and Human Values* 17.1: 36-56.

——, R. Hoogma and B. Elzen (1994) 'Strategies for shifting technological systems: the case of the automobile system', *Futures* 26.10: 1,060-76.

Sperling, D. (1995) *Future Drive: Electric Vehicles and Sustainable Transportation* (Washington, DC: Island Press).

Time (2000) 'The energy crunch', *Time*, 18 September 2000: 37-41.

Yergin, D. (1992) *The Prize* (New York: Touchstone Books).

Wells, P. (1998) *Automotive Materials: The Challenge of Globalisation and Technological Change* (London: Financial Times Automotive Publishing).

Whitelegg, J. (1993) *Transport for a Sustainable Future: The Case for Europe* (London: Belhaven).

4
Competing technologies and the struggle towards a new dominant design
THE EMERGENCE OF THE HYBRID VEHICLE AT THE EXPENSE OF THE FUEL–CELL VEHICLE?

Marko Hekkert
Utrecht University, The Netherlands

Robert van den Hoed
Delft University of Technology, The Netherlands

Once in a while, a radical breakthrough technology emerges that has a devastating impact on established industries. In comparison to existing technologies, such disruptive innovations deliver a dramatic leap in performance, and incumbent firms tend to respond either by ignoring the new technology or by trying to improve the performance of the established technology (the so-called **sailing ship effect**); as a result, they often perish (Christensen 1997; Utterback 1994). Established industry's reaction to the emergence of possible disruptive technologies is an intensively studied phenomenon in innovation studies (Tushman and Anderson 1986; Henderson and Clark 1990). Due to the unexpected nature of these events, they are often studied *ex post*.

While disruptive and radical technologies are highly imaginative, most technological progress has been made through incremental improvements in the available technology, products and processes (see, for example, Neij 1997). This difference is clearly demonstrated in the recent debates on transitions to more sustainable sociotechnical systems (Geels 2002; Kemp 1994; Schot *et al.* 1994). Although there is consensus over the fact that a transition to a more sustainable system of production and consumption needs to take place, there is no agreement on the role of radical break-through technologies in such a transition. Some consider that breakthrough technologies are necessary in order to reach a desired **final state** (e.g. Kemp 1994) while others stress the difficulties of such a transition and plead for more incremental routes.

Current technological developments in the personal transport system offer an excellent opportunity to compare these two strategies. Where environmental regulations require car-makers increasingly to look for technological alternatives, two major technological routes are currently proposed by the industry. The breakthrough route revolves around the fuel-cell vehicle (FCV), a radically new technology with zero emissions, high efficiency and independence from fossil fuels. The incremental route features the hybrid electrical vehicle (HEV) which is significantly more efficient and has much lower emission levels than conventional internal combustion engine (ICE) vehicles.[1]

Previously positioned as an intermediary staging post on the road to new technologies (such as FCVs), the HEV has always played a modest role in sustainable mobility. However, good environmental performance and recent commercial success are changing people's perspectives of HEV technology, to the extent that the HEV might, in fact, form a competitive threat to FCVs.

In this chapter we focus on the increased competition between these two automotive technology concepts. Based on a comparison of both technologies we will evaluate their chances of becoming the new dominant design. We will conclude by discussing the effect of these potential developments on the life chances of the competing technology.

Theory on competing technologies and transitions

The issues of competing technologies, technology substitution and dominant design are central topics in theories of **technology dynamics** and **technological forecasting**.

Technology dynamics theory frames competing technologies as a variation and selection process (Nelson and Winter 1982). In **variation processes**, many alternatives are developed by the technical community as an alternative to the current dominant design. In **selection processes**, through a series of smaller and larger choices by relevant stakeholders, one technology is selected and this then becomes the dominant design (Anderson and Tushman 1990). Anderson and Tushman (1990) indicate that the process towards a new dominant design can be divided into several stages. After the creation of a technological discontinuity (variation) a **stage of ferment** exists in which the new technology is in competition with the old one. During this period, **competition selection** takes place and the new technology becomes the **dominant design**. Then, an era of incremental change occurs in which the focus is on incremental improvements to the new dominant design. Based on this model, FCV and HEV can be

---

1 In FCVs, electricity is produced in a fuel cell, preferably fuelled by hydrogen. The HEV has a 'normal' ICE and, additionally, an electric motor: this combination makes the car more efficient.

characterised as **technological discontinuities**.[2] The HEV has already entered the stage of ferment, but the FCV has not yet done so. At this point it is unclear whether the FCV will ever actually enter the stage of ferment.

Both the variation and selection processes take place within a so-called **innovation system**. This is defined as the matrix of economic, social, political, organisational and other factors that influence the development, diffusion and use of innovations (Edquist and Johnson 1997). Innovation systems are often studied by taking a country as a unit of analysis. These studies take as their starting point the assumption that differences in the national system of innovation (NIS) influence the technology choices made by individual firms (Lundvall *et al.* 1992; Nelson and Winter 1982). For our purposes, it is more suitable to use the concept of **technological systems**. Also called **technology-specific innovation systems** (Jacobsson and Johnson 2000), these are systems built around a specific technology or product. The technology-specific nature of this model implies that there are many such systems under development at any one time. Each of these systems is unique in its ability to develop and utilise new technology. Where the focus is on competition between various technologies, this approach is much more suitable than the NIS model (Johnson 2001).

A technological system is formally defined as a 'network of agents interacting in a specific economic/industrial area under a particular institutional infrastructure for the purpose of generating, diffusing and utilising technology' (Carlsson and Stankiewicz 1995: 111).

Determining whether or not a new automotive technology stands a chance of becoming the new dominant design thus requires an analysis of the technological system in which competing technologies, such as ICE, HEV and FCV are developed and selected. Formally, a technological system is made up of organisations and institutions, and the interrelationships between them (Edquist 2001). Organisations can be seen as the players or actors in a system while institutions represent the rules (see Fig. 4.1).

Using this model, we will analyse the technological system around automotive technology in terms of the main actors and the common habits, regimes, rules or laws that regulate the relationships within the system. The relations between the actors themselves and between actors and institutions will be included in our analysis. Any consideration of competition between technologies also needs a thorough analysis of the technologies themselves. Therefore, our analysis will focus on:

- **Automotive industry:** to what extent do vested interests and organisational barriers support technological alternatives?

- **Oil industry/infrastructure:** to what extent do technological alternatives fit with the current infrastructure?

- **Institutional environment:** to what extent do regulations support the alternative technologies?

---

2   Note that the ICE vehicle fuelled by hydrogen or bio-diesel is a variation on the current dominant design. Note also that the electric vehicle is currently no longer considered by the automotive industry due to lack of commercial potential (van den Hoed and Vergragt 2003), which reflects an *ex post* selection process.

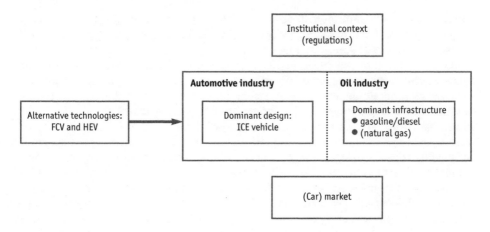

FIGURE 4.1 Technological system around the ICE vehicle and competing alternative
        technologies

- **Environmental performance:** to what extent do the alternatives compete with the current dominant design?
- **Market performance:** how does the market value the alternative technologies?

In the following sections, FCV and HEV technologies will be analysed in the context of these five factors in order to determine which is the most eligible to become the dominant design, and also to identify the key barriers to the overthrow of the current dominant ICE technology.

HEVs and FCVs in the technical system

In the following sections we will describe how well HEVs and FCVs fit with the actors and regulations in the automotive technological system.

HEVs and FCVs in relation to ICE and the fuel infrastructure

The current technological system for transport is based on the ICE and a gasoline/diesel fuel infrastructure. The introduction of the HEV and the FCV may require changes both at the level of the car and at the level of fuel infrastructure. For both car and infrastructure we discern two dimensions of change associated with the innovation: **technical novelty** and **organisational complexity** (requiring network change). The first dimension is defined as the extent to which the skills and expertise of organisations need to be adjusted to apply the novel technology. An example of such a change is a switch by a manufacturer from producing steel parts to plastic parts. Such a switch either requires hiring new personnel with prior experience or training, or it requires considerable retraining of the existing workforce. The second dimension concerns changes to the structure of the production and implementation network. For example, a shift from combustion-powered vehicles to battery electric vehicles (BEVs) requires changes in fuel supply and repair facilities, in addition to new engine components. Organisations not involved in the existing system will often provide such supporting facilities.

We use several concepts from the literature on innovation to indicate the level of change in these two dimensions: incremental; radical; modular; and system innovations (Henderson and Clark 1990; Tushman and Anderson 1986). Incremental and radical innovations represent the dimension of technical complexity of new innovations (incremental = low complexity; radical = high complexity) while modular and systems innovations represent, respectively, small and large changes in social networks. The two dimensions of change usually combine both technical and network dimensions. This can be seen in Figure 4.2 where technological change is depicted on the incremental–radical dimension and socioeconomic change on the modular–system dimension. The circle sizes indicate carbon emission reduction estimates relative to the gasoline–ICE fuel chain.

The four types of innovations can be placed in the two dimensional space framed by the technological complexity of the innovation and the necessary network change (Goverse *et al.* 2001). Figure 4.2 shows how alternative automotive concepts are placed in relation to conventional ICE vehicles.

The dominant ICE technology is situated at the reference case position in Figure 4.2. In the case of HEV, a battery is added to the conventional powertrain to store energy generated by the heat engine and recovered from braking; this allows buffer power to be used for acceleration and allows zero-emission running for brief periods. Its intro-

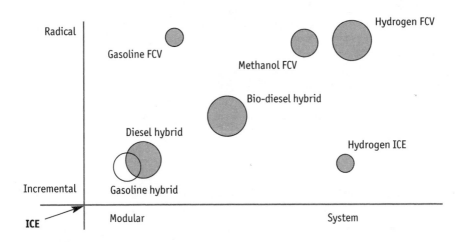

FIGURE 4.2 innovation characteristics of fuel chains

Source: Hekkert *et al.* 2005a

duction does not require changes in fuel supply since regular fuel can be the only energy input. This makes this innovation modular. Technically, this is an incremental innovation since the principles of the mechanical conventional powertrain remain the same in this vehicle, although the propulsion system is extended with an electrical drive.

Overall emissions of HEVs can be further improved by using bio-fuels. Production of bio-fuel requires a well-known, but totally different, fuel production method. The last stages of the fuel chain, distribution and end use, are the same as in the conventional ICE system. Therefore, this innovation is considered to have less systemic features than the other fuel–car systems in which the infrastructure is dramatically different from the current fuel infrastructure.

An alternative, where fuel supply remains unchanged, is the gasoline FCV. Here, the vehicle is the only component that changes. However, the gasoline FCV (in which new technologies are applied to convert gasoline into hydrogen to generate electricity for the electric motor) is technically a radical innovation. This radical innovation also implies that the vehicle's powertrain is fundamentally different, requiring completely new parts and maintenance. Furthermore, consumers will experience differences. Therefore, network changes will especially occur in the area of technology develop- ment and consumer information. In terms of network change, this innovation is regarded as being positioned between modular and system innovation.

The hydrogen FCV is placed in the upper-right corner of Figure 4.2, suggesting both technological and socioeconomic environment change. We have already argued that FCV is a radical innovation compared to ICE as the distribution and storage of hydrogen requires significant technical and infrastructure changes. Furthermore, more actors need to be involved in providing the necessary know-how for hydrogen distribution and fuelling.

The alternative option, to use methanol to fuel the FCV, is also situated in the upper- right corner. Although methanol, as a liquid, is easier to handle than hydrogen, a com- pletely new infrastructure would need to be developed requiring huge organisational change. Furthermore, on-board reforming of methanol is necessary to extract hydro- gen from it. Creating a small chemical factory within a car is a radical innovation com- pared to current ICE technology.

Figure 4.2 shows that FCVs with hydrogen fuel are in the upper-right corner and HEVs are in the lower-left corner. The latter is a much better place to be in terms of over- coming implementation barriers. The hybrid vehicle is compatible both with the cur- rent ICE system and the existing infrastructure, while the FCV requires changes both in car design and infrastructure. As a result, HEVs will experience far fewer barriers than FCVs.

Oil companies and the development of HEVs and FCVs

The oil companies are expected to play a decisive role in developing the vehicle of the future. As explained above, the relationship between vehicle design and energy infra- structure cannot be overlooked. The power of the oil companies in determining the fuel for FCVs is demonstrated by van den Hoed and Vergragt (2003). They explain that dif- ferent car manufacturers have different ideas regarding the ideal fuel for FCVs, ranging from methanol and hydrogen to regular gasoline. They argue that DaimlerChrysler had a significant technological advantage in methanol FCV development until 2000–2001, but lost its edge due to an oil industry 'boycott' of 'poisonous' methanol. Exxon has made the boldest statements about methanol not being the fuel of the future, and Shell has also tried to influence DaimlerChrysler to choose a fuel other than methanol (van den Hoed and Vergragt 2003).

The role of the oil companies is hard to predict since they show a strategic behaviour that anticipates different future fuel regimes. Suurs *et al.* (2004) have analysed the preferences of key actors for different fuel regimes. They quote statements from oil companies in which they state that they will sell any future fuel that society asks for (Suurs *et al.* 2004). The same research reveals that the oil companies see hydrogen as the fuel of the future but are more sceptical about its role in the short term. This fits with the variation strategy of Shell which involves the development of business initiatives focusing on both hydrogen and bio-fuels. Shell Hydrogen has been actively developing and installing a number of hydrogen filling stations in different countries.

It is worth noting that the resources devoted by the oil companies to alternative fuels are minuscule in comparison to fossil fuels. The reason for this is simple: even though oil companies anticipate a range of fuel regimes, their vested interests are embedded in gasoline. Any significant change in the fuel infrastructure would require massive investment and this acts as a huge incentive to keep the current fuel infrastructure intact. An example of this strategic behaviour is the development by Shell of an on-board fuel reformer to convert gasoline into hydrogen. The company claims that this option may very well be the ideal transition technology since it provides a means for FCVs to access the current fuel infrastructure. This has led to at least two joint development projects with DaimlerChrysler (Hekkert *et al.* 2005b). However, due to technical problems and the highly complex nature of the technology, Shell has not yet succeeded in convincing vehicle manufacturers that this is the ideal transition technology.

Conclusion

The vested interests of the oil companies are in gasoline, so their focus is on keeping the current infrastructure intact. However, the oil industry is starting to develop a portfolio of knowledge on alternative fuels that might make it more willing to change the infrastructure when there is sufficient pressure to do so. And it is clear that FCVs will also require large organisational changes from car-makers to develop the technology and create the fuel infrastructure.

Environmental performance of different vehicle technologies

Carbon emissions

The reason why FCV technology is considered so promising is hidden in the circles in Figure 4.2. The circles represent the reduction in carbon emissions per kilometre for the different options, based on Hekkert *et al.* (2005a). Thus, the hydrogen FCV shows a large emission reduction potential compared to the hydrogen ICE. However, the figure also clearly shows that HEVs also score well, especially when diesel is used as the fuel. And when diesel is partly replaced by bio-diesel carbon emissions come down even more. In terms of carbon emissions, Hekkert *et al.* (2005a) expect that the bio-diesel HEV very closely approaches the FCV. This is in line with the findings of Weiss *et al.* (2003). Thus, one of the main advantages of FCVs (i.e. their zero emissions) is undermined. Figure 4.2 also shows that adapting the hydrogen FCV to the gasoline FCV in order to overcome infrastructure barriers is not advantageous in terms of carbon emissions. This leaves the hydrogen FCV with just one advantage over HEVs in terms of emissions: it is a zero-emission vehicle (ZEV) under all circumstances while the diesel HEV is zero emission-only when the battery is used for driving.

Other advantages of electric drivetrains

Demand for additional auto features powered by electricity is likely to rise in the future. Examples of these are multimedia in-car entertainment devices, air conditioning to cool the car before the driver gets in and wireless communication with other cars. The FCV has the advantage of being a small power plant and this opens up numerous possibilities for additional features. However, the HEV also does well in terms of these new features since its battery capacity is extremely large compared to current ICE vehicles. Finally, additional small fuel cells can be added to any car exclusively to power these additional features.

Conclusion: environmental performance

The HEV scores better than the FCV in terms of technical and organisational implementation barriers. In terms of efficiency and providing support for additional car functions it can keep up with the FCV. But in terms of emissions the FCV scores much better than the HEV. This seems to be the most important advantage of the FCV. However, this applies only when the FCV is powered by hydrogen. All other FCV fuel combinations cannot compete with the HEV.

Institutional context for HEV and FCV

To what extent are FCVs and HEVs compatible with pressures originating from the institutional context? The following sections will discuss changes in regulatory regimes from 1990 to 2002, with particular focus on ZEV regulation in California.

ZEV regulation in historical perspective

The year 1990 marked an important shift in environmental regulations in the state of California with the passing of the ZEV regulation. In light of growing health problems caused by air pollution, the California Air Resources Board (CARB) decided to mandate sales of ZEVs. Large-volume manufacturers were obliged to bring 2% ZEVs to the market in the period 1998–2000 and 10% by 2003 (see Fig. 4.3). Intermediate-volume manufacturers were obliged to start bringing ZEVs to the market by 2003. The ZEV regulation entailed mandated sales of 60,000 ZEVs between 1998 and 2000 in California, and is expected to achieve 1.1 million ZEVs by 2010.

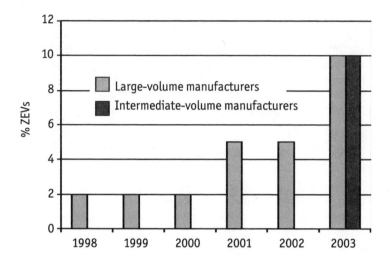

FIGURE 4.3 Original ZEV regulation

The ZEV programme stands out from previous emission controls by challenging the ICE paradigm. Given that, in 1990, battery electric vehicles (BEVs) were seen as the only viable zero-emission technology, the ZEV regulation became a major driver for the development of BEVs and other alternative technologies with zero-emission potential. Failure to comply with the regulation by manufacturers promised penalties of several thousand dollars per ZEV not sold. This proved a great incentive for ZEV development.

Over the years, ZEV standards have been postponed and watered down. In 1996, the pre-2003 ZEV obligations were skipped, although the 2003 requirement of 10% remained. An important argument in favour of omitting the early ZEV requirements related to the conclusions drawn by the Battery Panel—which was set up by the state of California to investigate the future potential of battery technology—that lead-acid batteries were not yet competitive while more promising technologies, such as nickel-metal-hydride (NiMH) batteries, required more development work.

By 1998, the 10% ZEV requirement had been watered down to 4% after fierce lobbying by vehicle manufacturers who argued that market opportunities for BEVs were low. A new category was proposed for the remaining 6%, the partial ZEV category (PZEV) (CARB 1998). Cars eligible for PZEV were required to reach the so-called SULEV (super-ultra-low-emission vehicle) standards, equivalent to what the emissions utilities produce for generating electricity for BEVs. The new category can be achieved by the most efficient HEVs.

In 2001, the ZEV regulation was changed again (CARB 2003), with the 4% ZEV requirement for 2003 reduced to 2%. For the remaining 2% another new category was introduced, the ZEV–AT (alternative technology). CARB's rationale for introducing a new category was to allow for the stimulation of new technologies which, although not necessarily achieving zero emissions, nevertheless offered strong advantages over ICE. The technologies eligible for the ZEV–AT category include HEVs, FCVs (methanol or gasoline) or natural gas vehicles. Thus, HEV and FCV technologies were further stimulated by CARB.

The last alteration made to the ZEV regulation occurred in 2003 (CARB 2004). The proposed amendments delayed the start of the ZEV requirements from the 2003 model year to the 2005 model year. An important element was a new mechanism allowing large-volume vehicle manufacturers to choose between the following two compliance paths in 2005 and subsequent model years:

1. A manufacturer is permitted to satisfy its ZEV obligations by meeting requirements similar to those in the ZEV regulation as amended in 2001 (2% 'gold' ZEV vehicles plus 2% 'silver' ZEV–AT and 6% 'bronze' PZEVs)

2. The manufacturer also has the option of electing a new alternative ZEV compliance path, by selling a number of FCVs by model year 2008 (the number is sales-dependent, but averages around 250 per vehicle manufacturer). This option relieves any ZEV obligations, but still requires the car-maker to sell a mix of 4% AT PZEVs and 6% PZEVs

Thus, by adding the second compliance path, the 2003 amendments provided further motivation for developing FCVs. Similarly, the HEV option remains an important route for achieving the ZEV obligations.

Carbon dioxide, energy efficiency, alternative fuels

Low- and zero-emission controls were the most demanding environmental requirements for the car industry in the 1990s. In recent years, however, issues around carbon dioxide emissions and energy efficiency have risen up the political agenda.

The 1992 Kyoto Protocol provided a key starting point, requiring governments to develop measures to curb greenhouse gas emissions at national level. In the EU this led, in 1995, to a collective voluntary agreement between the European, Korean and Japanese car industry to reduce carbon dioxide emissions by 25% in 2005 (in comparison to 1995 levels).[3] The standards are a major driver for car-makers to increase efficiency and develop new technologies. As a result, optimisation technologies for ICE vehicles have been developed (e.g. direct injection, common rail). HEV technology has also progressed, with the Toyota Prius accredited as the most efficient vehicle in its segment in 2001.

Furthermore, the 9/11 attack on the World Trade Center and the turmoil in the Middle East and Iraq has highlighted the dependence of the West (particularly the US) on oil and given the search for alternative fuels a new urgency. The quest for alternatives (for instance, natural gas- or ethanol-fuelled vehicles) was stimulated in the 1990s.

3   See europa.eu.int/comm/environment/co2/co2_home.htm.

However, in recent years, the **hydrogen vision** has generated so much momentum that the governments of Japan and the US, and those in Europe, have set up large hydrogen stimulation programmes. Indicative is the US$1.2 billion project set up by the Bush administration in 2002 under the significant name of FreedomCar. The programme entails a considerable push for hydrogen technology in transportation purposes. Unlike carbon dioxide emissions and energy efficiency, the unidirectional push to hydrogen is a strong supporting driver for FCV development; it does not, however, favour HEVs.

Conclusion: institutional context

Since 1990, the regulatory context, particularly in California, has stimulated the development of alternatives to the ICE vehicle. The emphasis has long been on zero emissions, providing a push for BEVs and FCVs, and limiting the potential for HEVs. Nevertheless, a shift can be discerned. The postponement and watering-down of zero-emission standards on the one hand, and the increased importance of energy efficiency and carbon dioxide emission reduction on the other, forms an increasingly favourable context for HEVs to co-exist alongside FCVs.

Market factors with respect to FCVs and HEVs

The costs of FCV technology are still hard to estimate given the limited data. Several studies have attempted to estimate costs, based on different assumptions leading to strongly varying results (van Dijkum 2003). This section looks at several studies on FCV stacks/systems costs.

Arthur D. Little (2000), under contract to the US Department of Energy (DOE), estimates that fuel-cell system costs are US$324/kW, assuming production volumes of 500,000 per annum for a 50 kW stack (total stack costs would thus be US$16,200). Similar values of US$195–325/kW (also assuming production volume of 500,000 units per annum) were found by Carlson *et al.* (2002). The Arthur D. Little research indicates that total fuel-cell system costs are dominated by stack costs, platinum loading and the material costs of the membrane electrode assembly (MEA). Costs for complementary components for cooling and pressurising the systems were minor. The study also estimates the cost of a reformer as around US$80/kW.

Another much cited study is that of Morisot (2002). This used real-time data of current fuel-cell costs (whereas the studies mentioned above used figures of projected material costs), but took volume production into account. The study concludes that total fuel-cell system costs can currently be estimated at around €8,100/kW, more than a factor of 20 higher than earlier studies: the fuel-cell stack being largely responsible for these costs (€5,320/kW) due to platinum and electrodes costs. Morisot (2002) makes a projection to 2005 and 2010 under assumptions concerning cost reductions of membranes (with Nafion assumed to be replaced by a different membrane altogether), electrodes and bipolar plates. Furthermore, a tenfold reduction in platinum loading in 2010 is assumed. As a result, cost estimates for a total fuel-cell system in 2010 is expected to be around €1,710/kW, still considerably higher than the other studies mentioned. Surprisingly, Morisot expects proton exchange membrane (PEM) fuel cell stacks to be €200/kW in 2010, but sees fewer opportunities to reduce costs for balance of plant, reformers and additional components (in total €1,510/kW). Also, Kalhammer *et al.* (1998) predict that balance of plant issues are underemphasised in current research and form big challenges for the FCV.

These figures give an indication of the costs of fuel-cell systems, being several hundreds of dollars per kW. In comparison, the current cost for an ICE system is US$25–35/kW: thus, fuel-cell technology faces enormous competitive challenges. An illustration of the costliness of FCV technology is demonstrated by the FCV prototypes delivered by Honda to the Japanese government in November 2002 and estimated at around US$1 million each. Nonetheless, FCVs have come a long way, with enormous cost reductions in the last decade, and further significant reductions expected in the future.

In contrast, the HEV has a relatively small price premium of 10–15% (based on sales prices). Although industry experts suspect that Toyota sold its HEV Prius at a loss in 1997–2000, in 2002 Toyota announced that it now made a modest profit.

With regard to drivability, the expectation is that the FCV will compete with ICE vehicles in the mid to long term (Kalhammer *et al.* 1998). Currently, the stacks are heavy, less energy-dense and the dynamic behaviour of the FCV still requires development (Hoogers 2003). Acceleration is a relatively strong asset due to a maximum torque available from 0 rpm. However, this comes at the price of a heavier motor. FCVs still require significant improvements to be competitive in performance, and it remains to be seen if they will succeed. HEVs, on the other hand, already compete on drivability with conventional cars.

Conclusions: market factors

Although difficult to predict the market value of the FCV, from a consumer point of view, the first signs do not seem favourable, particularly in terms of costs. HEVs, on the other hand, show considerable market success and are proving an increasingly robust competitor to ICE vehicles.

Overview of technological system indicators

Table 4.1 summarises the findings presented above. It shows that in terms of necessary technical change the FCV scores poorly. It can be considered as a radical technological change that needs much more development work to be competitive on the market. By contrast, the HEV has developed much further; it represents a less radical technological change and is already sold commercially. In terms of infrastructure change, the hydrogen FCV again scores very poorly. Building the hydrogen infrastructure will require massive effort and capital. The other FCV types (gasoline and methanol) are much more compatible with the current infrastructure but cannot be considered an alternative due to their poor emissions performance. The HEV is completely compatible with the current fuel infrastructure.

	Technical changes	Infrastructure changes	Regulation	Environmental performance	Market potential
FCV	– –	– – (hydrogen) + (gasoline) – (methanol)	++ → +	++ → + – → – – → –	?? → –
HEV	+ / ++	++	– → +	– → +/–	– → +

TABLE 4.1 Overview of factors influencing the viability of FCV and HEV over time

The ZEV regulation in California was a strong push for both HEV and FCV development. However, due to a postponement and relaxation of zero-emission targets, the influence of the regulatory environment on FCV development seems to be declining. The HEV, on the other hand, is likely to profit from this trend. Other types of regulation-based efficiency standards do not discriminate between FCV and HEV and therefore indirectly favour HEV due to its positive scores on the previous two criteria.

In terms of environmental performance, FCV has been seen as the best option for the future. However, recent studies have shown that in terms of efficiency and carbon emissions the FCV will have trouble competing with the HEV. The absence of non-carbon emissions is a very strong asset for the FCV. So the overall score on emissions is in favour of the FCV.

In terms of the market, expectations for the FCV are uncertain due to unknowable future costs. However, different car manufacturers claim that the costs are likely to stay very high for a long time. For HEVs, the market potential has improved considerably due to significant cost reductions and increases in profitability.

Industry activities in FCVs and HEVs

The above analysis, in which HEV is increasingly favoured over FCV, can also be observed in industrial activities. Based on patent analysis by automotive firms between 1990 and 2002, van den Hoed and Vergragt (see Chapter 5) came to the following conclusions. First, there was a rise and fall in BEV patents between 1990 and 2002, with a peak in 1996. Most BEVs were launched between 1996 and 1997, but the anticipation of a weak market led to a decline in patent activity and low R&D activity from 1996 on. Second, the data suggests a shift in research focus from BEV to both HEV and FCV after 1996. Patent activities of HEV and FCV accelerate around 1996–97 and, by 1998–99, they are acquiring more patents than BEVs. Third, HEVs receive increasingly more patents than FCVs, indicating their higher priority for car-makers. By 2000, nearly 50% of all alternative-fuel vehicle (AFV) patents were HEV-related, followed by approximately 35% for FCVs. Only 15% of all AFV patents were BEV-related.

The patent study illustrates how vehicle manufacturers have shifted attention from BEVs to HEVs and FCVs, and how HEVs and FCVs are competing for R&D funds at automotive research centres. By 2003, nearly all the major vehicle manufacturers had extensive FCV and HEV programmes. Where around 100 concept FCVs have been tested worldwide, HEVs are on sale and sell well. Initiated by Toyota and Honda, the market for HEVs exceeds 50,000 units and is rising rapidly, forming a formidable niche market. While large-scale commercial FCVs sales are not expected before 2008, HEVs have become a popular commercial alternative for achieving lower emissions and higher efficiency.

More importantly, a majority of vehicle manufacturers is currently involved in HEV development, thereby increasing the industry consensus that HEV has a future—possibly, even, as a dominant design rather than an intermediary step.

Conclusions

To understand the implications for the life chances of the FCV we fall back to lessons learned from innovation studies. We will discuss these implications in the context of **technological relative advantages** (Rogers 1984) and **technological trajectories** (Dosi 1982).

Rogers (1984) introduced the concept of relative advantages of one technology over the other as one of the factors that determine the chance of adoption. In other words: if a technology has large advantages over another, a customer is more likely to buy it. If the HEV becomes the new dominant design after ICE, the relative advantages (in terms of efficiency and emissions) of the FCV will be lower compared to the HEV than to ICE. This is likely to reduce the justification for large investments in technology development of the FCV.

Another important issue is the concept of technological trajectories. We have learned that a major transition from one technological system to another often takes place via so-called transition (or intermediate) technologies. These technologies form a bridge between the old regime and the new one. Some see the HEV as such a transition technology. However, this is questionable since HEV technology offers no experience of producing fuel cells or developing an alternative fuel infrastructure. A more logical transition technology is the gasoline FCV; this fits well with the current regime both in terms of fuel and technology. It is more efficient than current ICE cars and it offers an opportunity to create a mass market in fuel cells, thereby strongly reducing costs. When the FCV has outperformed ICE vehicles, the 'only' thing left is adaptation of the energy infrastructure. With HEV as the dominant design, there will be far fewer advantages to the gasoline FCV since HEVs are more efficient than gasoline FCVs. So now the argumentation will be that, due to better-performing reference technology, the opportunities for FCVs are drastically reduced.

Thus, when the HEV has become the dominant design, the step to the hydrogen FCV will have to be made directly. This will require a simultaneous effort to change both the infrastructure and engine technology. This is likely only under a very strict regulatory system focusing on non-carbon emissions, which is in opposition to the current trend.

References

Arthur D. Little (2000) *Cost Analysis of Fuel Cell System for Transportation, Base Line System Cost Estimate* (New York: Arthur D. Little).

Anderson, P., and M.L. Tushman (1990) 'Technological discontinuities and dominant designs: a cyclical model of technological change', *Administrative Science Quarterly* 35.4: 604-33.

CARB (California Air Resources Board) (1998) *Proposed Amendments to California Exhaust, Evaporative and Refuelling Emissions Standards and Test: Procedures for Passenger Cars, Light-Duty Trucks and Medium-Duty Vehicles-LEVII* (Sacramento, CA: CARB).

—— (2003) *Staff Report. Initial Statement of Reasons: 2003 Proposed Amendments to the California Zero Emission Vehicle Programme Regulations* (Sacramento, CA: CARB).

—— (2004) California Air Resources Board, Resolution 03-4, 24 April 2003, www.arb.ca.gov/regact/zev2003/reso304.pdf.

Carlson, E.J., J.H. Thijssen, S. Lasher, S. Sriramulu and G.C. Stevens (2002) 'Cost modelling of PEM fuel cell systems for automobiles', paper presented at the *SAE Future Car Congress*, Arlington, VA, 3–5 June 2002.

Carlsson, B., and R. Stankiewicz (1995) 'On the nature, function and composition of technological systems', in B. Carlsson (ed.), *Technological Systems and Economic Performance: The Case of Factory Automation* (Boston/Dordrecht/London: Kluwer Academic Publishers).

Christensen, C.M. (1997) *The Innovator's Dilemma: When New Technologies Cause Great Firms to Fail* (Boston, MA: Harvard Business School Press).

Dosi, G. (1982) 'Technological paradigms and technological trajectories: a suggested interpretation of the determinants and direction of technical change', *Research Policy* 11.3: 147-62

Edquist, C. (2001) 'Innovation systems and innovation policy: the state of the art', paper presented at *DRUID's Nelson–Winter Conference*, Aalborg, Denmark, 12–15 June 2001.

—— and B. Johnson (1997) 'Institutions and organisations in systems of innovation', in C. Edquist (ed.), *Systems of Innovation* (London/Washington, DC: Pinter): 41-60.

Geels, F.W. (2002) 'Technological transitions as evolutionary reconfiguration processes: a multi-level perspective and a case-study', *Research Policy* 31.8–9: 1,257-74.

Goverse, T., M.P. Hekkert, P. Groenewegen, E. Worrell and R.E.H.M. Smits (2001) 'Wood in the residential construction sector: opportunities and constraints', *Resources, Conservation and Recycling* 34.1: 54-73.

Hekkert, M.P., F. Hendriks, A.P.C. Faaij and M. Neelis (2005a) 'Natural gas as an alternative to crude oil in automotive fuel chains: well-to-wheel analysis and transition strategy development', *Energy Policy* 33.5: 579-94.

——, J. F. van Giessel, M. Ros, M. Wietschel and M. Meeus (2005b) 'The evolution of hydrogen research: is Germany heading for an early lock-in?', *International Journal of Hydrogen Energy* 30.10: 1,045-52.

Henderson, R.M., and K.B. Clark (1990) 'Architectural innovation: the reconfiguration of existing product technologies and the failure of established firms', *Administrative Science Quarterly* 35.1: 9-30.

Hoogers, G. (2003) *Fuel Cell Technology Handbook* (Boca Raton, FL: CRC Press).

Jacobsson, S., and A. Johnson (2000) 'The diffusion of renewable energy technology: an analytical framework and key issues for research', *Energy Policy* 28.9: 625-40.

Johnson, A. (2001) 'Functions in innovation system approaches', paper presented at *DRUID's Nelson–Winter Conference*, Aalborg, Denmark, 12–15 June 2001.

Kalhammer, F.R., P.R. Prokopius, V.P. Roan and G.E. Voecks (1998) 'Status and prospects of fuel cells as automobile engines: a report of the fuel cell technical advisory panel, Sacramento, CA', prepared for the State of California Air Resources Board.

Kemp, R. (1994) 'Technology and the transition to environmental sustainability: the problem of technological regime shifts', *Futures* 26.10: 1,023-46.

Lundvall, B., A.B. Johnson, E.S. Andersen and B. Dalum (2002) 'National systems of production, innovation and competence building', *Research Policy* 31.2: 213-31.

Morisot, O. (2002) 'EasyPac: technical and economical assessment of stationary PEM fuel cell systems', *European Fuel Cell News* 9.3: 12-19.

Neij, L. (1997) 'Use of experience curves to analyse the prospects for diffusion and adoption of renewable energy technology', *Energy Policy* 25.13: 1,099-07.

Nelson, R.R., and S.G. Winter (1982) *An Evolutionary Theory of Economic Change* (Cambridge, MA: Harvard University Press).

Rogers, E.M. (1984) *Diffusion of Innovations* (New York: Free Press, 4th edn 1995).

Schot, J., R. Hoogma and B. Elzen (1994) 'Strategies for shifting technological systems: the case of the automobile system', *Futures* 26.10: 1,060-76.

Suurs, R., M.P. Hekkert, M.T.H. Meeus and E. Nieuwlaar (2004) 'Assessing transition trajectories towards a sustainable energy system: a case study on the Dutch transition to climate neutral transport fuels', *Innovation: Management, Policy and Practice* 6.2: 269-85.

Tushman, M.L., and A. Anderson (1986) 'Technological discontinuities and organisational environments', *Administrative Science Quarterly* 31.3: 429-65.

Utterback, J.M. (1994) *Mastering the Dynamics of Innovation* (Boston, MA: Harvard Business School Press).

Van den Hoed, R., and P.J. Vergragt (2003) 'Technological shifts and industry reaction: shifts in fuel preference for the fuel cell vehicle in the automotive industry', paper presented at *Knowledge and Economic and Social Change: New Challenges to Innovation Studies' Conference*, Manchester, UK, 7–9 April 2003.

Van Dijkum, P.H. (2003) 'The path to handy, cost-effective fuel cells', *European Fuel Cell News* 9.4: 7-11.

Weiss, M.A., J.B. Heywood, A. Schafer and V.K. Natarajan (2003) *Comparative Assessment of Fuel Cell Cars* (Cambridge, MA: MIT Press).

5
Institutional change in the automotive industry
OR HOW FUEL–CELL TECHNOLOGY IS BEING INSTITUTIONALISED

Robert van den Hoed

Delft University of Technology, The Netherlands

Philip J. Vergragt

Tellus Institute, USA

Back in 1990, a number of car-makers set up extensive battery programmes. The battery electric vehicle (BEV) was generally seen as the most promising technology for achieving zero emissions—the possibility of a **battery society** was openly discussed and BEVs were expected to hit the market in the mid-1990s (Shnayerson 1996). Several car-makers visited the Vancouver-based pioneering fuel-cell company, Ballard. However, they dismissed Ballard's proton exchange membrane (PEM) fuel-cell technology as unrealistic (Motavalli 2000). For years to come, the fuel-cell vehicle (FCV) remained inconceivable for the automotive industry.

By 2004, literally every respectable car-maker worldwide had a fuel-cell programme. More than 15 car-makers have shown demonstration vehicles, joint estimated annual spending on FCVs by the industry is between US$700 million and US$1 billion[1] and the first fuel-cell buses hit the streets in 2002. By the end of this decade, FCVs are projected

---

1 Based on Kalhammer *et al.* 1998 complemented with more recent press releases from automotive giants such as Toyota and DaimlerChrysler.

to be commercially available, bringing the much-discussed **hydrogen society** a step closer.

This dramatic realignment in favour of fuel-cell technology demonstrates a seismic shift in the automotive industry's quest for **sustainable mobility**. In a period of 12–14 years, fuel-cell technology has been transformed from an unrealistic pipe-dream to a credible alternative to the internal combustion engine (ICE). How has this happened and what are factors involved? Furthermore, how is it that BEVs—once considered the design of the future—have been so completely sidelined?

This chapter examines the rise in popularity of fuel-cell technology in the automotive industry. It provides some insights into the processes by which industries select promising technologies and, more specifically, by which they transform into more sustainable practices. The chapter therefore describes an **institutionalisation** process in which fuel-cell technology gains momentum and becomes part of existing institutions. From this perspective, we hope to contribute to **institutional theory** by including the usually underexposed **treatment of technology**. Using institutional theory, the process by which fuel-cell technology is institutionalised is described, followed by an analysis of the sources of this technological institutionalisation and the factors that have contributed to the popularity of fuel-cell technology. We conclude by considering what might be further expected from this institutionalisation process, in order to shed light on potential barriers for the continuation of this process.

Institutional theory

Institutional theory is traditionally used to describe stability of organisations, industries or societies rather than change (Scott 2001). Institutional theory translates sociological theories to (among others) organisational level, to explain why organisations or industries look so much alike, a phenomenon dubbed **isomorphism** (DiMaggio and Powell 1983). The source of stability lies in the existence of so-called **institutions** that shape **organisational behaviour**. Scott (2001: 48) defines institutions as follows:

> Institutions are social structures that have attained a high degree of resilience. Social structures include norms, values, expectations, procedures, standards and routines.

In the case at hand (the automotive industry) institutions include the basic design of the car (e.g. internal combustion engine [ICE], four wheels, metal chassis and bodies), rules in traffic, standards set for safety and protection of cars, and also the network of automotive companies and suppliers. These are **social structures** that have existed for decades, subject only to small design changes over the years. The extent to which we are conscious of these norms and standards in the automotive industry differs, but a great deal of these institutions are taken for granted.

Using institutional theory to explain organisational behaviour has gained momentum only in the last two decades (Scott 2001). The main premise of institutional theory is that organisations tend to conform to institutions in the (external) **institutional context**. The institutional context consists of a set of regulations, norms, standards, values, codes and beliefs which prescribe appropriate and legitimate behaviour for an organisation (Scott 2001; DiMaggio and Powell 1983). Firms will tend to conform in order to obtain legitimacy.

Institutions can be categorised into three **pillars** (Scott 2001) leading to three types of pressures on organisations:

- **Regulative/coercive pressures**. These originate from powerful actors in the organisation's environment, and take the form of standards, mandates or rules. A central element is the fact that the actors can use their power to enforce these standards (which gives it their coercive character). Organisations comply out of expedience. Examples include regulations or mandates

- **Mimetic pressures**. These take the form of taken-for-granted practices or generally accepted appropriate behaviour for firms. Mimetic pressures originate from credible industry players, (traditional) role models and competitors with large resources, capabilities or a strong network. Firms comply out of social obligation and a fear of lagging behind. Examples may include particular car-makers proposing a new practice or technology

- **Normative pressures**. These take the form of beliefs, expectations, norms and values held by a larger community than the car industry itself (such as societal groups, regulators, consumers, suppliers). Firms' compliance is based on the taken-for-granted nature of normative pressures. Examples include the taken-for-granted nature of gasoline as car fuel

The three pillars are relatively stable; they apply external pressures on organisations that are not likely to change and tend to look alike.

Underexposed in institutional theory is the role of technology. We propose that, as with other sets of practices, technology can be described in institutional terms of norms, standards and values. In developing new products or technologies, companies are restricted by rules, routines and norms that guide them in making particular design choices. These design rules are functional in efficiently coming to end-results; but also provide hurdles in arriving at new solutions. Note that these terms correlate neatly with typical terms used in technology dynamics: design rules, dominant designs, technological expectations and technological regimes (Dosi 1982; Nelson and Winter 1982; Schot *et al.* 1994; Geels 2002). All emphasise stability and the continued use of this technology over technological innovations. Green *et al.* (1994: 1,056) use the term **technological institutions** which are described as being:

> sustained, not through any internal logic or intrinsic superiority to other institutions, but because of the interests that develop in its continuance and the belief that it will continue. Its continuance becomes embedded in technologists' and managers' frameworks of calculation and routines of behaviour, and it continues because it is thus embedded.

The authors (1994: 1,056) add:

> The (technological) regime will therefore constitute a set of 'socially' agreed objectives, as to what the parameters of an industry's products will be, how they would be typically made and, crucially for R&D, on which features of the product and process technological development should focus: in other words,

on which performance characteristics will serve as a heuristic for R&D attention.

We can thus consider technology as an institution (consisting of norms, beliefs, search heuristics and expectations); technological innovation can thus be seen as institutional change. Along these lines, **radical innovation** may be conceptualised both as a **de-institutionalisation** of the dominant trajectory and as an institutionalisation of a radically new technology located outside the current trajectory.

Institutional theory is useful in explaining stability and dominant paradigms. However it is less suitable for explaining (technical) change (Fligstein 1991; Greenwood and Hinings 1996). In recent years, several authors have argued that change does occur and that institutional theory should be altered to include these phenomena (Ventresca and Hoffman 2002; Brint and Karabel 1991; Levy and Rothenberg 2002). One way to explain the process of change is by looking at the sources of institutional change.

Institutional change refers to the phenomenon of institutionalisation (Scott 2001) defined as (Oliver 1996: 166):

> The process by which activities come to be socially accepted as 'right' or
> 'proper', or come to be viewed as the only conceivable reality.

This definition indicates how formerly unaccepted behaviour becomes accepted and internalised. A simple example is the airbag. Until 20 years ago airbags were not a part of the car, but now every new car has one. Airbags have become standard in the same way as seat belts, windscreen wipers, air conditioning and low-emission engines.

Parallel to the institutionalisation process, certain practices may become outdated, not applicable or out of line with changed regulatory standards. These practices can then become de-institutionalised (Scott 2001; Oliver 1992: 563):

> De-institutionalisation refers to the erosion or discontinuity of an institution-
> alised organisational activity or practice.

Where the former highlights the continuous process by which new routine legitimate behaviour is developed, the latter emphasises the replacing of old rules and routines by new ones.

Here, both institutionalisation and de-institutionalisation are at play. With regard to fuel-cell technology, new rules, routines, beliefs and expectations are constructed and supported by regulatory institutions, reflecting the institutionalisation process. At the same time, the legitimacy of the current dominant design—the ICE—is increasingly undermined, with the rules and standards surrounding it starting to be questioned in a process of de-institutionalisation. Indicators of de-institutionalisation range from weakened beliefs or changed interpretations of current practices (Greenwood and Hinings 1996) to outright abandonment of these practices (Scott 2001).

But what are the origins of (de-)institutionalisation? What factors make institutions change, and under which conditions? Recent institutional theorists propose that institutionalisation is a result of discourse and negotiation in the **organisational field** (Scott 2001: 56):

> A community of organisations that partakes of a common meaning system
> and whose participants interact more frequently and fatefully with one
> another than with other actors outside the field.

The organisational field can be seen as a network of organisations with different power positions and engaged in several coalitions with other field members. According to Hoffman (1999), an organisational field meets (or arises) around **issues**. Here, the issue is sustainable mobility. This comprises the ongoing discussion concerning the unsustainability of the ICE car and the problems associated with energy efficiency, carbon dioxide and local emissions, use of fossil fuels and the like. But the issue also encompasses discussions about available technologies and scrutiny of established technologies or practices. Field members negotiate over the **dominant problem definition** as well as **dominant solution directions** (Hoffman 1999; Vergragt 1988). It is within the organisational field that rules, regulations and norms are decided on, and technologies become accepted or dismissed. Note that this is a social process between field members in different power positions—(de-)institutionalisation is, therefore, inherently a political process (Ventresca and Hoffman 2002). An example of the organisational field at work is the dominant focus on technological solutions in order to attain sustainable mobility, largely as a result of corporate interests in the automotive industry. This is similar to the process by which the oil industry got gasoline accepted over methanol as the intermediate fuel for FCVs, through the building of coalitions with General Motors and Toyota, nicely illustrating how the organisational field works and how it results in changed institutions (van den Hoed and Vergragt 2003).

In the case of the automotive industry, apart from car-makers and oil companies, other field members include automotive suppliers, governmental agencies, research institutes, consumer groups and environmental organisations. With regard to sustainable mobility, other actors such as battery manufacturers, the chemical industry, hydrogen-related companies and fuel-cell manufacturers are also part of the organisational field.

Based on this model of the organisational field, five factors are likely to induce institutional change:

- **Exits and new entries.** Exits and entries can change the power structure in the field, leading to new coalitions and changed supported codes of conduct (Hoffman 1999; Oliver 1996)

- **External shocks or crises.** Fligstein (1991) argues that shocks are important mechanisms, leading to instability. According to Hoffman (1999), shocks provide the opportunity to reflect on established practices. Meyer (1982) shows how shocks can lead to uncertainty which in turn result in unorthodox experiments. Moors (2000) shows how a crisis, or the expectation of a crisis, puts pressure on a system and induces (radical) innovations

- **New technologies.** New technologies can provide answers to problems or **performance crises** (Oliver 1992) associated with the established technology or practice

- **New practices by established members.** Rather than being constrained by institutional pressures, organisations themselves are capable of influencing institutions by proposing new practices (Oliver 1992; Scott 2001; Ventresca and Hoffman 2002). This is often referred to as the **institutional entrepreneur** (Ventresca and Hoffman 2002)

- **Market changes**. Changes in the market can change demands for new practices, thus putting pressure on current practice (Oliver 1992)

The above five factors influence the negotiation process in the organisational field and the resulting outcomes of this process, namely the institutions. An analysis of institutionalisation of fuel-cell technology thus requires analysis of the above five factors and their influence on the organisational field. In the next section, the changed fuel-cell technology institutions (divided into coercive/regulative, mimetic and normative) will be assessed for the period 1990–2003. The data are gathered from governmental agencies (e.g. CARB), press releases from automotive companies[2] and influential research papers.

Institutionalisation of FC technology

In this section, we try to establish the extent to which fuel-cell technology has been institutionalised. This requires an analysis of coercive pressures, mimetic pressures and normative pressures.

Regulative institutions

Coercive pressures refer to strong forces mandating certain practices. In the case of the automotive industry, regulation is the strongest coercive force. To what extent have car-makers been coerced or even forced into developing FCVs?

Since the 1970s, environmental problems associated with the car have been increasingly regulated; for example, greenhouse gas emissions, energy efficiency, end-of-life scenarios and alternative fuels have been subject to regulation. However, none of these regulations has threatened ICE as the dominant technology or questioned its value to society. The only serious challenge to the ICE dominant design is the Californian zero-emission vehicle (ZEV) regulation (CARB 1996).

In 1990, the CARB included a passage in the ZEV regulation that mandated car-makers to sell ZEVs. Large car-makers were required to achieve 2% of their total sales in ZEVs by 1998, rising to 10% in 2003. Given that ICE vehicles cannot achieve zero emissions, alternatives were required. The only viable alternative at the time, according to the industry, was the BEV.

The ZEV regulation has been subject to change over the years. In 1996, the pre-2003 ZEV requirements were dropped in exchange for an industry commitment to bring a limited number of BEVs to the Californian market (CARB 1996). By 1998, the 10% target was lowered to 4%, with the remaining 6% to be achieved with extremely clean vehicles (CARB 1998).[3] In 2001, the 4% was further reduced to 2% and another a new category was added, the ZEV alternative technology (ZEV–AT). ZEV–AT was set up to stimu-

---

2   See www.fuelcells.org.
3   These vehicles would need to achieve SULEV (super-ultra-low-emission levels) emission standards, which are the equivalent of the emissions produced by utilities for generating electricity (CARB 1998).

late new technologies with very low emission levels, such as: natural gas vehicles (NGVs), hybrid electric vehicles (HEVs) and FCVs with an on-board reformer.[4] The last change, made in 2003, allowed car-makers to sell FCVs, thus giving them an alternative compliance route.[5]

Comparing the 1990 and the 2003 regulatory requirements, it is striking that the percentage of ZEVs that car-makers must sell has fallen significantly. Nevertheless, there is still an obligation to deliver vehicles with no emissions. Although car-makers have the option to fulfil the ZEV requirements with BEVs, the technical development of this vehicle has been so disappointing that FCVs are largely preferred by most car-makers, and this preference is being reinforced by the ZEV regulation.

Normative institutions

Normative institutions refer to the beliefs, expectations, norms and values associated with technology. To what extent does a consensus exist concerning the future of FCVs? How has the attractiveness of the FCV option changed through the years?

In the early 1990s, fuel-cell technology was not seen as a viable option for ZEVs. At that time, although technology was considered potentially suitable for stationary applications, mobile applications required much higher energy densities and cheaper fuel-cell stacks. Thus, the dominant alternative car design in the early 1990s was the BEV.

This paradigm began to change when, in 1994 and 1996, DaimlerChrysler (then called DaimlerBenz[6]) revealed two fuel-cell demonstration vehicles and expressed its commitment to pursue this technology. These events proved crucial in putting FCVs on the agenda of the automotive industry (Kalhammer *et al.* 1998; Maruo 1998). From the industry's perspective, fuel-cell technology has a number of attractions:

- In comparison to BEV technology, fuel cells offer greater future potential once obstacles such as the need for higher energy densities, lower weight and volume requirements, longer range and easier refuelling have been overcome. Cost issues remain a potential difficulty, but are not thought to be insurmountable (Kalhammer *et al.* 1998)

- Fuel-cell technology has a certain 'sex' appeal. The principle behind it is almost too simple for words (reverse electrolysis); its promise of maintenance-free and silent vehicles is very appealing, as is its flexible design potential (Nieuwenhuis and Wells 1997)

- The most important attraction of the FCV, however, lies in its environmental potential—it is energy-efficient, has low greenhouse gas emissions and is non-polluting. It represents the 'holy grail' of sustainable mobility (Hoogers 2003)

Thus, between 1996 and 1998, fuel-cell technology in vehicles generated a great deal of excitement, not only among car-makers, but also fuel-cell manufacturers, hydrogen

---

4   FCVs fuelled by direct hydrogen fall in the 'gold' ZEV–AT category.
5   The number of required sales is based on sales volume, but averages out at around 250 FCVs until 2008.
6   DaimlerBenz and Chrysler merged in 1998 to form DaimlerChrysler. Throughout this chapter, the company will be referred to as DaimlerChrysler.

companies (storage technology), oil companies (hydrogen infrastructure), chemical industry (catalysts and membranes for fuel cells) and governments (stimulation programmes, testing programmes). By the late 1990s, with the BEV market continuing to disappoint, fuel-cell technology became the new zero-emission alternative. The only question was: 'Could it be done?'

By 2003, the technology's technical viability was not in doubt. Test programmes with fuel-cell buses and cars had been under way for several years, the first FCVs had been sold and most of the critical technical problems had been solved (particularly cold start, water management and reforming technology), although it was acknowledged that further work was needed (Hoogers 2003).

Moreover, there is increasing international consensus among car-makers, oil industry, governments, environmental groups and research institutes on the viability of a future hydrogen society. The debate focuses on 'when' this transition will occur, rather than 'if'. Illustrative is Iceland's efforts to become the world's first hydrogen society in the next decade.

According to Dr Alan Lloyd, chair of CARB: 'Fuel cells offer our nation the double benefit of clean air and energy independence.'[7] The long-term vision of FCVs and hydrogen (generated by photovoltaics or wind) remains a strong one, to which a growing fuel-cell community adheres. By the early 2000s, oil companies had set up extensive hydrogen programmes, stock prices of fuel-cell manufacturers were booming and fuel-cell stimulation programmes by governments were too numerous to mention.[8]

In recent years, however, the rosy hydrogen FCV picture has developed some cracks. Energy efficiency and emission levels are not as favourable as once thought (Weiss *et al.* 2003; see Chapter 2), while the safety of hydrogen FCV buses operating in Amsterdam has been called into question.[9] Thus, the vision of a gleaming hydrogen society still exists, but its sheen has been slightly tarnished.

Mimetic institutions

What are the mimetic institutions for the automotive industry? What are considered good and legitimate practices for the industry to adopt? One relatively objective method of assessing company R&D activities is by analysing patents. A study was carried out using patent data from the US Patent Office complemented with that from the European Data Office.[10] Figure 5.1 shows the dominant role of BEV technology in R&D

---

7   See www.cafcp.org/releases/2001-10-16_Study_Quotes.html, accessed 19 September 2003.

8   Kalhammer estimates investments until 1998 in fuel-cell technology to be US$1.5–2 billion. Based on press releases, the programmes of DaimlerChrysler and Toyota had annual investments of more than US$200 million in fuel-cell technology in the period 2000–2003.

9   RTL-4 News 10 September 2003, 7.30 pm.

10   See www.uspto.gov, gb.espacenet.com. As a main data source the US Patent Office was used, given the size of the US market (propensity to patent in the US is high), the presence of ZEV regulation in California (the US thus provides an important market to secure ZEV-related patents) and the high costs for having US patents (thereby securing the quality of patents; in comparison in Japan costs for patenting are much lower leading to high patent activity for decoy purposes). Nevertheless, European companies such as DaimlerBenz, BMW, Volkswagen, Renault and Peugeot-Citroën are not active in the US (and thus show little patent activity there); to compensate patents of the European Patent Office (EPO) complement the US data.

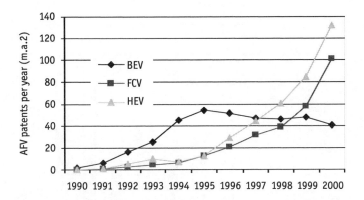

These data include all large car-makers worldwide: DaimlerBenz/Chrysler, General Motors, Honda, Toyota, Ford, Nissan, Mitsubishi, BMW, Volkswagen, Fiat, Renault, PSA (Peugeot, Citroën), Daihatsu, Daewoo and Hyundai.

FIGURE 5.1 Patents in BEVs, FCVs and HEVs applied for by car firms (1990–2000: moving average 2)

priorities until 1997 (this was in line with disappointing BEV sales at around this time) with a shift from BEV to FCV (and HEV) taking place around 1997. In 1998, there were more patents for FCV and HEV technologies than for BEV. By 2000, the number of FCV and HEV patent applications were, respectively, two and a half to three times higher than BEV applications. Figure 5.2 reveals that, by 2000, nearly 35% of all alternative-fuel vehicle (AFV)-related patents were FCV-related, 50% were HEV-related and just 15% were BEV-related. Figure 5.3 shows that, by 2000, close to 9% of all patent applications were related to AFVs. More than 3% of all patents in 2000 were FCV-related (compared

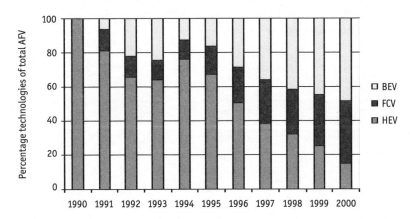

For the purposes of the analysis, AFVs include only technologies such as BEV, HEV or FCV.

FIGURE 5.2 Patents in BEVs, FCVs and HEVs as percentage of total AFVs applied for by car firms (1990–2000: moving average 2)

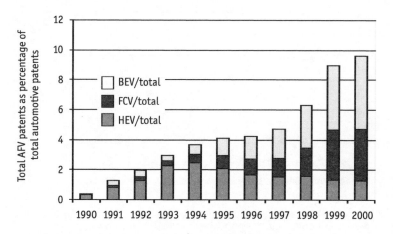

FIGURE 5.3 AFV patents as percentage of total automotive OEM (original equipment manufacturer) patents (1991–2000: moving average 2)

to no more than 0.4% in 1994)—in other words, one out of every 33 patent applications made by car-makers was fuel cell-related in 2000.

The patent study shows the increased R&D activities in fuel-cell technology, and the integral place fuel-cell research has captured in automotive R&D. The institutionalisation of FCV as common practice in the auto industry is further illustrated by an analysis of the introduction of demonstration FCVs. Figure 5.4 shows how, for nearly two years (1994–96), DaimlerChrysler was the only car-maker with a FCV model. Then, in less than three years (late 1996 until early 1999), seven other firms issued their first demonstration FCV. Another two years later, 14 (most of the industry) had demonstrated a FCV arising from an in-house fuel-cell programme. This majority reflects the consensus on this technology.

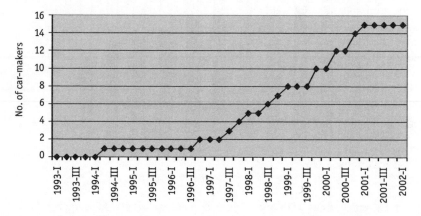

FIGURE 5.4 Cumulative number of car-makers showing FCV demonstration models

As the world's leading car-makers initiated fuel-cell programmes, so they terminated BEV programmes. Fuel-cell programmes are now an integral element in auto R&D, as demonstrated by the following statements:

- B. McCormick, co-director of General Motors' Global Alternative Propulsion Centre (GAPC) states that fuel-cell technology is 'no longer a science project; the fuel cell is getting to be real'[11]

- Dr E. Shubert, co-director of General Motors' GAPC notes: 'Hydrogen is the only energy carrier that will satisfy the need for a lasting reduction in carbon dioxide emissions despite a steady increase in the number of motor vehicles on the road'[12]

- Ford states: 'We believe fuel cells are the only technology today with the potential to someday replace the internal combustion engine'[13]

Thus, in the last decade, fuel-cell technology has gained remarkable momentum and has been accepted by a wide range of societal groups (including the oil/automotive sectors) as the future car propulsion system with hydrogen as the fuel. How can this popularity be explained?

Sources of institutionalisation of FCVs

Using the five change factors described earlier, the sources of the institutionalisation of FCV technology will be examined.

Exits and new entries in the organisational field

The organisational field is not a stable set of organisations and coalitions—exits and entries occur which impact on progress towards sustainable mobility, leading to different norms, beliefs and expectations (in other words, to different institutions).

The most notable new entrant is, of course, Ballard, the leader in fuel-cell technology. By increasing energy density combined with more powerful membranes while at the same time reducing platinum load, Ballard has made the PEM fuel cell eligible for applications in cars (Motavalli 2000). In the slipstream of Ballard's pioneering work, a whole range of new fuel-cell companies have flourished, such as International Fuel Cells, Plug Power, H-Power and DeNora. The competition among these firms has created further momentum. With DaimlerChrysler showcasing its NECAR models and the FCV now well and truly on the map of the auto industry, a range of related industries jumped aboard—hydrogen-related companies for storing and handling hydrogen (e.g. Quantum, General Hydrogen), chemical companies for developing membranes and catalysts (e.g. Johnson Matthey, DuPont, 3M, Hoechst) and, of course, fuel companies

---

11   See www.evworld.com, March 2001.
12   See www.fuelcells.org, August 2001.
13   See www.evworld.com, May 2001.

(Methanex for methanol, StatOil, BP, Shell). These firms developed their own coalitions, both with each other and with car-makers. Again, momentum increased.

By contrast, and illustrating the working of the organisational field, the late 1990s saw the exit of battery developers, BEV developers and related industries as a result of disappointing sales and the shift to FCVs.

But to what extent did Ballard put fuel-cell technology on the map? Remarkably, the crucial inventions Ballard made to the fuel cell originated from 1985 and 1986, years before the ZEV regulation, and more than eight years before the first prototype FCV appeared. In this period Ballard was unable to get fuel-cell technology on the agenda. Motavalli (2000) describes how several car-makers tested Ballard stacks in the early 1990s, but dismissed the technology as being too costly and too bulky.

The ZEV regulation and the early improvements in stack performance did not seem to raise Ballard's profile or get FCVs on the agenda. In fact, it could be argued that this happened only when DaimlerChrysler decided to engage in collaborative research with Ballard.

External shocks or crises

Two external shocks or crises were important factors in the rise of fuel-cell technology. First, by challenging the ICE paradigm, the Californian ZEV regulation was a shock to the automotive industry. The central message sent by this regulation was that, in the future, polluting emissions from cars would no longer be tolerated. A zero-emission vision, an alternative to ICE, was born. For car-makers, ICE could no longer be taken for granted. So, although auto R&D continued to develop ICE technology, it also started to include non-ICE alternatives. Another impact of the ZEV regulation was to provide a boost for zero-emission technology companies, such as battery developers and pioneers such as Ballard who saw the potential to form fruitful new coalitions with car-makers (Motavalli 2000).

Second, the attack on the World Trade Center in New York in 2001 had a profound impact on the institutionalisation of fuel-cell technology and, in particular, the hydrogen society (see Chapter 4). As a result of 9/11, the Iraq conflict and continuing instability in the Middle East, oil security and dependency have become important issues for the US government. In his 2003 State of the Union address, President Bush announced US$1.2 billion investments for research into hydrogen for car propulsion,[14] further illustrating the widespread expectation of a hydrogen FCV society.

New technologies

The performance characteristics of the fuel cell have most definitely contributed to its success. One of its most important characteristics is **power density** (measured in kW per litre). According to Kalhammer et al. (1998), Ballard's fuel-cell power density showed a factor ten increase between 1990 and 1998. By 1998, 1 kW/litre had been achieved. This doubled the target of 0.5 kW/litre set by the Partnership for Next Gen-

---

14   See www.eere.energy.gov/hydrogenfuel.

eration Vehicles (PNGV)[15] in 1994 (see Fig. 5.5). The Partnership's 1998 goal of 1.4 kW/litre was nearly achieved in early 2000 with Ballard's Mark 900 series achieving a 1.3 kW/litre output,[16] while its successor reached more than 2.0 kW/litre in 2002.[17]

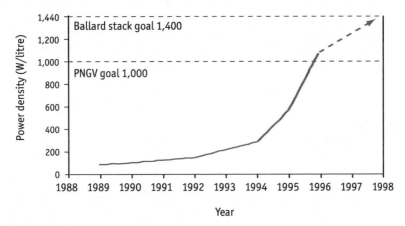

FIGURE 5.5 Evolution of Ballard stack performance

Source: Kalhammer *et al.* 1998

With this progress, the power density of fuel-cell technology approaches that of the ICE; and whereas, formerly, the fuel-cell stacks used the complete compartment space of a vehicle (in NECAR I), the system now fits the floor of the Mercedes A-class, not compromising passenger space. Furthermore, the weight of the stacks has come down by several factors (Hoogers 2003; Kalhammer *et al.* 1998). Similar progress has been made with regard to low-temperature operation, dynamic behaviour, and water and heat management (Hoogers 2003).

It is safe to say that, without this remarkable technological progress, fuel-cell technology would not now be on the agenda of the automotive industry. With the technical aspects under control, more commercial aspects have become important, the key one being cost. Although costs have undoubtedly come down, this remains one of the more difficult challenges.

Institutional entrepreneur

Institutional entrepreneurs are those companies within the institutional context itself that are the source of novel practices. Although car-makers are constrained by their institutional context, they can nevertheless influence the institutions in their context by proposing new, unorthodox practices or technologies. History shows how the automotive industry has taken on this role.

---

15 PNGV was initiated by the Clinton administration with the objective of developing vehicles capable of achieving 80 miles per gallon; see www.pngv.org.

16 See www.hfcletter.com/letter/februaryoo/feature.html.

17 See www.eere.energy.gov/news/archives/2001/oct31_01.html.

A good first example is General Motors' showcase of its EV1 in 1990 and its simultaneous announcement to commercialise the BEV in 1995. This announcement formed an important push for CARB to adopt the ZEV regulation. General Motors positioned the BEV as a **viable technology** (i.e. one commercially available in the mid to long term). This optimism concerning BEVs was unprecedented (Shnayerson 1996): it illustrated a shift in normative pressures, namely in the commercial beliefs and expectations of BEV. Whereas formerly regarded as a study project, BEVs began to gain perspective due to General Motors' activities. As a result, other car-makers also started investing in BEV programmes.

Similarly, DaimlerChrysler's showcasing of the NECAR I (in May 1994) and, in particular, the NECAR II (in May 1996) had a similar effect. Before these events, the viability of fuel-cell technology as a car propulsion unit had generally been seen by the automotive industry as unrealistic. The progress made by DaimlerChrysler projected fuel-cell technology as a viable alternative to ICE. Possibly even more important was the reputation of DaimlerChrysler as a well-known innovator in the industry, with a strong and innovative R&D department and culture. Furthermore, the company's links with subsidiaries in aerospace (DASA, Dornier) and electronics (AEG) also provided a source of innovative technologies. It was no accident that DaimlerChrysler's belief in fuel-cell technology originated from its aerospace subsidiary Dornier which had experimented with the technology in the late 1980s as part of a space-related project (Motavalli 2000). Thus, DaimlerChrysler was a likely candidate for an institutional entrepreneur, creating normative expectations and beliefs for the industry as a whole.

A final example of the institutional entrepreneur phenomenon is in Toyota's HEV activities. Although considered by other car-makers, HEV technology was generally seen by the industry as too expensive and too complex for commercial application. With the risky market introduction of the Prius in the late 1990s, Toyota dispelled that myth. The success of the Prius not only provided a role model for the rest of the industry, it also influenced the regulatory institutions—in California the HEV is now classified in the ZEV–AT category, and provides a possible extra push to develop more stringent energy efficiency standards (see Chapter 4).

General Motors, DaimlerChrysler and Toyota are institutional entrepreneurs proposing new and unorthodox practices. Three technologies previously considered unrealistic or commercially unviable have become serious options to be considered by the rest of the industry. Regulatory standards have also changed as a result of these technological proposals. Thus, these three firms have changed the institutional context in which they operate. They did this, not for altruistic purposes, but for sound business reasons, having built strong foundations for their respective technologies. Further support from others in the sector and from regulators has helped to improve their competitive position. By acting strategically, firms can position themselves in the driver's seat of innovative practices and technologies.

Innovation and strategic behaviour may not, however, be sufficient, as is shown by BMW whose endeavours to get its hydrogen ICE vehicle accepted by the industry and regulators have not succeeded (as yet). It stands alone in its approach, as it does in its application of fuel-cell technology as a battery replacement. BMW's relatively small size and lack of resources seem to affect its ability to influence other players. Institutional entrepreneurs need:

- Some level of credibility derived from a strong resource position (e.g. General Motors, Toyota)

- A strong R&D department (e.g. DaimlerChrysler and, to a lesser extent, General Motors and Toyota)

- A strong knowledge position in the technology (e.g. DaimlerChrysler and General Motors)

- A strong network (e.g. General Motors and Toyota with Exxon, Daimler-Chrysler with Ballard)

Institutional entrepreneurs are a strong force in shaping the institutional environment.

Market changes

Rather than solely looking at technological opportunities or regulatory climates, markets are also subject to change (Christensen 1997). While markets change, 'old' technologies can become obsolete or insufficient to fulfil market needs. Consequently, 'new' technologies can become more attractive. To what extent could the changing market environment have been the reason for the success of fuel-cell technology? Only to a limited extent, so it seems.

On dominant market criteria such as costs and performance, the FCV is unlikely to provide better value than the current ICE (van den Hoed and Brezet 2003). It is more likely that any added value will be derived from the electric nature of FCVs, as conventional batteries can hardly keep up with the increasing energy demands of modern cars. Fuel-cell technology not only solves this problem, it can also provide electric power when the motor is not running. Hoogers (2003) and Kalhammer *et al.* (1998) concede that this application of fuel-cell technology is interesting, but suggest that it does not offer sufficient added value to propel FCVs into the market alone. Similarly, silent cars are, at this stage, not a serious market driver.

Furthermore, the history of environmentally benign cars has not been comforting. Several models boasting better efficiency or low emissions, but sold at a price premium, have remained niche markets.[18] The first model to show some market success is the Toyota Prius, despite its price premium. By 2002, more than 100,000 models had been sold,[19] an unprecedented amount for an environmental car. The FCV will have to display qualities other than its environmental performance to gain market acceptance.

Conclusions

This chapter has described how fuel-cell technology has become an accepted technological alternative to the ICE. The FCV is in the process of becoming institutionalised,

18   This includes models such as the VW Lupo, Opel Ecotec motors, Honda Insight, nearly all BEVs on the market.
19   Toyota press release, 24 April 2002.

manifested in the form of: regulatory support systems (e.g. ZEV and carbon emissions regulations); expectations/beliefs in a hydrogen FCV society (normative); and a sense of what is considered appropriate behaviour by car-makers in order to achieve sustainable mobility (mimetic). This process of institutionalisation is described both as a process of gaining momentum and growing acceptance for a technology, and also as a political process through which stakeholders and coalitions of stakeholders try to collect support and achieve consensus for their particular (technological) interests. Based on this assumption, the factors that influence this institutionalisation process have been discussed, using the organisational field as the locus of institutional change.

A combination of change factors is at play in explaining the current popularity of fuel-cell technology in the automotive industry. The remarkable technological progress displayed by the technology has been a dominant reason for car-makers to invest in it. Without this progress it is unlikely that the technology would ever have made it to the demonstration stage. However, technological progress alone seems insufficient to explain its success. The 'shock' of the Californian ZEV mandate provided car-makers with a powerful incentive to look for, and invest in, alternatives. But ZEV has had another effect: it has attracted new entries with innovative technologies (e.g. battery developers and fuel-cell manufacturers) to the organisational field, thereby laying the foundations for new coalitions and shifting the power structures. ZEV has been a second crucial condition for the success of fuel-cell technology. Less influential, but nevertheless supporting the development of alternatives such as FCVs, has been the increasing international concern regarding terrorism and oil supply.

The case also shows how car-makers themselves have been instrumental in getting their own industry to adopt new technologies. Ballard's technology had been available since the mid-1980s, but only DaimlerChrysler's investments (in 1993) put the company and its technology on the map. Similarly, General Motors' adoption of AeroEnvironments' BEV technology illustrates how large car-makers play a crucial role in technology acceptance.

Thus, we conclude that the combination of an attractive technology, shocks and institutional entrepreneurialism have all played key roles in getting fuel-cell technology onto the R&D agenda of the global automotive industry.

Whether this is sufficient to secure the future commercial success of FCVs remains uncertain. Although an institutionalisation process has taken place, we can only conclude that fuel-cell technology is only slightly institutionalised. Similarly, and possibly more importantly, the ICE is only slightly de-institutionalised. The case shows how market factors have had a very small role in raising the popularity of FCVs, and might well dampen the potential for future success. This suggests that, although the current combination of change factors favours ongoing R&D on fuel-cell technology, it does not guarantee its commercialisation. Whereas in the R&D stages, competitive advantage and the acquisition of valuable resources are important drivers for car-makers (in order to safeguard their knowledge positions), commercialisation requires cost-effectiveness as well as significant resources to build manufacturing capacity. A similar scenario to that seen with BEVs is conceivable, in which poor sales lead the industry to retreat from further development and investment. Thus, without significant market incentives the further institutionalisation of FCVs might well be hampered.

This chapter shows how institutional change is the result of discussions at organisational field level, with the ZEV regulation providing a good example of how several stakeholders can influence the outcome. Furthermore, the powerful negotiating role of car-makers (as well as the oil industry) is striking. It is the large car-makers, such as DaimlerChrysler and General Motors, who put fuel-cell and BEV technologies, respectively, on the agenda, rather than small firms such as Ballard. An estimated US$200–300 million annual budget is available for car-makers such as General Motors and DaimlerChrysler for research on fuel-cell technology, providing a strong knowledge resource based in research institutes, academia, pressure groups or regulators. This resource can influence the technological decision-making, technological trajectories and success or failure of technologies in the automotive industry. Given the strong role of the automotive industry, and conflicting economic incentives and sustainable objectives, the existence of a large knowledge gap between the car industry and those who regulate it is undesirable if sustainable mobility solutions are to be achieved.

Based on these assessments, the following recommendations to regulators are made:

- Regulators should continue focusing on long-term desired objectives for sustainable mobility, such as zero emissions. Over time, such objectives may well become institutionalised, thus creating normative pressures to adopt new and sustainable practices, and simultaneously attracting new companies with innovative technologies. Furthermore, it will further commit car-makers to the sustainable mobility track

- Apart from institutionalising new technologies such as fuel-cell technology, de-institutionalisation of the ICE should be targeted. As long as the ICE is perceived as an unproblematic technology, it will be very hard to replace it with alternatives

- Progress in fuel-cell technology should be fostered, particularly with respect to market criteria such as costs and performance. Currently, the FCV is not yet able to provide market value, and promoting it too soon could endanger its long-term success. Patience should be exercised together with experimentation. Although breakthroughs remain necessary, it seems wise to initiate small-scale experiments to foster learning with respect to consumer acceptance and technological requirements, thereby paving the way towards viable FCVs (Brown *et al.* 2003)

References

Brint, S., and J. Karabel (1991) 'Institutional origins and transformations: the case of American community colleges', in W.W. Powell and P.J. DiMaggio (eds.), *The New Institutionalism in Organisational Analysis* (Chicago: University of Chicago Press): 337-61.

Brown, H.S., P.J. Vergragt, K. Green and L. Berchicci (2003) 'Learning for sustainability transitions through bounded socio-technical experiments in personal mobility', *Technology Analysis and Strategic Management* 15.3: 291-13.

CARB (California Air Resources Board) (1996) *Staff Report. Final Statement of Rule-making: Amendments to the Zero Emission Vehicle Requirements for Passenger Cars and Light Duty Trucks* (Sacramento, CA: CARB).

_____ (1998) *Proposed Amendments to California Exhaust, Evaporative and Refuelling Emissions Standards and Test: Procedures for Passenger Cars, Light-Duty Trucks and Medium-Duty Vehicles-LEVII* (Sacramento, CA: CARB).

Christensen, C.M. (1997) *The Innovator's Dilemma, When New Technologies Cause Great Firms to Fail* (Boston, MA: Harvard Business School Press).

DiMaggio, P.J., and W.W. Powell (1983) 'The iron cage revisited: institutional isomorphism and collective rationality in organisational fields', *American Sociological Review* 48.4: 147-60.

Dosi, G. (1982) 'Technological paradigms and technological trajectories', *Research Policy* 11: 147-62.

Fligstein, N. (1991) 'The structural transformation of American industry: an institutional account of the causes of diversification in the largest firms, 1919–79', in W.W. Powell and P.J. DiMaggio (eds.), *The New Institutionalism in Organisational Analysis* (Chicago: University of Chicago Press): 311-37.

Geels, F.W. (2002) 'Technological transitions as evolutionary reconfiguration processes: a multi-level perspective and a case-study', *Research Policy* 31.8–9: 1,257-74.

General Motors (2001) *Well-to-Wheel Energy Use and Greenhouse Gas Emissions of Advanced Fuel/Vehicles Systems: North American Analysis: Executive Summary* (Argonne, IL: Argonne National Laboratory).

Green K., A. McMeekin and A. Irwin (1994) 'Technological trajectories and research and development for environmental innovation in UK firms', *Futures* 26.10: 1,047-59.

Greenwood, R., and C.R. Hinings (1996) 'Understanding radical organisational change: bringing together the old and the new institutionalism', *Academy of Management Review* 21.4: 1,022-54.

Hekkert, M., and R. van den Hoed (2003) 'Competing technologies and the struggle towards a new dominant design: the emergence of the hybrid vehicle at the expense of the fuel cell vehicle?', paper presented at *Greening of Industry Conference: Innovating for Sustainability*, San Francisco, CA, 12–15 October 2003.

Hoffman, A.J. (1999) 'Institutional evolution and change: environmentalism and the US chemical industry', *Academy of Management Journal* 42.4: 351-71.

Hoogers, G. (2003) *Fuel Cell Technology Handbook* (Boca Raton, FL: CRC Press).

Kalhammer, F.R., P.R. Prokopius, V.P. Roan and G.E. Voecks (1998) 'Status and prospects of fuel cells as automobile engines: a report of the fuel cell technical advisory panel, Sacramento, CA', prepared for the State of California Air Resources Board.

Levy, D.L., and S. Rothenberg (2002) 'Heterogeneity and change in environmental strategy: technological and political responses to climate change in the automotive industry', in M.J. Ventresca and A.J. Hoffman (eds.), *Organisations, Policy and the Natural Environment: Institutional and Strategic Perspectives* (Stanford, CA: Stanford University Press): 173-93.

Maruo, K. (1998) *Strategic Alliances for the Development of Fuel Cell Vehicles* (Goteborg, Sweden: Goteborgs Universitet).

Meyer, A. (1982) 'Adapting to environmental jolts', *Administrative Science Quarterly* 27.4: 515-37.

Motavalli, J. (2000) *Forward Drive: The Race to Build 'Clean' Cars for the Future* (San Francisco: Sierra Club Books).

Moors, E.H.M. (2000) 'Metal making in motion: technology choices for sustainable metals production', PhD thesis, Delft University of Technology, The Netherlands.

Nelson, R.R., and S.G. Winter (1982) *An Evolutionary Theory of Economic Change* (Cambridge, MA: Harvard University Press).

Nieuwenhuis, P., and P. Wells (1997) *The Death of Motoring? Car Making and Automobility in the 21st Century* (Chichester, UK: John Wiley).

Oliver, C. (1992) 'The antecedents of deinstitutionalisation', *Organisation Studies* 13.4: 563-88.

—— (1996) The institutional embeddedness of economic activity', *Advances in Strategic Management* 13: 163-86.

Scott, W.R. (2001) *Institutions and Organisations* (London: Sage).

Schot, J., R. Hoogma and B. Elzen (1994) 'Strategies for shifting technological systems: the case of the automobile system', *Futures* 26.10: 1,060-76.

Shnayerson, M. (1996) *The Car That Could: The Inside Story of GM's Revolutionary Electric Vehicle* (New York: Random House).

Van den Hoed, R., and P.J. Vergragt (2003) 'Technological shifts and industry reaction: shifts in fuel preference for the fuel cell vehicle in the automotive industry', paper presented at *Knowledge and*

Economic and Social Change: New Challenges to Innovation Studies Conference, Manchester, UK, 7–9 April 2003.

—— and J.C. Brezet (2003) 'Incumbent's curse in the automotive industry: prospects for fuel cell vehicles from the automotive industry perspective', paper presented at *Sustainable Innovation*, Stockholm, Sweden, 27–28 October 2003.

Ventresca M.J., and A.J. Hoffman (2002) *Organisations, Policy and the Natural Environment: Institutional and Strategic Perspectives* (Stanford, CA: Stanford University Press).

Vergragt, P.J. (1988) 'The social shaping of industrial innovations', *Social Studies of Science* 18.3: 483-513.

Weiss, M.A., J.B. Heywood, A. Schafer and V.K. Natarajan (2003) *Comparative Assessment of Fuel Cell Cars* (Boston, MA: MIT Press).

Wells, P., and P. Nieuwenhuis (2001) *The Automotive Industry: A Guide* (Cardiff, UK: Centre for Automotive Industry Research).

6

System innovation in the automotive industry
ACHIEVING SUSTAINABILITY THROUGH MICRO–FACTORY RETAILING

Andrew Williams

BRASS Centre, Cardiff University, UK

In recent years, the automotive industry has been characterised by relatively poor economic performance in comparison to many other sectors. Most companies still return very slim profit margins when compared to turnover and some (e.g. Fiat) have even incurred heavy losses in recent years. In addition, negative expectations over share value have led to poor share price performance in many companies, including Nissan, DaimlerChrysler and General Motors (Wells and Nieuwenhuis 2001). In response to these problems, a combination of strategies such as global consolidation, platform sharing, outsourcing of non-core competences and the employment of financial incentives have ensured that most companies have maintained some form of economic viability.

As well as financial concerns, the industry must respond to a range of negative environmental effects caused by the production, use and disposal of vehicles (DTI 2000; Motavilli and Spencer-Cooke 2000; Carley and Spapens 1998). Here, too, the industry has successfully adopted a wide range of environmental improvements and achieved a variety of eco-efficiency gains (SMMT 2001). Moreover, there is growing evidence that manufacturers are considering the life-cycle environmental implications of car production, use and end-of-life management in the design of new vehicles and models (Leone 2000).

Even given these ongoing and large-scale efforts, however, the economic and environmental problems associated with the industry continue. Many companies are still forced to close plants and cut jobs in an effort to improve profitability. Furthermore, emissions of carbon dioxide to the atmosphere as a consequence of car usage continue to rise, as do overall levels of fuel consumption. This situation has led some commentators (Nieuwenhuis and Wells 1997, 2003; SustainAbility and UNEP 2001) to suggest that, for a variety of reasons, the types of product, process and other improvements achieved by companies are not adequate to effect lasting long-term sustainability improvements in the industry.

Limitations of the current approach

In terms of improving the sector's profitability, the prevailing global system of vehicle production—based on the all-steel monocoque body—limits the scope of companies to adopt new strategies. This is because the current paradigm drives the industry to manufacture the maximum amount of vehicles in the pursuit of economies of scale to recoup the investments made in capital-intensive technology. As a result, the current economic strategies of most global automotive companies are based on the reconfiguration of production and technological systems in order to realise maximum profits from the manufacture of cars based on the dominant design. However, such strategies do little to challenge the underlying logic of oversupply and inherent limits to profitability. It is clear that such a technocentric approach is, at present, unlikely to deliver radical improvements in economic prospects.

As far as the environmental domain is concerned, it has been observed that incremental improvements in the environmental performance of vehicles are often negatively counterbalanced by increases in overall consumption or more intensive usage patterns. In this respect, the prevailing economic strategy based on the maximisation of unit sales and consumption has direct implications for the overall environmental impact of the industry. Eco-efficiency gains are more than offset by the fact that more cars are in use.

Functional and system innovation

When these phenomena are taken into account, it is clear that a more integrated approach to economic and environmental strategies is required in order to achieve genuine sustainability gains. Such an approach will need to ensure that a wider array of stakeholders are involved in the required change processes. It has been recognised by some that, on the basis of current thinking, it is unlikely that the major global automotive manufacturers can deliver sustainable mobility solutions on the scale required (SustainAbility and UNEP 2001). Moreover, the limited focus on incremental technological improvements, however innovative, must be accompanied by a broader focus on elements such as behavioural and system-level changes. The logic of these criticisms suggests that lasting change in the automotive industry can be achieved only via radical improvements in resource efficiency, accompanied by changing consumption patterns. The realisation of this interdependence between sustainable modes of production and consumption is closely linked to earlier theoretical models which have suggested that, in the generic sense, change needs to be effected at the level of function and system innovation, rather than at the product level, in order to achieve sustainability (Brezet 1997).

In this sense, improvements in the automotive industry need to shift from a focus on improvements in product environmental performance or end-of-life management towards a perspective that takes the underlying function of the car as the starting point for an investigation of new and innovative ways to deliver this functionality. Such a radical shift may also require changes in the entire system associated with the product. This may imply changes in the underlying economic or market dynamics as well as in infrastructure and the behaviour of related organisations and stakeholder groups.

At present, such notions do not tend to be considered as part of the corporate strategies of the major manufacturers. It is in the context of this logic of function and system innovation, however, that innovative new solutions must be sought to address the sustainability issues faced not just by the automotive industry, but also by industry as a whole. It is also evident that in order to realise such solutions, a much wider array of stakeholders associated with a given product or industry—in particular, policy-makers and consumers—must become actively involved in ongoing change processes. As well as collaborating with other organisations within its sector and throughout product supply chains, companies must now consider the role of consumers, retailers and other stakeholders outside their traditional sphere of influence to move towards the functional and systemic improvements necessary for sustainability.

Product-service systems

The challenge now is to devise ways in which such sustainability improvements might be achieved at the practical level. In this respect, the concept of product-service systems (PSSs) offers an interesting perspective. A PSS has been described as 'a system of products, services, supporting networks and infrastructure that is designed to be: competitive, satisfy customer needs and have a lower environmental impact than traditional business models' (Mont 2002a: 239). At its core, the PSS concept is based on a fundamental shift in the relationship between the producers of a product or service and its consumers. Instead of being centred on 'traditional' forms of sale, ownership, consumption and disposal of products, a PSS focuses on the delivery of a 'function' to the customer that might, in practice, mean the provision of any combination of products and services that are capable of 'jointly fulfilling a users need' (Goedkoop *et al.* 1999: 10). In doing so, it embraces a range of elements relating to the management of products throughout their life-cycle in an effort to minimise environmental impacts and to identify alternative profitable revenue streams.

In practice, many of the elements of a PSS can and do form part of existing business-to-business or business-to-consumer interaction. However, it is only when each of the components are unified into a coherent whole that a 'full' PSS can be said to exist. These components are described in more detail below.

New notions of ownership

Within the prevailing production and consumption paradigm, the economic relationship between the manufacturer and ultimate consumer of a product is very limited. In most cases, once they leave manufacturing sites, products are distributed to a network of retail outlets to be purchased by consumers. This intermediate retail function means that there is rarely any direct contact between producers and purchasers. Following purchase, the responsibility for product use and disposal tends to lie with the consumer, and manufacturers have no further involvement with the management of a product following its sale. There are, of course, exceptions. Some companies sell their products via mail order or the internet and deal directly with consumers in the management of product returns. In addition, maintenance contracts or warranties sometimes oblige manufacturers, or their subcontractors, to undertake repair activities if any faults occur to a product within a specified time-scale. Furthermore, the advent of **producer responsibility** legislation in the EU (European Commission 2000) and elsewhere has imposed physical and often financial responsibility on manufacturers for the management of products at the end of their useful life.

Although such examples provide some evidence of an ongoing relationship following the sale of a product, they do little to alter the underlying nature of the economic relationship between producer and consumer. In the main, consumers continue to 'own' products after purchase and the responsibility of manufacturers is limited. The PSS concept challenges this fundamental logic. Within a PSS, a product is rented and/or leased to a consumer instead of being sold. In such a way, the ownership of the product is retained by the manufacturer and utility is provided to consumers through the sale of functional units. Although the idea of such **functional sales** is not entirely new (see, for example, Mont 2002b), when employed as part of a broader PSS, such an approach has the potential to radically change the behaviour of both manufacturers and consumers.

Design of products and services

The fact that manufacturers retain ownership of products within a PSS means that instead of representing profit centres, products become cost centres instead. Since producers become responsible for the physical and financial management of a product throughout its life-cycle, they have an incentive to minimise the associated costs. For example, if manufacturers assume responsibility for product take-back systems, particularly when also subject to regulations that set targets on the percentage of waste products that are recycled or re-used, they are motivated to explore ways of reducing the costs of managing the process and of recycling or refurbishing products at end-of-life.

This changed incentive structure could have a number of implications for the way in which companies approach the design of products and services. To begin with, they will benefit financially by designing products that are easier, and therefore cheaper, to disassemble, refurbish or recycle after the initial use phase. In addition, manufacturers will be motivated to improve the durability of products in order to realise the maximum amount of revenue through using the minimum amount of resources. If the lifetime of a product is extended, more potential profit is available via the increased sale of functional units.

Within this context, concepts such as the modularity and upgradability of products become an important part of the design process. If individual components or modules of a product can be regularly repaired, replaced or upgraded as part of an ongoing contract between producer and consumer, the concept of providing entirely new products and disposing of used ones becomes increasingly obsolete.

New forms of producer–consumer interaction

Another aspect of a PSS is the importance of new forms of dialogue between the supplier and the user of products and services. The fact that manufacturers enter into a long-term contract to provide required levels of functionality means that there is a greater opportunity to enhance the depth and quality of the relationship between them and consumers. While delivering many of the economic and operational benefits identified in the field of customer relationship marketing (Vavra 1995; Gronroos 1990; Addis and Holbrook 2001), it is also envisaged that within the PSS context such channels of communication will further improve the environmental benefits that might be attained. For example, in many product groups it is during the use phase that a significant proportion of negative environmental impacts occur. As shown above, this is the case for a car, where carbon dioxide and other pollutants continue to be emitted throughout its life. The types of long-term producer–consumer relationships facilitated via a PSS present opportunities for the provision of information to users on how to minimise the environmental consequences of product use. The manufacturers of products are likely to possess better information on the conditions of usage under which such impacts might occur and, within a PSS, can provide users of products with guidance on how to best avoid such types of usage.

Another facet of producer–consumer interaction that might be facilitated within a PSS is the reverse flow of information relating to aspects of a product's environmental performance. It is possible that, through long-term usage of a product or service, consumers might discover important facts relating to how best to reduce environmental impacts or improve design. Via formal feedback loops, this information could be conveyed to manufacturers and be considered as part of the ongoing process of continuous PSS design and improvement.

It is likely, at least within conventional modes of product manufacture, distribution and re-use, that retailers would form a pivotal role in facilitating such exchanges of information between producers and consumers. At the point of sale, retailers might provide users with information on environmentally optimised product use. They might also act as first point of contact for users when they make suggestions for product improvements intended for manufacturers.

The PSS concept represents an example of an innovative practical approach to moving beyond simple product environmental innovation and towards innovation at the functional and systemic level. Table 6.1 summarises some of the benefits, and also the potential limitations, of adopting such an approach.

Benefits	
Customer relationship management	By entering into a contract with consumers, companies are provided with opportunities to communicate with them on a regular basis. Within a PSS this might entail the provision of information on new products, services or upgrades. New forms of producer–consumer interaction are also facilitated (see above)
Product acquisition	The establishment of a system of regular product take-back for upgrades or replacement allows companies to benefit from a continuous and predictable source of materials and components
Environmental benefits	Environmental benefits include: dematerialisation; reduced impact during use phase via improved availability of information; regular upgrades to more environmentally benign technology; better end-of-life management of waste; and provision of economic incentives to re-use, repair and remanufacture
Legislative compliance	A PSS approach assists manufacturers in meeting obligations for the collection and treatment of waste products (e.g. as imposed by the EU End-of-Life Vehicles Directive; European Commission 2000)
Limitations	
Over-reliance on existing infrastructure	In order to function optimally, a PSS must often make use of existing infrastructures and networks. For example, the provision of product take-back systems might oblige companies to make use of existing collection services (such as those provided by local authorities or retailers) or the local recycling infrastructure. Such systems may face capacity constraints or lack appropriate technology
Negative environmental impacts	The establishment of product take-back and reverse logistics systems may result in an increase in transport mileages and associated emissions, especially if producer and consumer locations are dispersed across large geographical areas
Management of retail function	The central role of retail and sales staff in liaising between producers and consumers, and facilitating flows of information, may be difficult to manage in practice
Company-related barriers	These include an unwillingness to divulge technical information or outsource support functions; internal systems inertia (e.g. reluctance to introduce necessary changes to accounting methods); capacity constraints; cost; and internal conflict of functions

TABLE 6.1 Some benefits and limitations of PSSs

Source: Mont 2001: 20-25, modified by author

Micro-factory retailing in the automotive industry

It is clear from the above analysis that the adoption of the PSS concept within the auto-motive industry could represent an interesting and effective means of addressing some of the economic and environmental concerns outlined earlier. If the merits of such an approach are to be accepted by the industry, there is a need to explore how such concepts might be implemented at the empirical level. In this light, the analysis below describes how the notion of micro-factory retailing (MFR) might provide a potential means of undertaking such practical steps.

As mentioned earlier, the core technology of most of today's automobiles is the all-steel welded or monocoque body first developed by E.G. Budd in the US in the 1910s (Nieuwenhuis and Wells 2003). The production technology, including press technol-ogy, body build and paint plants, required to manufacture these bodies is highly capi-tal-intensive and forces businesses to make large volumes of cars in order to achieve economies of scale and recoup initial investments (Nieuwenhuis and Wells 1997, 2003; Wells and Nieuwenhuis 1999, 2000, 2001). The outcome is the prevailing market struc-ture, characterised by large-scale manufacturing plants tied in to global distribution and logistics systems, resulting in a host of associated economic and environmental problems.

The MFR concept is founded on the idea that the all-steel body vehicle design is replaced by one based on a separate chassis onto which a variety of different body shapes may be mounted. The cost of the production technology associated with this type of design is much lower than that needed for the monocoque body. It is therefore possible to break even or achieve a profit via greatly reduced manufacturing volumes. For example, it is estimated that a MFR site would incur investment costs of only around £50 million compared to approximately £1.5 billion for a traditional site (Nieuwenhuis and Wells 2003). This departure from the prevailing manufacturing paradigm allows increased flexibility in areas such as plant size, location and function as well as in vehi-cle design and relationships with consumers. In many ways, the MFR concept is closely aligned with many of the ideas associated with PSS, particularly those relating to prod-uct-based services (Bartolomeo *et al.* 2003). Furthermore, it might also represent a means of delivering such a system in the automotive industry that is capable of address-ing some of the potential limitations outlined earlier (see Table 6.1). This idea is explored in more detail below.

Plant size and location

The fact that high manufacturing volumes are no longer economically necessary within the MFR system means that there is more scope to experiment with the size and capac-ity of production sites. Break-even points can be achieved at an order of magnitude lower than is currently possible, meaning that an average MFR site is more likely to pro-duce around 5,000 units per annum rather than 250,000. The smaller scale of manu-facturing operations means that plants can be located much closer to the market than is currently possible, without the need to occupy large areas of land or to be linked to extensive distribution systems. In fact, MFR sites might be based at the local level, thus doing away with the need for comprehensive distribution systems altogether. Similarly, although more generic components and sub-assemblies could be sourced from central locations operating to economies of scale, there might be a greater capacity to source other parts and materials locally. It would be more economically and environmentally efficient to supply components via logistics systems as opposed to entire vehicles.

Innovative vehicle design

Freedom from the constraints of the all-steel body means that manufacturers would have the capacity to be more experimental in their approach to vehicle design. In practice, the separation of body from chassis provides opportunities for the introduction of modular concepts. This opportunity is further enhanced if the chassis is based on alternative powertrain technology such as electric or fuel cell systems. In theory, components, sub-assemblies, body panels or even an entire body could be removed and repaired or upgraded with relative ease. Examples of vehicles based on such modular designs already exist: for example, General Motors' AUTOnomy concept vehicle (Nieuwenhuis and Wells 2003; Burns *et al.* 2002; see also Chapter 16). In addition, concepts such as the Ridek system (see Chapters 7 and 8) show that interchangeability between a variety of body shapes and chassis designs is a realistic aim (Wells 2003; Dower 2001). This possibility means that a MFR site would be in a position to produce such vehicles as the central element of a PSS. Furthermore, it would be possible for users to use a vehicle with an electric or fuel cell-based powertrain for urban travel and easily change to an internal combustion powertrain for inter-urban journeys while still keeping the same body and interior. Such an arrangement means that infrastructural limitations to the use of hydrogen or electric vehicles could be overcome incrementally through initial provision of recharging or refuelling facilities at the local level, allowing a phased transition from a solely petroleum-based system.

Plant function

The small-scale and locally based nature of a typical MFR site means that it would not be limited solely to carrying out manufacturing activities. Proximity to the market means that facilities could also perform a retail function. It is possible that consumers could visit a MFR site and, together with qualified manufacturing or design staff, specify the exact nature of the vehicle they require. They could then collect the car from the site when it is finished.

Such a set-up offers much more choice for consumers over vehicle design and specification. Crucially, the arrangement also facilitates the type of enhanced producer–consumer interaction envisaged as part of a PSS. In addition, such communication processes can occur without the need to involve independent or franchised dealerships or retailers. Users have direct access to qualified staff involved in the design and manufacture of vehicles and vice versa.

All of the above factors combined mean that a MFR site is ideally placed to offer a full repair and modular upgrading service on vehicles leased to consumers as part of a long-term contract. Within such a system, it is likely that the type of vehicles produced would continue in usage beyond currently viable mechanical or economic limits. In fact, it is possible that many would never become end-of-life vehicles in the traditional sense. However, localised MFR sites would still be capable of managing take-back and reverse logistics systems that handled complete vehicles, modules or components for servicing, repair, upgrades or end-of-life management. Particularly when based in urban locations, a micro-factory's proximity to consumers would also mean that some of the economic and environmental shortcomings of such systems could be overcome.

Advantages of the MFR approach for establishing a PSS in the automotive industry

The variety of elements associated with a MFR approach to vehicle manufacture and producer–consumer interaction demonstrate that it could represent a viable option for the introduction of PSS concepts in the car industry and facilitate a transition towards sustainability through system-level innovation. Table 6.2 illustrates how a MFR approach might both enhance the envisaged benefits of a PSS and also help to address the potential limitations.

Conclusions and directions for future research

At the conceptual level, the discussion above has shown that the adoption of MFR concepts in the automotive industry could facilitate the implementation of a full-scale PSS at local levels. Furthermore, Table 6.2 shows that the MFR approach may also offer distinct advantages compared with prevailing visions of PSS. However, although examples exist of MFR-type initiatives in the automotive industry (Wells and Orsato 2003a, 2003b), there is currently no evidence that the concept has been employed to its full potential, particularly in terms of its contribution towards the establishment of a complete PSS. In this light, there is a need for more research into how MFR might realise this potential and, in particular, pilot projects aimed at testing the concept in practice. In addition, it is important that such initiatives seek to test the thesis through a rigorous evaluation of the likely sustainability impacts of the visualised change processes and the particular effect of localisation and the unification of manufacturing and retail functions.

It must also be understood that such radical changes present considerable challenges to a wide range of actors both within and outside the industry to enable success at the practical level. The implementation of system innovations such as MFR and PSS requires awareness of not just network and infrastructural factors but also of the importance of involving a wide range of stakeholders in the necessary change processes. It is crucial that such awareness informs and underpins future theoretical and empirical research. In particular, it is vital that the key role of potential users and local communities is both accounted for and understood. Without consumer or market acceptance, any initiative, despite the potential sustainability benefits, is likely to struggle.

In fostering the levels of commitment and expertise necessary to effect real change in the industry, the challenge now is to involve the relevant stakeholders in a structured

Customer relationship management	New manufacturing and retail paradigm results in location of manufacturing sites much closer to customers. This localisation facilitates easier planning and management of the type of producer–consumer information feedback loops envisaged by the PSS concept
Product acquisition	Combination of localisation and modular approach to vehicle design allows better management of product upgrades, thereby facilitating the efficient planning of product, component and material acquisition via reverse channels (Heiskanen and Jalas 2000)
Environmental benefits	Decrease in manufacturing volumes and resource usage. Reduced environmental impact during use phase. Lower total stock of products and higher rate/quality of utilisation of end-of-life vehicles, components and modular sub-assemblies (Heiskanen and Jalas 2000; White *et al.* 1999; Stahel 1996; Scholl *et al.* 1998; Littig 1999). Body-chassis separation and interchangeability facilitates selection of vehicles more suitable for mobility needs (e.g. use of electric/fuel-cell chassis for urban usage and conventional ICE technology for longer journeys).Manufacturer retention of vehicle ownership maximises incentives to dematerialise, intensify product use, extend product life and improve product function
Legislative compliance	MFR approach is a potentially profitable and proactive means of responding to emerging patterns of legislation, in particular, producer responsibility regulations such as the EU End-of-Life Vehicle Directive (European Commission 2000)
Reliance on existing infrastructure	MFR sites' acceptance of vehicles and components for repair, replacement, upgrade or end-of-life management reduces dependence on existing recycling and remanufacturing infrastructure. Localisation means that it would be cheaper, and therefore more feasible, to arrange collection and transportation 'in-house' without the need to contract externally. Body-chassis interchangeability might also help to address challenges of alternative-fuel infrastructure provision (e.g. via the use of alternatively powered chassis for urban use to help facilitate the incremental introduction of local recharging or hydrogen refuelling stations, while in the short term allowing inter-urban transport to remain powered by the current infrastructure via the use of a replacement ICE chassis)
Impact on take-back systems	Proximity of manufacturing sites to users means operation of reverse logistics and product take-back systems is likely to be more economically and environmentally sustainable. Reduced mileages mean less expenditure on fuel and energy. In addition, associated emissions could be reduced, or even eradicated, if collection vehicles incorporated environmentally benign powertrain technology
Management of retail function	The unification of the commercial and retail functions at MFR sites means that manufacturers could interact directly with vehicle users, thus eliminating the need to rely on external dealerships to liaise between producers and consumers and fostering the easier management of information flows. Such an approach redirects production towards customer needs, rather than following the logic of mass production (Jackson 1996), and is more closely aligned with notions of a 'customised economy' (Schmidt-Bleek and Lehrner 1999)
Company-related barriers	Reduced dependence on capital-intensive production technology improves prospects for higher profits at reduced output levels, helping to overcome internal resistance based on cost concerns. Small-scale operations make necessary changes in accounting methods easier to manage

TABLE 6.2 **Advantages of the MFR approach for establishing a PSS in the automotive industry**

process of research, evaluation and testing, at both the conceptual and empirical level. In this respect, there are important roles for industry actors, along with governments, users and a broad range of associated interests. There is also a need for a deeper investigation of these roles, including how they might evolve within the wide variety of transition contexts, to assist stakeholders in further understanding the actions required to promote and realise sustainable change in the automotive industry.

References

Addis, M., and M.B. Holbrook (2001) 'On the conceptual link between mass customisation and experiential consumption: an explosion of subjectivity', *Journal of Consumer Behaviour* 1.1: 50-66.

Bartolomeo, M., D. dal Maso, P. de Jong, P. Eder, P. Groenewegen, P. Hopkinson, P. James, L. Nijhuis, M. Örninge, G. Scholl, A. Slob and O. Zaring (2003) 'Eco-efficient producer services: what are they, how do they benefit customers and the environment and how likely are they to develop and be extensively utilised?', *Journal of Cleaner Production* 11.8: 829-37.

Brezet, H. (1997) 'Dynamics in eco-design practice', *UNEP/IE Industry and Environment* 20.1-2, January–June 1997: 21-24.

Burns, L.D., J.B. McCormick and C.E. Borroni-Bird (2002) 'Hydrogen fuel cell cars could be the catalyst for a cleaner tomorrow', *Scientific American* 287.4: 64-73.

Carley, M., and P. Spapens (1998) *Sharing the World: Sustainable Living and Global Equity in the 21st Century* (London: Earthscan).

Dower, G.E. (2001) *Modular Vehicle Construction and Transportation System*, US Patent Number 6,059,058.

DTI (UK Department of Trade and Industry) (2000) *The Environmental Impacts of Motor Manufacturing and Disposal of End-of-Life Vehicles: Moving towards Sustainability* (London: Cleaner Vehicles Task Force Report, HMSO).

European Commission (2000) 'Directive 2000/53/EC of the European Parliament and of the Council on 18 September 2000 on end-of-life vehicles', *Official Journal of the European Communities*, 21 October 2000.

Goedkoop, M.J., C.J.G. van Halen, H.R.M. te Riele and P.J.M. Rommens (1999) *Product Service Systems: Ecological and Economic Basics* (The Hague: Den Bosch & Amersfoort: Pi!MC, Stoorm C. S. & PRé Consultants).

Gronroos, C. (1990) *Service Management and Marketing: Managing the Moments of Truth in Service Competition* (Lexington, MA: Lexington Books).

Heiskanen, E., and M. Jalas (2000) *Dematerialisation through Services: A Review and Evaluation of the Debate* (Helsinki: Finnish Ministry of the Environment).

Jackson, T. (1996) *Material Concerns: Pollution, Profit and Quality of Life* (London: Routledge).

Leone, F. (ed.) (2000) *Regulation and Innovation in the Area of End-of-Life Vehicles*, report commissioned by the European Commission Joint Research Centre-Institute for Prospective Technological Studies (JRC-IPTS) and Enterprise DG (Seville, Spain: IPTS).

Littig, B. (1999) *Gemeinsame Nutzung und Ökoeffiziente Dienstleistungen im Privaten Haushalt* (Bestandaufnahme und Weiterführende Fragestellun Sociological Series No. 36; Vienna: Institute for Advanced Studies).

Mont, O. (2001) *Introducing and Developing a Product-Service System (PSS) Concept in Sweden* (Lund, Sweden: International Institute for Industrial Environmental Economics [IIIEE], Lund University, and Nutek).

—— (2002a) 'Clarifying the concept of product-service system', *Journal of Cleaner Production* 10.3: 237-45.

—— (2002b) *Functional Thinking: The Role of Functional Sales and Product-Service Systems for a Function-Based Society* (report 5233; Lund, Sweden: Naturvardsverket/International Institute for Industrial Environmental Economics [IIIEE], Lund University).

Motavilli, J., and A. Spencer-Cooke (2000) 'The road ahead', *Tomorrow* 10.5 (September/October 2000).

Nieuwenhuis, P., and P. Wells (2003) *The Automotive Industry and the Environment* (Cambridge, UK/Boca Raton, FL: Woodhead Publishing/CRC Press).

—— and —— (1997) *The Death of Motoring?: Car-Making and Automobility in the 21st Century* (Chichester, UK: John Wiley).

Schmidt-Bleek, F., and F. Lehrner (1999) *Die Wachstumsmaschine* (Munich: Droemer).

Scholl, G., B. Hirschl and F. Tibitanzl (1998) *Produkte länger und intensiver Nutzen zur Systematisierung und Okologischen: Beurteilung alternativer Nutzungskonzepte* (Berlin: Schriftenreihe des IÖW 134/98).

SMMT (Society of Motor Manufacturers and Traders) (2001) *Towards Sustainability: The Automotive Sector: Second Annual Report* (London: SMMT).

Stahel, W.R. (1996) 'Conditions of demand and supply with dematerialisation as a key strategy', paper presented at *Dematerialisering: En Strategi för Uthållig Utveckling [Dematerialisation: A Strategy for Sustainable Development]* (Stockholm: Avfallsforskningsrådet, 16 June 1996).

SustainAbility and UNEP (United Nations Environment Programme) (2001) *Driving Sustainability: Can the Auto Sector Deliver Sustainable Mobility?* (London/Paris: SustainAbility/UNEP).

Vavra, T.G. (1995) *Aftermarketing: How to Keep Customers for Life through Relationship Marketing* (Chicago: Irwin Professional Publishing).

Wells, P. (2003) 'Reinventing the battery electric car: the Ridek', *Automotive Environment Analyst* 100: 24-26.

—— and P. Nieuwenhuis (2001) *The Automotive Industry: A Guide* (Cardiff, UK: Centre for Automotive Industry Research and British Telecommunications plc).

—— and —— (2000) 'Why big business should think small', *Automotive World*, July/August 2000: 32-38.

—— and —— (1999) 'Micro-factory retailing: a radical business concept for the automotive industry', *Sewells Automotive Marketing Review* 5: 3-7.

—— and R.J. Orsato (2003a) 'Product, process and structure: redesigning the industrial ecology of the automobile', *Proceedings of the International Society for Industrial Ecology Conference*, Ann Arbor, MI, 29 June–2 July 2003.

—— and —— (2003b) 'The ecological modernisation of the automobile industry', *Proceedings of the Berlin Conference on the Human Dimensions of Global Environmental Governance for Industrial Transformation*, Berlin, 5–6 December 2003.

White, A.L., M. Stoughton and L. Feng (1999) *Servicising: The Quiet Transition to Extended Product Responsibility* (Boston, MA: Tellus Institute, www.tellus.org).

7

Business models for relocalisation to deliver sustainability

Peter Wells and Paul Nieuwenhuis

ESRC Centre for Business Relationships, Accountability, Sustainability and Society, Cardiff University, UK

A number of years ago we proposed the concept of micro-factory retailing (MFR) as a possible future business model for a sustainable car industry (Wells and Nieuwenhuis 2000; Nieuwenhuis and Wells 2003). This posits a gradual replacement of the large centralised facilities that currently dominate the industry by a dispersed network of small local assembly, sales and repair facilities. We argued that this would entail abandoning certain key technologies and practices that dominate traditional car-making— notably Budd's all-steel body and its attendant massive capital investment needs— which are major contributors to the sector's chronic lack of profitability. The argument was first advanced in print in Wells and Nieuwenhuis 2000, and was subsequently refined through various iterations and treated in more detail in Nieuwenhuis and Wells 2003. It is currently the subject of a research project within Cardiff University's Economic and Social Research Council (ESRC) Centre for Business Relationships, Accountability, Sustainability and Society, under the aegis of which some of the details will be investigated.

The key elements of MFR involve a moving of economies of scale up the supply chain and well away from assembly. Assembly involves configuring the vehicle to the needs of the customer, and this is best done in the most flexible, usually most labour-intensive, and most localised manner to ensure sound communication between the final assembler and the customer. Economies of scale can be achieved in key modules, components or other elements that are of less interest to the customer, such as basic powertrain and chassis items, rather than in that most visible element—the car body. Once this move has been made, a host of other possibilities are opened up. In this chapter we focus on the impact of this alternative business model on local economies.

This chapter demonstrates the interconnections between product, process, scale, structure and consumption. We side with those who argue that **relocalisation** is the basis for viable alternative business models, providing economic resilience to local communities, and a key route to sustainability. Those working from a cultural and social perspective have sought to emphasise the significance of local economic structures in engendering a sense of belonging and mutuality (Douthwaite 1996; Korten 1999; Hines 2000; McIntosh 2002). The key has been to find business models to supplant those currently in place (Hart 1997). Critics of unsustainable business find little difficulty in identifying the problems (Korten 1995, 1999; Gray 1998; Shrybman 1999; Klein 2000), but arriving at remedial solutions has proven more difficult. We argue that sustainable business must change the terms of competition and create a new **vernacular economics**—an inclusive **economics of the people** (Schumacher 1973; Daly 1999; Hawken *et al.* 1999; McIntosh 2002; Desai and Riddlestone 2002). Schumacher (1973) subtitled his book, 'economics as if people mattered'—something our current dominant economic paradigm seems to have forgotten.

Seen in a historical perspective, mass production via large-scale facilities and concentrated ownership structures can be seen as a necessary but temporary phase (Batchelor 1994). Our proposed vision for automotive MFR is radically different to the current structure of multi-brand, multi-location companies founded on the logic of mass production and its associated economies of scale.

As a theoretical concept, **local** defies precise definitional boundaries. It is a dynamic, socially embedded concept that embraces elusive phenomena such as a sense of place and belonging. **Locality** has meaning that is contextual and relative (and so may therefore appear elusive); yet it is also persistent and surviving, presenting a challenge to the more modern nation-state (Stephens 1976). We conclude that the decentralised economy constructed from micro-businesses can provide the skeleton on which the body politic of localities can, at last, be rebuilt.

The socio-cultural basis of locality

Our spatial world operates at several levels: global, international, national, regional, metropolitan and local. These terms combine distinct characteristics: physical size, natural geographic boundaries, cultural aggregations, legal entities, political entities and domains of economic power. In between these levels, geographers have constructed other plausible concepts: for example, the **hinterland** concept or the notion of the **triad countries/regions** (Ohmae 1985). The environmental dictum of 'think global, act local' embraces the two extremes of spatial scale, but in practice both extremes are rather fluid in definition. Hence, any call, such as that made here, for relocalisation forces us to consider what we mean by 'local' at all. Hines (2000: 30) claims:

> The parameters of the area within which each industry would site would be predominately the nation state, although for some goods (e.g. agricultural products), the area might be sub-national. For very large industries, such as

aeroplane production, the delineation might be the actual grouping of countries which make up the geographical bloc.

Locality is a discourse, continually redefined and contested in many different domains. While it may be analytically helpful to separate the many strands of that discourse into more manageable portions, it is important to be mindful that cultural impulses for new thinking can come from many sources. This suggests that attempts to undertake the journey of sustainability must consider the issue of locality and the meaning that the concept of locality has in people's lives.

The environmental basis of locality

Environmental problems can become manifest over a variety of spatial scales: from the highly localised pollution incident, to regional questions over biodiversity, to transnational concerns over boundary-crossing polluting emissions and discharges, and, finally, to the global impact of ozone depletion or greenhouse gas emissions.

In certain instances, the incidence of local environmental problems is simply a function of geography. Only certain locations have iron ore, or can support cotton plants and, therefore, only these places can experience the particular problems associated with ore extraction or cotton farming. Problems arise when people in a locality feel that they are taking on an unfair environmental burden on behalf of the wider society as a whole: for example, waste incinerators, airports, mines, wind generators or new housing developments.

Large-scale high-throughput production tends to be capital-intensive and inflexible. A potential consequence is over-production. The pressure to achieve high output is considerable and may override actual market demand. Moreover, in the search for ever-greater levels of production efficiency, it may be the case that optimum production capacity grows over time. As well as allowing higher unit throughput per unit of capital investment, large-scale production usually also reduces variable costs (notably labour). Lower unit costs in production lead to lower unit prices in markets, and—all things being equal—market expansion. Over-production may be masked by technological innovation to increase the unit value of the product and by expansion of the market which forces a re-evaluation of the 'normal' level of consumption.

The automotive industry shows symptoms of over-production. These include high rates of discounting for new products, high rates of product value depreciation, ownership rates that greatly exceed the ability of people to use the product and premature scrapping of the product. Over-production, a strong possibility with capital-intensive plant, is undesirable because it constitutes a waste of resources and unnecessary pollution.

The economic basis of locality

The ecological perspective presents a challenge to the predominance of production in both mainstream economics and in Marxist thinking. While there have been attempts to formulate a new **environmental economics** (Pearce 1989, 1991), radical critics argue that this is a deeply flawed project (Hayward 1994).

Still, the localisation of a distributed economy is not just a statement of how to do things 'better' from an economic perspective. On the contrary, it is a deliberate attempt to reintegrate economics with the concerns of politics and society. The basic principles outlined here are derived from Schumacher (1973: 26-35):

- Material wealth, particularly as measured by metrics such as GDP, has no correlation with individual happiness or peacefulness

- Continued 'growth' on such measures is doomed to meet the physical limitations of the natural world

- Contemporary economics is based on the non-valuation of natural 'free' goods or the short-term valuation of irreplaceable natural resources

- The distributed economy is founded on the notion of the economics of permanence

- Science and technology should be oriented towards the peaceful, the non-violent, the gentle, the organic and the non-invasive

- Technologies should be cheap enough to be accessible to everybody, suitable to deployment on a small scale and capable of fostering creativity

- Work should be enriching and rewarding, not enslaving humanity to the regimen of the machine

- Wealth and power should not be concentrated into the hands of the few; in particular, the capital cost of a workplace should not be substantially more than the average annual wage

It is clear that the latter principle poses a particular challenge. The broader social and cultural dimensions of locality are beyond the scope of this chapter, although the comments above argue that they must be part of the wider definition of sustainability. The focus is on the economic dimensions of locality. Embedded within this is the idea that relocalisation is a dynamic process of progression towards local (economic) self-sufficiency. For some, therefore, relocalisation can be achieved only by economic protectionism against the adverse effects of free trade, with a strategy that (Hines 2001: 45):

> centres on the replacement of the present political and economic theology of globalisation with an emphasis on local production and the rebuilding of local economies . . . Localisation means, very simply, that everything that could be produced within a nation or region should be.

Note, however, that 'nation' and 'region' are quite different geographic entities. Moreover, within the same short article other phrases are used, all of which have different meanings; examples include 'domestic markets', 'local economies', 'nations', 'local governments', 'communities' and 'community life'. Furthermore, there is a logical limit to the ability of a 'locality', however defined, to provide for economic self-sufficiency if it is to exist beyond the level of subsistence. It cannot be expected that every village, town or region could possibly provide all the materials and products that necessary in contemporary society. Similarly, Hines's (2000: 30) suggestion quoted earlier that the nation-state may be the optimum unit in most cases has different implications for Luxembourg and the US. Daly (1999: 68) quotes John Maynard Keynes on this issue:

> I sympathise therefore, with those who would minimise, rather than those who would maximise, economic entanglement between nations. Ideas, knowledge, art, hospitality, travel—these are the things which should of their nature be international. But let goods be homespun whenever it is reasonably and conveniently possible; and above all, let finance be primarily national.

Is a decentralised economy more robust? The implication is that such an economy is self-sufficient, autonomous, able to withstand the vagaries of global economic turbulence, the people within it masters of their own destiny and therefore genuinely free. There may also be analogies with biodiversity in that an economically diverse society may be more resilient, in the same way as a biologically diverse ecosystem.

The significance of scale in sustainable business

It is inevitable that relocalisation raises the issue of the **scale** of capital investment. Local patterns of production and consumption mean a fragmentation of economic effort with smaller markets for products and services. The congruence between economies of scale, centralisation (or concentration) of capital and globalisation represents the dominant mode of organisation for production and consumption, although not the only possible one. Put in terms of business models, the profitability opportunities afforded by sector consolidation and the creation of monolithic corporate entities are apparently immutable and inevitable; but they are also historically specific (Post 1961; Wells 2001c). In this case, as the business context changes, so the business models may also change.

Perhaps the single dimension that is most relevant to the analysis of the automotive industry is that of scale. The anarchist theorist Murray Bookchin (1980: 92) has sought to emphasise that technology per se is insufficient. What is of equal importance is that, from an ecological perspective, the organisation of economic and social life also needs to approach a human scale:

> Simply put, this means that corporate gigantism with its immense, incomprehensible industrial installations would have to be replaced by small units which people could comprehend and directly manage by themselves.

And as Schumacher (1973: 31) argued:

> Small-scale operations, no matter how numerous, are always less likely to be harmful to the natural environment than large-scale ones, simply because their individual force is small in relation to the recuperative forces of nature.

In the automotive industry, perhaps the best-known single example of large-scale manufacturing and the pursuit of centralised economies of scale, there are clear signs that limits are being reached. Generic diseconomies of scale include, for example, the costs of co-ordinating and managing very large, multicultural organisations. Specific internal diseconomies of scale that apply to the automotive industry might include the negative market consequences of product standardisation with all-steel vehicle bodies (Nieuwenhuis and Wells 1997, 2003). This, in itself, suggests that scale is being used in two senses here. First, there is the question of scale with respect to manufacturing facilities, an issue closely related to the characteristics of product design and process technology. Second, there is the question of scale with respect to the corporation as a whole. Typically, in the automotive industry, economies of scale derive from activities such as purchasing and R&D that can be spread over several models or manufacturing plants.

Profitability in the automotive industry has declined over a long period dating back to about 1930 (cf. Haglund 2001). Moreover, there appears to be no more room for traditional inter-company consolidation. The consequence, in markets such as the US, is a market artificially boosted by discounts and incentives with consumers locked into finance deals on cars that will be virtually worthless when it comes to the trading them in (Kiley 2003).

Being small in scale does not guarantee robustness for individual companies or for the decentralised economy as a whole. Indeed, because each individual economic entity is relatively weak there is a clear danger that, under some strong competitive challenge, they will simply all collapse at once. Economic history is full of examples of rapid structural change of this type, as in the automotive sector in the 1930s when high investment in new technologies for mass production conspired with the world economic crisis to condemn scores of car manufacturers (Nieuwenhuis and Wells 1997: 196-99; Nieuwenhuis and Wells 2003: 100-15; Raff 1991, 1994). This is why it is important to have business models that are deeply rooted in their local economies, to have sources of competitive advantage that cannot be replicated or bypassed by other competitors.

A further issue to consider is that of scale and ownership. This must be a part of the analysis of relocalisation and the business models presented below. It appears to be generally assumed that small-scale, local manufacturing means a 'more democratic' ownership structure without undue concentrations of wealth and power. Even where such enterprises are privately and individually owned, the relative concentration of wealth is not great and the business is presumed to be better embedded in the locality through many formal and informal mechanisms.

Illustrations of local sustainability: business models for a new era

Local assembly facilities within our MFR model could be centrally owned by corporations, under a franchise system, be jointly owned by a MFR collective or be locally owned by a local business (e.g. a former car dealer) or individual. In rejecting mass manufacturing it is important that the alternative business models are based on concepts such as product stewardship and producer responsibility, as well as on localisation. The operationalisation of these concepts is by no means straightforward. Moreover, as Gillespie (2001: 54) warns:

> green consumerism is spreading the message that by substituting good materials and designs for bad ones, then it is possible to marry the growth economy and protection of the environment. Many green theorists are profoundly sceptical as to whether this is in fact the case.

Thus, making cars more efficiently, with less waste and even making fewer of them does not, in itself, make automobility sustainable. This issue is explored and developed in more detail in Nieuwenhuis and Wells 2003. The following examples give some indication of the manner by which relocalisation may be achieved. The over-arching concept is that of MFR which is a business model for the automotive industry in a distributed economy (Wells and Nieuwenhuis 2000; Wells 2001a; Nieuwenhuis and Wells 2003). Importantly, this approach makes feasible alternative materials and design concepts that are viable only at low volume. In many ways, this allows significant improvements in the industrial ecology of automobile production and distribution, but which in traditional thinking are not economically viable at 'high volume'.

Example 1: TH!NK

The basic design concept of TH!NK was a two-seat city battery electric vehicle (BEV) for urban commuters and utilities (Wells and Nieuwenhuis 1999). Up to the point when Ford stepped in and bought the company, this BEV required an investment of only US$35–40 million compared to the US$1 billion thought to have been spent by Daimler-Chrysler on the two-seat Smart car (Automotive Industries 2000).

The business plan included two aspects of relevance to relocalisation. The first was for the factory to use internet sales and mobile service delivery to obviate the need for dealerships; hence, the factory would be the point of retail and service delivery, giving the company a broader income base. The second was the intention to supply potential new markets (such as California) by locating 'cloned' factories in those markets. The spatial scale of such markets (i.e. the definition of 'local' in this example) and the extent of such cloning were seen as dependent on the success of the product, perhaps envisaged as one plant per national territory.

Example 2: Ridek

The Ridek, as described by its inventor in Chapter 8, consists of two parts—a motorised deck (termed the Modek) that combines the chassis with the powertrain in one integral unit, and a self-contained body module (termed the Ridon) that is mounted onto the motorised deck via four fixing points (Wells 2003). The Modek is intended to be battery-powered, at least in urban areas. However, because the design range is quite small (approximately 50 miles between recharges) it is possible to keep costs and weight down. The battery can be recharged while in the Modek or, if time is of the essence, the entire Modek can be swapped.

Under the proposed business model only the Ridon would be purchased and owned by the consumer. The Modek would be owned by the municipal authority which would have to retain sufficient numbers to allow Modeks to be exchanged as required. Modeks would then be rented or leased out to consumers, but could be serviced, repaired, maintained or upgraded at a central urban facility.

Localisation in this model is defined at the urban level. It is envisaged that the Ridek would be produced by small companies in the urban area, while the Modek would be owned by the local government and located at municipal level. In the case of the US, city authorities usually have responsibility for transport within their territory.

Example 3: OScar

OScar is a UK-based entrepreneurial start-up company that is seeking to bring to market a vehicle concept based on the Hypercar of Amory Lovins. It combines a carbon-fibre body structure with fuel-cell powertrain to create a lightweight zero-emissions vehicle (ZEV). However, one of the most interesting aspects of this particular project is the use of **open-source design**, as in Linux software (Wells 2001b), although it is also proposed to adopt **materials leasing** in the supply chain.

The idea at the moment is for a small-scale manufacturing effort simply because the product is going to be a niche application. Hence, one MFR-type unit could supply a market such as the UK. Again, market expansion would be met by multiplying the number of plants rather than building one larger plant.

Example 4: MDI Air Car

The company Moteur Développement Internationale (MDI) was formed to bring to market the ideas of the inventor of the compressed-air engine, Guy Nègre (Wells 2002). The technical concept and the business plan have generated much controversy in the automotive industry, and doubts over both remain. The car is positioned in the market, and performs rather like a BEV but without the weight and cost penalty of high-performance batteries. Compared with contemporary petrol and diesel cars the range, top speed and acceleration are limited.

MDI has tried a quite different approach with respect to its business model, and one that has interesting pointers to achieving relocalisation. The core of the MDI approach is to grant licences to third parties that in effect take on an MDI franchise for a defined territory in return for the investment needed to create the factory to serve that territory. In addition, the standardised factory includes office space and a showroom, because in the MDI concept the point of manufacturing is also the point of retail and service/maintenance delivery. The scale of territory or definition of locality in the MDI approach appears to be approximately equal to a European sub-national region or US metropolitan area.

Example 5: GM AUTOnomy and HY-wire

These are described in considerable detail by Borroni-Bird in Chapter 16. Designed by General Motors (GM), the brief for these concept cars was essentially to reinvent the automobile in the light of the fuel cell and drive-by-wire. The result is a truly revolu-tionary concept, and an important reminder that notwithstanding the constraints that bind existing industrial organisations it is possible for radical thinking to be nurtured within them also.

In concept, the GM AUTOnomy has certain similarities with the Ridek outlined in example 2. The vehicle is split, with a running chassis on which a body can be mounted. The chassis contains the fuel cell and all related powertrain components, as well as the physical and electronic docking points for the body. With drive-by-wire there is scope for the redesign as demonstrated by the Hy-wire concept vehicle (General Motors 2003).

From the perspective of centralisation and relocalisation the GM concept offers ele-ments of both. It could be envisaged that the core chassis and powertrain would be assembled at a large-scale, centralised facility gaining huge economies of scale and thereby making the fuel cell economically viable. Small-scale local enterprises could add the bodies.

Conclusions

There is no definitive concept of relocalisation that captures all types of economic activ-ity and all types of locality. Rather, it is an organising concept, a philosophy, a way of thinking about the world that guides analysis and action. Thus, what might be consid-ered as 'local' for car production might be quite different to that for computers or houses or paper.

There are some clearly discernable trends towards Schumacher's (1973) 'small is beautiful' philosophy in a range of industrial sectors, amid public concern over global-isation (Klein 2001). However, on a macro-level the World Trade Organisation (WTO) agenda of global free trade encourages ever-larger units of production and business. This is actually a relatively new phenomenon; only a few years ago protectionism was still common and, even now, many so-called barriers to trade are still in place (Wood 1994). It is therefore not surprising that even the WTO itself feels compelled to admit in its 1998 annual report that (Gray 1998: 3):

> Empirical evidence tends to show that trade liberalisation may entail non-trivial adjustment costs for certain groups.

Korten (1995, 1999) and, particularly, Hines (2000) both suggest that a re-emphasis of the 'local' may well provide the answer. Hines (2000) sets out a new world trade regime which emphasises relocalisation—an idea promoted by a growing body of lit-erature focusing on the revitalisation of local communities (e.g. Shuman 1998; Shiva 1998; Douthwaite 1996; Hines 2000). The Rio Earth Summit of 1992 also emphasised the local in its Agenda 21, by encouraging the implementation of local equivalents on the basis of 'think global, act local'. How is this relevant for our MFR concept? Shuman (1998: 6) explains that localisation:

> means nurturing locally owned businesses which use local resources sustain-ably, employ local workers at decent wages and serve primarily local cus-

tomers. It means becoming more self sufficient, and less dependent on imports. Control moves from the boardrooms of distant corporations and back to the community where it belongs.

The main aim is that any move towards the local (Hines 2000: 31):

> has at its core the aims of providing basic needs sustainably, improving human rights, reducing the power gaps between different groupings and genders, and increasing equity and democratic control over decision-making.

We could add that in the automotive case it would also enable a better response to genuine customer demand, while restoring profitability to the sector and thus making an important move towards rendering it economically, as well as socially and environmentally, sustainable.

References

Automotive Industries (2000) 'Smart thinking?', *Automotive Industries* 37.180: 9.

Batchelor, R. (1994) *Henry Ford: Mass Production, Modernism and Design* (Manchester, UK: Manchester University Press).

Bookchin, M. (1980) *Toward an Ecological Society* (Montreal: Black Rose Books).

Daly, H. (1999) *Ecological Economics and the Ecology of Economics: Essays in Criticism* (Cheltenham, UK: Edward Elgar).

Desai, P., and S. Riddlestone (2002) *Bioregional Solutions for Living on One Planet: Schumacher Briefing No. 8* (Totnes, UK: Green Books).

Douthwaite, R. (1996) *Short Circuit: Strengthening Local Economies for Security in an Unstable World* (Totnes, UK: Green Books).

Gillespie, A. (2001) *The Illusion of Progress: Unsustainable Development in International Law and Policy* (London: Earthscan).

General Motors (2003) *Hy-wire and HydroGen3* (Zurich: GM Europe, Mediainfo CD).

Gray, J. (1998) *False Dawn: The Delusions of Global Capital* (London: Granta).

Haglund, R. (2001) 'Tell-all tome: GM-published history includes company's woes', book review reprinted from *The Flint Journal* in *Society of Automotive Historians Journal* 191: 8.

Hart, S. (1997) 'Beyond greening: strategies for a sustainable world', *Harvard Business Review*, January/February: 66-76.

Hayward, T. (1994) *Ecological Thought: An Introduction* (London: Polity Press).

Hawken, P., A. Lovins and L.H. Lovins (1999) *Natural Capitalism: The Next Industrial Revolution* (London: Earthscan).

Hines, C. (2000) *Localisation: A Global Manifesto* (London: Earthscan).

—— (2001) 'The new protectionism', *The Ecologist* 31.2: 44-50.

Kiley, D. (2003) 'Lack of trade-in value burns car buyers', *USA Today* 7 July: 1A.

Klein, N. (2000) *No Logo* (London: HarperCollins).

Korten, D. (1995) *When Corporations Rule the World* (San Francisco: Berrett-Koehler).

—— (1999) *The Post-Corporate World, Life after Capitalism* (West Hartford, CT: Kumarian Press).

McIntosh, A. (2002) *Soil and Soul: People versus Corporate Power* (London: Aurum Press).

Nieuwenhuis, P., and P. Wells (1997) *The Death of Motoring? Car Making and Automobility in the 21st Century* (Chichester, UK: John Wiley).

—— (2003) *The Automotive Industry and the Environment: A Technical, Business and Social Future* (Cambridge, UK: Woodhead Publishing).

Ohmae, K. (1985) *The Rise of Triad Power* (New York: Harper & Row).

Pearce, D. (1989) *Blueprint for a Green Economy* (London: Earthscan).

—— (1991) *Blueprint 2: Greening the World Economy* (London: Earthscan).

Post, D.R. (1961) *A Tour of the Remarkable Ford Industries During the Days when the End Product was the Matchless Model A* (facsimile edition of 1929 original by Ford Motor Co.; Arcadia, CA: Post Motor Books).

Raff, D. (1991) 'Making cars and making money in the interwar automobile industry: economies of scale and scope and the manufacturing behind the marketing', *Business History Review*, Winter 1991/92: 721-53.

—— (1994) 'Models of the evolution of production systems and the diffusion of mass production methods in the American motor vehicles industry', paper presented at 2nd International Meeting of GERPISA (Groupe d'Études et de Recherches Permanent sur l'Industrie et les Salariés de l'Automobile), Paris, France, 12–16 June 1994.

Schumacher, E.F. (1973) *Small is Beautiful: Economics as if People Really Mattered* (London: Abacus).

Shiva, V. (1998) *Globalisation, Gandhi and Swadeshi* (New Delhi, India: Research Foundation for Science, Technology and Ecology).

Shrybman, S. (1999) *A Citizen's Guide to the World Trade Organisation* (Ottawa: Canadian Centre for Policy Alternatives).

Shuman, M. (1998) *Going Local: Creating Self-reliant Communities in a Global Age* (New York: The Free Press).

Stephens, M. (1976) *Linguistic Minorities in Western Europe* (Llandysul, UK: Gomer).

Wells, P. (2001a) 'Micro factory retailing: a business model and development trajectory for emerging economies', paper presented at *Greening of Industry Network Conference, 'Sustainability at the Millennium: Globalisation, Competitiveness and the Public Trust'*, Bangkok, Thailand 22–25 January 2001.

—— (2001b) 'Not invented here: the future of car design', *Automotive World Opinion* 5: 15-17.

—— (2001c) Wide strip steel and the automotive industry: welded together by destiny?', paper presented at conference *The History of the Wide Strip Mill*, Manchester University Department of Classics and History, 27–28 April 2001.

—— (2002) 'The Air Car: symbiosis between technology and business model', *Automotive Environment Analyst* 92: 25-27.

—— (2003) 'Reinventing the battery car: the Ridek', *Automotive Environment Analyst* 100: 24-26.

—— and P. Nieuwenhuis (1999) 'TH!NK: the future of electric vehicles?', *Automotive Environment Analyst* 53: 20-22.

—— and —— (2000) 'Why big business should think small', *Informa Automotive World*, July/August 2000: 32-38.

Wood, A. (1994) *North–South Trade, Employment and Inequality: Changing Fortunes in a Skill-Driven World* (Oxford, UK: Oxford University Press).

8
Modularity for greening the automobile

Gordon Dower

The Ridek Corporation, Washington, DC, USA

Like the camel that was allowed to put its nose into the Bedouin's tent and by degrees took it over, the internal combustion engine (ICE) has taken over our cities, clogging and polluting them to an unacceptable degree. Dependent though we are upon it, the ICE has to go. But what is there to replace it? The electric motor? There is plenty of electricity, especially at night, and a grid system for distributing it. Much of it comes from renewable and non-polluting sources. Even the 60% we get from coal can, if we insist, be obtained with zero pollution in clean coal generators.

Until recently, electric drives for cars were largely ignored because of the difficulty of storing electricity. A report issued by the California Air Resources Board (CARB) in 2000 concluded that a major breakthrough in battery technology would be needed before the battery electric vehicle (BEV) could be cost-effective (CARB 2000). Following that, hybrid electric vehicles (HEVs) and fuel-cell vehicles (FCVs) have come to the fore. These electric vehicles (EVs) generate electricity within the car. However, the HEV is not a zero-polluting vehicle. It has an ICE that pollutes, albeit much less in city stop-and-go driving than a conventional car. It also tends to be more expensive and is, at best, a stopgap. Although the FCV is a zero-polluting EV, it is not a feasible solution, at least not in the short to mid term. A competitively priced FCV is probably a decade away, and the infrastructure to supply it with hydrogen will probably require a score of years, and enormous expenditure—far beyond the resources of all but the wealthiest of countries (Wallace 2003).

The BEV offers a more complete solution to vehicular pollution because it is a zero-polluting EV and has the infrastructure to support it. If a BEV was as economical and convenient as conventional cars, it would soon replace them. BEVs are pleasant to drive, quiet and can be fast, but they don't go very far. Unfortunately, where a car has a range of about 300 miles on a tank of gasoline, a BEV's range is perhaps only half or a quarter of that. Energy, in the form of gasoline or diesel fuel, can be reloaded in minutes, but quick-charging a battery takes five to ten times longer. Also, batteries wear out in a few years and are expensive to replace. For these reasons, despite it being the vehicle of choice when gasoline cars were unreliable and required hand-cranking to start them, the BEV has almost disappeared. Consequently, it has been denied the extensive R&D underlying the highly evolved and sophisticated fossil fuel-burning car. However, the winds of change are veering and beginning to blow the other way. The metamorphosis of the fossil fuel-burning car has already begun, with the apparently successful hybrid car—still burning fossil fuel, still with its ICE, but also electric.

Today, HEVs and FCVs receive the most attention. However, if a good, cheap battery were available, this could quickly change, and better batteries are on the way. While we wait for that better battery, can we adapt the automobile so that even today's lead-acid battery suffices to make it acceptable and attractive? Then, when better batteries emerge, the BEV becomes a winner.

The key is to reduce the range requirement and improve the working conditions (and thus the life) of the battery. If we can accept a modest range, we have a lighter vehicle with a cheaper battery. One suggestion to compensate for the limited range of a BEV is to change its batteries instead of waiting for them to be recharged. In theory this is sound, but in practice it is difficult, and batteries may be damaged in the process (Rader-Olsson 2000). Rather than disconnecting and removing the battery, sliding it onto a sturdy carriage, to replace it with another, why not change the battery, wheels and running gear in one piece?

Ridek

The author holds patents for a modular vehicle, the Ridek, composed of a motorised deck (the Modek) with a passenger compartment (the Ridon) riding upon it (Dower 2000a, 2000b). In an attractive business paradigm, the Modek would be supplied under a rental contract to the owner of the Ridon. For urban use, the readily exchanged Modek would run on its battery, making the Ridek a zero-polluting electric vehicle (ZEV). For inter-urban use, the Modek could be quickly exchanged (at a Modek exchange station) for a fuel-burning ICE Modek. The Ridek concept turns out to have unexpected advantages and economies that combine to render the BEV potentially competitive, using off-the-shelf components.

What range would be acceptable to most drivers? For urban driving a daily range of 50 miles would suffice most of the time. On those occasions when it did not, exchange of the Modek for one that is fully charged could be carried out in less time than that needed to refill the gas tank of a conventional car, while the driver and passengers remain in the Ridon. Normally, recharging the Modek would take place overnight from a domestic supply so that visits to an exchange station would be infrequent—perhaps monthly.

Setting the range at 50 miles instead of, say, 150 miles, reduces the battery size, and hence the cost, to less than one third—less because the lighter vehicle needs less energy to propel it. An important factor affecting battery life is battery management. Good management can more than double a battery's life, but this is normally awkward and unlikely. However, it becomes easy and convenient when a rented Modek is exchanged because the Modek without a Ridon affords easy access to the battery which can be serviced without disturbing it or its connections. It turns out that the saving from using electricity from the grid instead of gasoline is sufficient to cover battery replacement costs (Dower 2002a, 2002b). So we have a paradigm in which the BEV becomes cost-effective. Furthermore, there are other savings and advantages with the Ridek. Indeed, if the perfect battery should become available so that constructing a BEV on traditional lines was cost-effective, the Ridek design would have sufficient additional merits to promote and justify its continued use.

Although, over the years, the development of the BEV has not received much encouragement, it can now incorporate many significant advances from the electronics industry (Westbrook 2001). High-speed switches give more efficient motor controllers. The motors themselves are considerably more efficient and lighter. Regenerative braking has become common practice in hybrids, and super capacitors offer highly efficient energy storage without compromising battery life. Lightweight materials for chassis and body construction help to increase range.

EV1

The sophisticated EV1 electric car produced by General Motors (now mysteriously withdrawn to be broken up, despite the earnest pleas of happy users and eager buyers; see Goldstein 2003), is a far cry from the elegant, though primitive, electric brougham that Henry Ford bought for his wife in 1910. However, for all its excellent engineering, the EV1 reflects a mind-set that appears to pervade auto-makers and designers. This dictates that cars should appear excessively streamlined to cater to a desire for speeds that are illegal on most highways. The roofs of such cars are low and their passengers sit as close as possible to the surface of the road, to be packaged with the machinery and gas tank, and level with the bumper of another car impacting from the side at an intersection! Reinforced doors and side-impact airbags do not entirely reassure the majority of car buyers, who show their concern by preferring sports utility vehicles (SUVs), light trucks and minivans. The roofs of many low-slung cars are often so low that doors must be cut into the roof to avoid striking one's head during entry or exit. It is not convenient or elegant to jack-knife oneself into these streamlined marvels.

Similar streamlined thinking slants the windshield, side and rear windows so that, from above, the roof shades only half the area of the passenger compartment. In California, this greenhouse needs a powerful air conditioner to make any car that has been standing in the sun habitable before the passengers lose their grooming and composure. Running a powerful air conditioner while stalled in traffic could deplete a battery of the energy to continue when the flow of traffic is restored—a taxing proposition for a BEV! Poor design of both dwellings and cars has led to the extravagant use of air conditioners and the neglect of principles well known to ancient architects and builders. Consider the design of a simple shed in which a gardener might choose to sit, out of the glaring sun. This is no greenhouse. The roof and walls would be reflective and insulated, the windows shaded and there would be ventilation. To make it a little high-tech, there might be a solar panel on the roof to drive a fan inside.

A new class of vehicle

Just as the early car-makers had to realise that they were not making horseless carriages but a new form of transportation, so must the Ridek maker realise that this is a new class of vehicle, not to be restricted by mind-sets based on form rather than function.

The EVI was a substantial vehicle, yet it carried only two people. A family BEV must do better than that. Streamlined it certainly was, to minimise drag, especially at highway speeds. This, with tyres having a low resistance to rolling, contributed to its 150 mile range. The Ridek, on the other hand, was conceived with urban driving, convenience and utility in mind. Minimising drag is important, but as a compromise rather than an ethic. Any design must be a compromise encompassing perceived or assigned priorities. When we emphasise convenience, we must not ignore the inconvenience of frequent re-energising because that will subtract from the overall convenience equation.

Overnight recharging is clearly less inconvenient than having to divert to a petrol station in the middle of a journey to fill up. Modek exchange will be required occasionally, but this can be quicker than filling up, provided there is a convenient Modek exchange station. Another benefit would be freedom from routine servicing—required only for the Modek and carried out after it had been exchanged. Instead of a courtesy car, users keep their own Ridon.

In keeping with our emphasis on convenience and utility, the Ridek's dimensions are based on the commodious Astrovan or the Eurovan that has the same profile, although is slightly narrower. Today, these serve as family cars, taxis, delivery vans and service vehicles. With suitable Ridons, Rideks could find similar employment. This makes the Ridek zero-polluting EV more useful than the unambitious and diminutive so-called 'neighbourhood vehicles' presently wearing the zero-polluting EV escutcheon. Because the Modek determines only the footprint, not the profile, the Ridek can have various configurations, such as a light van.

The deck of the Modek is 63.5 cm above the ground. This allows the driver to sit at the same height as the driver of an Astrovan, with the same excellent view of the road and positional safety from side impact—the same as that of an SUV, but without the latter's high centre of gravity and tendency to roll over. Although a Ridek is unlikely to roll over, it has rollover bars that securely lock into the Modek. To these the floor, seats, seat belts, controls, windows, roof and doors of the Ridon are attached. When the Ridon is lifted, for storage or Modek exchange, the roll bars are raised, either by jacks or from hooks on the roof. This design gives great freedom for constructing and covering the Ridon without compromising safety or exchangeability.

An important feature of the Ridek design is that it lends itself to local manufacture and, therefore, the support of local industry. Instead of the conventional unitary body, requiring huge stamping machinery, the Modek has a simple chassis that can be locally fabricated according to specifications provided by The Ridek Corporation, which ensures standardisation so that all Ridons will fit. The Modek chassis can be fitted out with off-the-shelf components, updated as required. This ensures that Modeks need not become obsolete for many years. Apart from reducing depreciation, the potentially very long life of a Modek helps to address a growing environmental problem: the disposal of old cars. A recycling charge, similar to that for batteries, is now being considered for new cars.

In a crash, the conventional automobile absorbs kinetic energy by progressive crumpling. While it is clearly preferable to crumple the car rather than its contents, there is no need for this to be so expensive. This was demonstrated by the five-mile-per-hour bumpers mandated some years ago but discontinued in favour of today's shiny plastic bumpers that belie their name. Without the need to rely on a lucrative aftermarket for replacement parts, Modeks can be designed to be crash-resistant and easily repairable. Eventually, insurance rates would take favourable accident statistics into account.

The Ridek is a new class of vehicle subject to different rules and considerations from the conventional car, van or lorry. Although offered as a viable BEV, it can be a HEV, FCV or an ICE vehicle.

The benefits of renting

Whatever its motive power, by separating a privately owned environment (Ridon) from machinery that may have multiple users and greater utilisation, several benefits accrue. For these to be fully realised, the Modeks should be rented. Licence plates for this new class of vehicle would be attached to the Modek, not the Ridon. Although third-party rental agencies could be used, the licensing authority could still require the installation of various sensors and devices needed for traffic control and law enforcement. The rental agreement would supply, with the Modek, a computer to be used in the Ridon to communicate with the Modek and control it. A card reader resembling the automatic teller at a bank would establish the driver's authority. Without a valid card, the Modek could not be driven and so could not be stolen. Sensors within the Modek would respond to signals from law-enforcement officers thereby eliminating the high-speed car chase. Other devices that would be a boon to traffic control could be installed: for example, to ease traffic congestion, reduce accidents and help the commuter. Transponders could be installed, as they are in airplanes, to indicate position, movement and speed to a traffic control centre. Tolls and parking fees could be charged automatically. Ultimately, this could lead to charges for road use according to the time of day—already necessary in some cities. Speeds could be adjusted according to road conditions. Reckless or poor driving could be discouraged, as they should always be. On-board cameras could survey other drivers and provide valuable liability data following accidents, just as fixed cameras already do.

At first, perhaps, not all of these 'benefits' might find favour, suggesting that Big Brother is watching. However, the reward of faster and safer driving should win over the majority of drivers who wish only to reach their destination quickly and safely. Traffic would be more civilised, as it increasingly has to be. In many cities, congestion is a bigger problem than pollution. The Ridek concept addresses both.

The production of Rideks through local manufacture and entrepreneurship in various regions or cities could lead to Ridon–Modek incompatibility with advances made in one city overlooked by others. Therefore, the enterprise of converting to Rideks should be co-ordinated. This is easy to achieve with manufacture under patent licence.

Since the award of the author's US patent (Dower 2000b), there has been extensive press coverage for a scheme, attributed to a leading auto-maker, of 'separating the powertrain and chassis from the body structure' heralding 'the death of the unitary body' by creating 'a completely new basis for business strategy in the automotive industry' in which 'vehicle bodies could be interchangeable, adapted to local conditions, provided by third parties, subject to modular refit and exchange, of endless variety dedicated to specific purposes (and hence more efficient purposes) and unconstrained in design except . . . where body meets the chassis' in a design that will be seen 'as an entirely new design paradigm' (Wells 2002: 106). The reader will perceive obvious similarities to the Ridek concept, which such comments serve to endorse. Interestingly, whereas Ridek is presented as a practical means for making the BEV cost-effective and acceptable, the motivation of the other seems to be to further the FCV. While the facility of battery exchange (through Modek exchange) appears to be a particularly valuable merit of the Ridek concept, the other foreseen advantages of the Ridek concept are therefore endorsed.

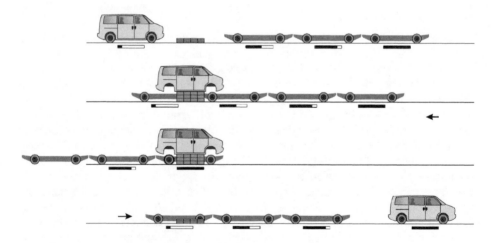

FIGURE 8.1 One of several possible means for Modek exchange

A method of exchange is illustrated in Figure 8.1. A Ridek joins a file of Modeks charging themselves from conducting rails beneath (not shown). The Ridon is lifted off its Modek by a jacking mechanism (rectangles). The Modek file backs up to put the lead Modek, by now fully charged, beneath the Ridon which then is lowered onto it. The reconstituted Ridek drives away and the Modek file advances for the next exchange.

The whole process takes less time than filling a petrol tank. For the purposes of illustration, horizontal bars indicate the state of charge of the corresponding Modeks.

To allow for such exchanges, it might be expected that there would be more Modeks than Ridons, but the reverse may be true. When a Ridek is parked at an airport's long-term lot, its Modek could be detached and used to carry other Ridons, as car rentals, taxis and commercial vehicles. Thus, idle machinery in the lot could find other uses. Instead of several cars, a Ridon owner may have several Ridons, some of which may be used seasonally. Modeks could be obtained only when needed—a considerable saving. Minimising idle machines through shared use, without sacrificing the environmental privacy of one's personal Ridon, would be an important saving. Motor vehicles should not stand idle for long, but Ridons can do so indefinitely without harm. Ridons may show little depreciation, compared with a car. Depreciation of Modeks should also be low because of their low rate of obsolescence. Being simple affairs without running gear, Ridons should not be expensive, although they could be elaborate and expensive if desired. Consequently, the outlay to acquire Ridek transportation should be relatively small. More important, perhaps, they could be highly customised and personalised.

Modek construction

Figure 8.2 shows a prototype Ridek. The abundant space within the Modek makes this an ideal vehicle to prototype. The patent describes how electrical connections between the Modek and Ridon can be avoided. Air conditioning or cooling would take place in the Modek and be sent to the Ridek through ducts. A small gasoline or natural gas heater would supply heating from the same system. This makes sense because heat from the motor can be used for passenger comfort and the batteries may need warming in very cold weather. Purists can observe that, when its heater is running, the Ridek is no longer zero-polluting, but that applies to most dwellings and buildings. The brake and steering controls are mechanically linked from the Ridon. The vertical steering column between the Ridon and Modek is interrupted and coupled with a dog clutch. The brake pedal in the Ridon bears on a plate on the Modek which then actuates the brakes. An infrared data link communicates the accelerator control and other information in both directions. In the Ridon, a small battery energises its electrical circuits, including the computer. It is charged from the Modek via an inductive link. Headlights are located in the Modek.

Ridon design

It is interesting to consider a 'garden shed' design to avoid the greenhouse effect of sloping windows. Windshields that slope forward instead of backward are common in marine craft because they give excellent visibility. Outwardly sloping windows do the same in many buildings. The windshield and other windows slope slightly outward. In profile view, the resulting Ridek would appear non-aerodynamic. There are some fish that look like this. However, they are beautifully streamlined when viewed from above. The East German Trabant was a car that exhibited this form of streamlining. Following this, the windshield should form a deep V to deflect the air that would normally pass over the roof to the sides That a forward-sloping, V-shaped windshield need not produce excessive drag is demonstrated by its use in some aircraft.

FIGURE 8.2 Prototype Ridek, shown at EVS-20, Long Beach, California, November 2003

Exchanging the Modek

Various methods of Modek exchange are possible. The method described in the patent (Dower 2000b) would be quick, and would require only a simple standing structure. However, it needs four retractable side wheels in the Ridon, and some means for moving the old Modek away and replacing it with a new one. The method shown in Figure 8.1 allows exchange Modeks to be parked bumper-to-bumper in a file overlying charging rails. When the Ridek joins the back of the file, its Ridon is lifted and the file backs up to bring the lead Modek beneath the Ridon which is then lowered to form a fully charged Ridek ready to be driven away. If a Ridon is to be stored at home, it could be lifted off the Modek by hooking onto the roll bars from the top.

Customer appeal

Customers have the final say. They have to like the Ridek for it to succeed. Its practicality and safety features will appeal, especially to parents who will like to think that, when the teenager borrows the Ridek, it will be under the watchful eye of 'traffic control'. They will feel safer knowing that help can be dispatched if there is an accident and that the other driver's fault can be readily established. Besides, overall running costs are less. This is essential if the Ridek is to receive acceptance. Let us review the reasons why it should be cheaper to run. We shall allow that the saving in fuel costs by using electricity balances the periodic cost of battery replacement. Factors reducing operating expenses are:

- Low initial investment (for the Ridon)
- Zero maintenance
- Reduced insurance costs

- Minimal depreciation and recycling charges (if any)
- Reduced idle time (of the Modek) through shared use

Quicker commuting and easier parking are likely bonuses to be offered by grateful authorities who are saving on crime, law enforcement and traffic control, while local industry will also benefit. Some congested urban centres may give additional incentives—such as access where gasoline and diesel cars are banned—to make room for a camel with sweeter breath.

References

CARB (California Agency Air Resources Board) (2000) *Zero-Emission Vehicle Programme Biennial Review* (Sacramento, CA: CARB).

Dower, G.E. (2000a) 'The Ridek: a new class of vehicle splits the hybrid spatially and temporally', paper presented at the *Electric Vehicle Symposium EVS-18*, Berlin, October 2000.

—— (2000b) *Modular Vehicle Construction and Transportation System*, United States Patent Number 6,059,058.

—— (2002a) 'The Ridek: a vehicle that separately and separatively packages machinery and passengers', paper presented at the *IBEC 2002 Automotive and Transportation Congress*, Paris, July 2002.

—— (2002b) 'Ridek: a renaissance of the battery electric vehicle', paper presented at the *Electric Vehicle Symposium EVS-19*, Busan, South Korea, October 2002.

Goldstein, D. (2003) 'Commentary: overcharged and underserved', *EAA Current Events*, May/June 2003: 3.

Rader-Olsson, A. (2000) *Clean Vehicles with Electric Drive* (Stockholm: KFB-Rapport, Final Report from the Swedish Research, Development and Demonstration Programme on Electric and Hybrid Vehicles 1993–2000).

Wallace, J. (2003) 'Market drivers and barriers to the commercialisation of advanced vehicles', paper presented at the *Advanced Automotive Battery Conference,* Nice, France, 11–13 June 2003.

Wells, P.E. (2002) 'GM skateboard: the revolution is here', *Automotive World,* 12 November 2002, www.AWKnowledge.com.

Westbrook, M.H. (2001) *The Electric Car* (Power and Energy Series 38; London: Institution of Electrical Engineers).

9

Social learning through technological inventions in low-impact individual mobility
THE CASES OF SPARROW AND GIZMO

Halina Szejnwald Brown and Catherine Carbone

Clark University, USA

> I see us as being in the art business. Art, entertainment and mobile sculpture which, coincidentally, also happens to provide transportation.[1]
>
> *Robert Lutz, General Motors executive*

The search for sustainable mobility systems has high visibility on the policy, research and business agendas. Interest in innovative technologies for individual mobility that can lower our dependence on the automobile is high. Consumer acceptance is one of the many obstacles these innovations face. The traditional car is a powerful cultural symbol. It represents such attributes as speed, power, freedom, versatility, convenience and individuality. These attributes have, over the years, created a particular frame through which we consider ways of satisfying our individual mobility needs. When people judge alternative vehicles through the same **interpretive frame** as that used for traditional internal combustion engine (ICE) cars, the results are often unfavourable for new entrants.

Society thus faces a dilemma—the dominant sociotechnical regime of the automobile, with its associated cultural, industrial, built and institutional structure, resists the changes necessary for a more sustainable individual mobility solution. Previously, we have argued that small-scale experiments aimed at developing, testing and introduc-

---

1 *The New York Times*, 28 April 2002.

ing new technologies and services offer one way out of this dilemma. They do so in three ways: by generating opportunities for developing and testing new technologies and services; by creating conditions conducive for higher-order learning among the participants; and by facilitating a collective act of social learning and institutional innovation towards sociotechnical regime shifts (Brown *et al.* 2003, 2004).

Numerous authors refer to the importance of higher-order learning in sociotechnical experiments, and often note its absence (Hoogma *et al.* 2002). Yet little systematic study has been done on defining the learning processes in experiments, monitoring them, assessing their societal impacts or examining the conditions under which learning occurs (or not), and by what mechanisms. We believe that gaining a better understanding of the learning processes occurring both within small-scale experiments and beyond can provide crucial input for advancing the theory of sociotechnical regime shifts.

Previously, we analysed two cases of innovations in personal mobility conducted by consortia of public and private interests, including a university (Brown *et al.* 2003, 2004). One of them entailed an innovative three-wheel power-assisted **bike-plus**; the other consisted of creating mobility chain services on the Dutch island of Texel. We classified these initiatives as bounded sociotechnical experiments (BSTEs). We use the term BSTE to denote a project exhibiting several characteristics. It is an attempt to introduce a new technology or service on a small scale. It is often a collective endeavour, carried out by a coalition of diverse actors, including business, government, technical experts, educational and research institutions, non-governmental organisations (NGOs) and others. There is a cognitive component to a BSTE in that at least some of the participants explicitly recognise the effort to be an experiment, in which learning by doing, doing by learning, trying out new strategies and technological solutions, and continuous course correction, are standard features.

BSTE is driven by a long-term and large-scale vision of advancing society's sustainability agenda, although the vision need not be equally shared by all participants. Its goal is to try out innovative approaches as a means of solving larger societal problems of unsustainable technologies and services. This latter characteristic distinguishes a BSTE from, for example, initiatives to address a particular environmental problem or to introduce a strictly market-driven new mode of transportation. A successful experiment creates a functioning, socially embedded new configuration of technology or service that then serves as a starting point for further innovation or for diffusion, or that can inform the policy-making process. A BSTE is more than an effort to develop a winning technology or service. It is also an incubator of ideas, a focus for diffusion of new conceptions of mobility and access, an accumulator of empirical experiences with technologies and services, and a place for social learning. It also provides an opportunity to draw into the sustainability agenda actors who would otherwise not see a place for themselves in these types of projects, which are often sponsored by powerful corporate, governmental or NGO entities. An obvious indication of a success is when this new configuration diffuses beyond the experimental boundaries and is widely adopted. But other ways to measure success in BSTEs include 'spawning' other BSTEs and inducing higher-order learning both among its participants and in the wider societal sphere.

This chapter examines two cases of technological innovation in individual mobility that are driven by purely entrepreneurial spirit. They entail the commercial introduction of innovative, low-impact vehicles in the US—Sparrow, produced by Corbin Motors of Hollister, California; and Gizmo, produced by Neighborhood Electric Vehicle Company (NEVCO) of Eugene, Oregon. Both are three-wheeled electric vehicles with seating capacity for one adult. They were first produced as prototypes and then moved to a small commercial scale.

Three broad questions drive this analysis. The first focuses on the extent to which the manufacturers understand, and respond to, the production, infrastructure, and social and cultural barriers they face in commercialising their vehicle. The second focuses on the role of various societal actors (in addition to the producers and consumers) in the process of adoption and large-scale diffusion. The third question explores the impact of the innovation on social learning. In particular, we ask whether the diffusion of these innovations influences how society—on both the individual and collective level—conceptualises its mobility needs and ways to satisfy them.

We conclude that social learning is relatively limited in both cases, largely because of inadequate involvement of the many stakeholders in the fate of the inventions. While the producers of Sparrow and Gizmo understand well the technical and infrastructure issues related to the successful introduction of the vehicles, they have little understanding of, or appreciation for, the influence of the social context on diffusion of technological innovations. Conceptualising these two entrepreneurial efforts as BSTEs will, in our opinion, lead to a change in the marketing strategies for the vehicles and will facilitate social learning. In short, the entrepreneurial and social objectives will coincide. We suggest how such BSTEs might be designed.

Bounded socio-technical experiments as agents of social learning

Higher-order learning is a radical change in approach to interpreting observations (interpretive frames) and to solving problems and advancing objectives. It entails changes in the assumptions, norms and interpretive frames that govern the decision-making process and actions of individuals, communities and organisations. It occurs through reflection and self-evaluation. Higher-order learning contrasts with lower-order learning, in which problems are corrected or policies altered without changes in problem definition, interpretive frames or in norms and values.

Learning occurs through a **feedback–stimulus** mechanism, when the existing, well-accepted, time-tested and trusted interpretive frames and competences receive feedback on their performance in solving a problem or advancing specific objectives. If, as a result of this feedback, it becomes apparent that the desired results are not forthcoming, these cognitive constructs become subject to reassessment and, if necessary, are replaced with new ones. This broad concept of feedback–stimulus is consistent across a wide range of disciplinary writings about learning, from cognitive sciences to organisational sciences to policy sciences (Argyris 1977; Argyris and Schön 1978; Sitkin 1992; Wenger 1998, 2000; Lee 1993; van Eijndhoven et al. 2001; Sabatier 1999; Wildawski 1990; Glasbergen 1996; Schön 1983; Schön and Rein 1994; Senge 1990; Easterby-Smith 1997; Fischer 1994).

The feedback process takes place by way of interaction and discourse among professional groups or **communities of practice** (the latter term was introduced by Wenger 1998) working on a particular project. Schön (1983) and Schön and Rein (1994), Fischer (1994) and, more recently, Grin and van de Graaf (1996a, 1996b) identify four increasingly abstract orders of discourse, with higher-order learning occurring most effectively at the second and third levels of discourse:

- Discourse is centred on the technical aspects of solving a previously-defined problem

- The definition of the problem is questioned

- There is confrontation between different interpretive frames

- There is a clash of fundamental ideas about preferred social order

Several factors can enhance learning through interaction and discourse:

- Presence of participants representing a range of problem definitions and interpretive frames

- Having something to interact about, such as a specific project or a problem to solve

- Ability to communicate in a common language

- Presence of individuals who serve as brokers of new ideas among different participants and beyond the boundaries of the discourse

A sense of urgency is an important facilitator of learning because it forces the repeated trying (and failing) that is central to the learning process (Sitkin 1992; Birkland 1997). Exercises in mental model-building, scenario-building, role-playing, visioning, system-thinking and other group techniques that generate feedback on the accepted assumptions and behaviours, as well as emergence of knew knowledge, are also effective in some contexts in producing higher-order learning (Senge 1990; Green and Vergragt 2002; van Eijndhoven *et al.* 2001; Paquet 1999; Gertler and Wolfe 2002).

BSTEs have several inherent characteristics that are conducive to higher-order learning. Participation by heterogeneous actors who represent different organisations, communities of practice and institutional affiliations assure the presence of a range of interpretive frames and belief systems. Moreover, the very act of choosing to participate in the experiment suggests a willingness on the participants' part to interact with one another and with each other's interpretive frames. The vision of sustainability (the driving force for at least some participants) has the potential to provide a platform for reframing the clashing interpretive frames, should conflicts arise. By evolving around a tangible specific (i.e. the innovative product or service), the project has a focal point and a shared language for the discourse. The two previous Dutch case studies have shown that other features, such as structured visioning exercises, a sense of urgency (rooted in market pressures) and information brokering by some of the participants, are often present or can be built into a BSTE. The studies also showed that lack of pressure was the greatest deterrent to learning (this was most evident in the bike–plus experiment). In this particular case, the pressure was low for two reasons—public funding for the experiment reduced the financial risks; and the participants in the experiment were risk-averse.

The Dutch BSTEs in mobility also uncovered a considerable degree of higher-order learning. This consisted of several actors:

- Redefining the core business of the organisations they represented in relation to personal mobility

- Discovering new couplings between problems and solutions

- Redefining their relationships with other participants around mobility services

- Discovering new business opportunities in mobility services

- Formulating new policy approaches

We conceptualise the process of social learning beyond the boundaries of a BSTE as a diffusion of ideas from the experiment into the wider societal sphere. Social learning is a collective change in prevalent views, norms, problem definitions and relationships among groups. It involves both social interactions and cognitive processes. The social component entails transmission and diffusion of new ideas and knowledge while the cognitive components include reflection, reassessment and reframing on the individual or group level, (see, for example, such social theorists as Storper 1996; Luthans and Kreitner 1985; Granovetter 1973; Bandura 1977; Hamblin *et al.* 1979; Minstrom 1997; see also Rogers 1985 on diffusion of technological innovation).

The central idea of the diffusion framework is that an individual learns by observing the behaviour of others and then decides to do (or not) something similar. In this process, an adopter (or rejecter) of an innovation passes through a stage of reassessing the usefulness of the new idea in the context of his/her values, norms, lifestyle, needs and wants. The behaviour of the group to which the individual belongs, the group's opinion leaders and other external factors, influence this process. In our adaptation of the diffusion framework, the participants in BSTEs serve as **idea brokers** who transmit ideas and knowledge into their own professional groups, communities of practice and personal networks. Learning occurs as a result of interactions and discourse between the new ideas and those that are already well established within that group. The discourse can occur on any of the four levels we identified above in relation to BSTEs but, as before, it is most productive on levels two and three in producing higher-order learning.

Two case studies of alternative vehicles for individual mobility

Sparrow and Gizmo are each four foot by eight foot in size, one passenger, three-wheeled electrically powered vehicles, designed for use on secondary and urban roads. The case descriptions presented here are based on extensive interviews with a NEVCO

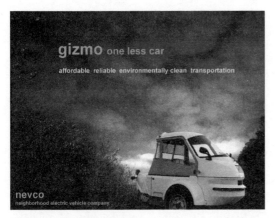

FIGURE 9.1 Gizmo promotion

FIGURE 9.2 Promotional shot of the Sparrow

representative and a Corbin Motors dealer in Rochester, New York, as well as documentary and website analysis. Since the completion of these case studies, in 2003, Corbin Motors has filed for bankruptcy and the Sparrow line of vehicles has been discontinued; it is not clear whether the production of other, more profitable three-wheeled electric models, such as Merlin, will continue.

Corbin Motors, the manufacturer of Sparrow, specialised in designing and creating unique, efficient and environmentally friendly vehicles of high quality. The company produced numerous niche-designed, alternative vehicles; over 250 Sparrows have sold. At its peak, there were over 40 Corbin dealerships throughout the US, Canada, Mexico and Singapore. NEVCO, the manufacturer of Gizmo, specialises in environmentally friendly vehicles for city use that are easy to park and are safer to pedestrians than traditional vehicles. The company has sold several dozen Gizmos.

Gizmo's and Sparrow's greatest challenge has been to break into the traditional automobile and motorcycle markets, and those using alternative fuel and propulsion technologies. The competition between the two is indirect because the new entrants seek to create specialised niches and existing ICE car manufacturers do not to see them as true competitors. Corbin Motors formed partnerships with many well-established companies, including Kilovac (which designs and creates electronic systems for Sparrow) and Progressive Suspension (which engineers suspension systems for both Sparrow and Ford Motor Company).

The two cases are similar on several counts. In the technological and production realm, both vehicles have similar design features which are radically different from traditional cars while aiming for some of the same infrastructure. Being small and electrically powered both address the problems of pollution, traffic congestion, parking and dependence on fossil fuels. Their electricity use corresponds to approximately one cent per mile. Both vehicles confront various technical challenges, such as power, battery recharging time, maximum speed (70 mph for Sparrow and 20–40 for Gizmo), driving range between charges (15 miles for Sparrow and 45 for Gizmo) and safety. Gizmo's steel perimeter and roof frame, a very rigid body of fibreglass with a crush zone in front and absence of a steering wheel are important safety features. Sparrow is equipped with automotive safety glass, a spherical body design that provides additional strength and an emergency power-off button. Both companies claim that their vehicles are very reliable and require little maintenance. Their simple design, combined with the use of off-the-shelf parts, make these vehicles relatively easy to repair. Nonetheless, both companies readily acknowledge that the shortage of qualified service stations around the country is problematic.

At the time of this analysis Sparrow was priced at less than US$15,000 and Gizmo below US$9,000. At these prices and production volumes, the vehicles were, unfortunately, not profitable. Neither company has entered into joint ventures thus far. However, in the case of Corbin Motors, the company's diversified products, including ICE vehicles, allowed it to finance the development of vehicles (such as Sparrow) with the profits from its better-selling vehicles (such as Merlin).

Another similarity between the two cases is their poor fit with existing institutional and policy contexts. Neither Corbin Motors nor NEVCO received public subsidies. While their customers do qualify for various federal and state credits and incentives, these are inconsistent and unreliable. For instance, Oregon offers US$1,500 for an individual and US$2,800 for a business in the form of a tax credit; California offers US$1,000 (but requires a three-year guarantee on the battery pack, which has been an obstacle for Gizmo); and Georgia offers US$5,000 incentive. Other government incentive programmes disqualify Gizmo and Sparrow because of the three-wheel design. These include: the 10% electric vehicle (EV) credits; Energy Policy Act (EPACT), which requires federal fleets to invest in alternative-fuel vehicles (AFVs); and the Californian zero-emission vehicle (ZEV) credits (in California, ZEVs are classified as motorcycles).

Both vehicles also have difficulty in obtaining insurance in some states, partly because they do not fit into the existing vehicle categories and because the rigorous safety tests required of cars do not apply to them. A motorcycle licence is required in some states but not others. Businesses and public fleets have, additionally, been unable to get business insurance for Gizmo and Sparrow because of their classification as motorcycles and their electric propulsion.

In general, no large-scale advertising of either vehicle has occurred. Both Sparrow and Gizmo are clearly advertised as alternative vehicles, and as an addition to customers' transportation options. This is evidenced in the case of NEVCO by the phrase on their website: 'Gizmo, one less car'.[2] The benefits of using a small EV, rather than a traditional car, are pointed out throughout the NEVCO website, which is currently the company's only form of advertising. Both vehicles are advertised in a similar way, with the emphasis on the vehicles' convenience, high quality and environmental credentials; these attributes confer a number of benefits on their owners by allowing them to travel more efficiently, park more easily because of the small size, and forgo some taxes and tolls. In other words, the marketing portrays the vehicle as a 'smart' alternative to traditional modes of personal transport.

Both manufacturers appear to be well aware of the importance of the cultural and functional meanings that consumers attach to alternative vehicles, and the challenge they encounter when comparisons are made. In an effort to counter this tendency, which may disadvantage the innovations, both emphasise the differences between their inventions and the traditional automobile. The marketing messages on the companies' websites do, however, differ in some important respects. In the Sparrow case, the marketing of the vehicle is largely environmentally neutral. Facts about the vehicle are presented and environmental undertones can be discerned but, for the most part, people are left to associate their own values with the vehicle and define it in a way that makes them feel comfortable. Thus, Corbin Motors made no large social statements about Sparrow. The message is, therefore, an individual one that Sparrow owners are smart. This is, perhaps, why the company saw such a large range of cultural niches emerging among its customers. This wide range of consumer types enabled people from many segments of society to be exposed to Sparrow and gain familiarity with it. It also increased the range of meanings attached to Sparrow which might, in turn, increase the probability of a dominant meaning to emerge and gain wider acceptance. While some customers may be interested in Sparrow primarily because of its environmental benefits, others may be attracted by its uniqueness. These individuals may not even be aware of the environmental benefits of the vehicle.

Corbin's 2001 business plan for Sparrow identified several classes of consumer:

- **Early adopters:** people who like to own cutting-edge innovative products

- **Urban professionals:** people who tend to be educated and socially responsible, living and working in an urban environment

- **College students:** who are attracted to the vehicle's affordability, environmentally friendly features and compact size (a bonus for campus parking)

- **Financially prudent:** people who are attracted to the low maintenance and recharging costs, low registration costs, and time-saving features

- **Small business owners:** people who are attracted by the unique and eye-catching design, along with the vehicle's environmentally friendly attributes

- **Motorcycle enthusiasts:** people who enjoy riding motorcycles but who appreciate an enclosed cabin and other comforts

- **Retirees:** retired people who value the cost-efficiency and low maintenance of Sparrow

In contrast, marketing of Gizmo focuses heavily on its environmental benefits, targeting the green consumer first and other types second. NEVCO's customers are roughly equally divided into environmentally conscious commuters and businesses seeking publicity and attention by putting their logo on the innovative vehicle. A few individuals bought Gizmo simply because of the unique nature of the vehicle.

Both companies marketed their vehicles as distinctly different from traditional cars while showing that they perform many of the functions of the traditional vehicle, only better. This creates a paradox of being simultaneously similar and different. The paradox extends to other social dimensions of individual mobility. Both vehicles suffer from the classification problem, being neither a car nor a motorcycle. This has advantages and disadvantages: for example, the classification as a motorcycle exempts the vehicles from the numerous safety and performance standards to which traditional cars are subject (such as crash testing). On the other hand, this may be a problem for safety-conscious consumers. The unresolved classification problem prevents some insurance companies from providing coverage for Gizmo and Sparrow, and excludes both vehicles from applying for government funding for environmentally benign vehicles. Notably, both companies performed very little market analysis before introducing the two vehicles.

Another similarity between the two is that both companies pursued their inventions in a relatively solitary manner with neither participating in joint ventures or seeking local government involvement. Support from local governments and businesses can be helpful in facilitating diffusion, as the project gains the reputation of having the acceptance of trusted and long-standing leaders in the community. Companies and local governments are more likely to be supportive if they feel they can benefit from the association with the new technology, such as environmental gains.

Nevertheless, some business partnerships have taken place. In certain regions, Domino's Pizza uses Sparrow for delivery while Nike and Etrade use Sparrow for self-promotion purposes. NEVCO has sold Gizmo to Eugene Water and Electric Board and to Portland Gas and Electric. Both companies present vehicles on a limited basis at various conventions. In general, however, societal actors other than individually motivated consumers played a minimal role in the adoption and diffusion of the vehicles.

Sparrow and Gizmo as BSTEs

The success of Sparrow and Gizmo can be conceptualised in two ways—as a commercial and environmental success in a competitive marketplace and as a facilitation of social change towards alternative mobility systems. The first perspective centres specifically on the two inventions and concerns itself with their popularity, profitability and staying power. It considers ways of gaining visibility and interests, building support, finding the best fit with existing social and physical infrastructures, and finding ways to identify and meet existing needs and to couple problems with solutions. Here, success is measured by the rate of diffusion and the commercial and environmental gains achieved.

The second approach views the two innovations as seeds of social and institutional innovation toward a personal mobility system that is convenient, economical and less energy-intensive. This approach values the individual and social learning that occurs when individuals and organisations use the vehicles.

Rogers's theory of **diffusion of innovation** (1985) is suitable for considering the ways of facilitating commercialisation of Gizmo and Sparrow. This states that diffusion of technological innovation results from communication of new ideas through various channels in a social system. Greater visibility is central to fostering the communication channels and to cultivating the social system. This can be accomplished through, among others, identifying and deploying appropriate opinion leaders and by small-scale advertising. The fact that people actively seek out these vehicles, despite the absence of advertising, signifies that a market for them must exist. Targeting alternative technology exhibitions, environmental symposia and the like, are some of the options for advertising. Another method is to encourage their use by businesses. Because of their unique and memorable features, both Sparrow and Gizmo have been utilised by businesses seeking visibility. By increasing the number of companies using these vehicles, familiarity and confidence in them can be raised. Another benefit of this approach is enhanced interactions with the vehicle by way of providing hands-on experience for the drivers. Other forms of interactions are possible, such as demonstrations and test drives.

The initiatives outlined above are not easy, nor do they guarantee commercial success because of the many other factors involved. Furthermore, they create a number of dilemmas—how to communicate without predetermining the message; how to offer solutions to existing problems without presupposing what the problem is; how to appeal to potential audiences through powerful symbols without, at the same time, narrowing down the range of meanings that the new technology may take on. Because there is a large sociological and cognitive component to the social acceptance of these vehicles, and because different segments of society impart different meanings to it, advancing one meaning as the dominant one carries with it the risk of alienating the other segments who may not wish to be associated with that particular meaning. It also carries the risk of missing out on a key diffusion pathway.

Partly for these reasons, we argue in this chapter that the social functions of Gizmo and Sparrow should be given greater weight in evaluating their success. More specifically, we should ask whether the two inventions influence the way consumers and institutions define their mobility needs and seek out the means to satisfy them. In other words, do the innovative vehicles stimulate individual and social learning about alternative mobility systems and thus indirectly contribute to social change?

Based on an analysis of the two Dutch experiments in personal mobility (Brown *et al.* 2003) we concluded that small-scale experiments with new technologies and services have the potential to facilitate such learning, especially when conceptualised and carried out as BSTEs, with an emphasis on individual and social learning. Several characteristics make the Sparrow and Gizmo cases prime candidates for pursuing this objective. One of them is a sense of urgency, owing to the financial risks taken by the manufacturers. Another is the innovations themselves—unusual and challenging artefacts around which interactions and discourse can take place. In fact, the marketing strategies for the vehicles recognise this potential for higher-order learning. The marketing message is that, in short-distance driving, the need for mobility and access can be satisfied without sacrificing speed and freedom, while simultaneously solving parking problems, saving money, reducing environmental impacts, and projecting the image of pioneer and adventurer.

What is in short supply in these two cases is active participation by a wide range of actors who would collectively represent a range of problem definitions and interpretive frames. Both are necessary for productive discourse and learning. Neither company has done much to engage external actors. Corbin Motors engaged in a limited number of partnerships with manufacturing companies and businesses interested in advertising their services by way of an attention-grabbing vehicle, while NEVCO has participated in a handful of conventions; but neither involved local or regional governments, universities, existing mobility companies or other potentially crucial actors. Nor did they seek out systematic feedback from their customers in order to understand why they purchased the vehicles, what symbolic meaning they attached to them, if any, and how their views on alternative mobility solutions evolved. Such initiatives could create a fruitful discourse and generate new ideas about the role of sustainable individual mobility solutions.

A better understanding might also emerge on the diffusion of the knowledge about Sparrow and Gizmo beyond the experimental boundaries into society at large. An additional benefit would be to improve both the technical design of the artefacts and their fit into the physical and social infrastructure. These initiatives would also allow us to map up the learning processes and thus contribute to a better understanding of how sociotechnical experiments induces such learning. Finally, widening the circle of participants would create opportunities for implementing structured visioning exercises.

Drawing on a larger set of actors could be accomplished by engaging a wider group of stakeholders, including:

- Local government
- Citizens' groups
- Universities
- Non-governmental organisations
- Businesses

These stakeholders should be encouraged to study the fate of Gizmo and Sparrow in the marketplace, adopt the vehicles on experimental basis, and include them, as well as other such mobility solutions, into long-term planning. Designing a programme for mapping out and interpreting the learning processes would also be constructive. A promising approach would be to introduce a system for obtaining systematic feedback from the purchasers of the vehicles and other stakeholders. Notably, the above changes would also facilitate the market diffusion of these innovations. In short, the business and social agendas would reinforce each other.

References

Argyris, C. (1977) 'Double-loop learning in organisations', *Harvard Business Review* 55.5: 115-25.

—— and M. Schön (1978) *Organisational Learning: A Theory of Action Perspective* (Reading, MA: Addison-Wesley).

Bandura, A. (1977) *Social Learning Theory* (Englewood Cliffs, NJ: Prentice Hall).

Birkland, T. (1997) *After Disaster: Agenda Setting, Public Policy and Focusing Events* (Washington, DC: Georgetown University Press).

Brown, H.S., P.J. Vergragt, K. Green and L. Berchicci (2003) 'Learning for sustainability transition through bounded sociotechnical experiments in personal mobility', *Technology Analysis and Strategic Management* 13.3: 298-315.

——, ——, —— and —— (2004) 'Bounded sociotechnical experiments (BSTE): higher-order learning for transition toward sustainable mobility', in B. Elzen, F.W. Geels and K. Green (eds.), *System Innovation and the Transition to Sustainability: Theory, Evidence and Policy* (Cheltenham, UK: Edward Elgar): 191-219.

Easterby-Smith, M. (1997) 'Disciplines of organisational learning: contributions and critiques', *Human Relations* 50.9: 1,085-113.

Fischer, F. (1994) *Evaluating Public Policy* (Boulder, CO: Westview Press).

Gertler, M.S., and D.A. Wolfe (eds.) (2002) *Innovation and Social Learning: Institutional Adaptation in an Era of Technological Change* (New York: Palgrave Macmillan).

Glasbergen, P. (1996) 'Learning to manage the environment', in W.M. Lafferty and J. Meadowcroft (eds.), *Democracy and the Environment: Problems and Prospects* (Cheltenham, UK: Edward Elgar): 175-212

Granovetter, M.S. (1973) 'The strength of weak ties', *American Journal of Sociology* 78.6: 1,360-80.

Green, K., and P.J. Vergragt (2002) 'Towards sustainable households: a methodology for developing sustainable technological and social innovations', *Futures* 34: 381-400.

Grin, J., and H. van de Graaf (1996a) 'Technology assessment as learning', *Science, Technology and Human Values* 20.1: 72-99.

—— and —— (1996b) 'Implementation as communicative action: an interpretive understanding of interactions between policy actors and target groups', *Policy Sciences* 29: 291-319.

Hamblin, R.L., J.L. Miller and D.E. Saxton (1979) 'Modelling use diffusion', *Social Forces* 57: 799-811.

Hoogma, R., R. Kemp, J. Schot and B. Truffer (2002) *Experimenting for Sustainable Transport: The Approach of Strategic Niche Management* (London: Spon Press).

Lee, K.N. (1993) *Compass and Gyroscope: Integrating Science and Politics for the Environment* (Washington, DC: Island Press).

Luthans, F., and R. Kreitner (1985) *Organisational Behaviour Modification and Beyond: An Operant and Social Learning Approach* (Glenview, IL: Scott, Foresman & Company).

Minstrom, M. (1997) 'Policy entrepreneurs and the diffusion of innovation', *American Journal of Political Science* 41.3: 738-70.

Paquet, G. (1999) *Governance through Social Learning* (Ottawa: University of Ottawa Press).

Rogers, E.M. (1985) *Diffusion of Innovation* (New York: The Free Press, 4th edn).

Sabatier, P. (ed.) (1999) *Theories of the Policy Process* (Boulder, CO: Westview Press).

Schön, D.A. (1983) *The Reflective Practitioner: How Professionals Think in Action* (New York: Basic Books).

—— and M. Rein (1994) *Frame of Reflection: Towards the Resolution of Intractable Policy Controversies* (New York: Basic Books).

Senge, P.M. (1990) 'Building learning organisations', *Sloan Management Review* 32.1: 7-23.

Sitkin, S.B. (1992) 'Learning through failure: the strategy of small losses', *Research in Organisational Behaviour* 14: 231-66.

Storper, M. (1996) 'Institutions of the knowledge-based economy', in OECD, *Employment and Growth in the Knowledge-based Economy* (Paris: OECD): 255-83.

Van Eijndhoven, J., W. Clark and J. Jager (2001) 'The long-term development of global environmental risk management: conclusions and implications for the future', in J. van Eijndhoven, W. Clark and J. Jager (eds.), *The Social Learning Group: Learning to Manage Global Environmental Risk* (Boston, MA: MIT Press): 281-97.

Wenger, E. (1998) *Communities of Practice: Learning, Meaning and Identity* (Cambridge, UK: Cambridge University Press).

—— (2000) 'Communities of practice as social learning systems', *Organisation* 7.2: 225-46.

Wildawski, A. (1990) 'Choosing preferences by constructing institutions: a cultural theory of preference formation', *American Political Science Review* 81: 3-21.

Thanks to Richard Newman, HTP Video, for use of the Sparrow image; and to Carl Watkins, NEVCO, for use of the Gizmo image.

10

The seven characteristics of successful sustainable system innovations

Tom van der Horst

Organisation for Applied Scientific Research (TNO), The Netherlands

Philip J. Vergragt

Tellus Institute, Boston, USA

Car transport is a mass of unsustainable activities: fossil fuel consumption; polluting emissions (including greenhouse gases); accidents and injuries; occupying precious space; and congestion. Moreover, personal car transportation is increasing worldwide, especially in the fast-growing economies of former developing countries such as China and India. Car companies tend to innovate in terms of bigger cars with more features and power, rather than in fuel-saving smaller city vehicles. Of course, these innovations are driven by consumer preferences which are induced by advertising, perceived need, and a desire to demonstrate prestige and status.

Minor incremental innovations are not sufficient to yield the required reduction in the car's environmental and societal impacts. To break through to a more sustainable society, we are faced with the challenge of accomplishing transitions—major societal changes in which a new lifestyle and/or new technology is introduced and adapted to by society. An example of such a transition is the shift from a coal-based energy infrastructure to natural gas for households in the Netherlands (Rotmans and Kemp 2000). Here, we investigate a possible transition towards a sustainable personal transportation system.

Innovations to produce transitions, aimed at creating breakthroughs to sustainable development, offer many different and challenging opportunities. There are chances for new and existing companies throughout the chain to create new business, and opportunities for new technology, products and services that benefit the consumer. This would give governments the opportunity to encourage prosperity and well-being from entirely new perspectives, resulting in a breakthrough in terms of energy efficiency and sustainability.

The challenge lies in identifying, explicating and concretising the opportunities that transitions may create. Against the background of that challenge, this chapter intends to give an initial impetus to the elaboration and application of the concept of sustainable system innovation (SSI).

The starting point is that SSIs may be a first step towards transitions aimed at an energy-efficient and sustainable society. In the concept of SSI, the main dimensions for innovation (such as scope, duration and sphere of action) are deliberately formulated in more limited terms compared with transitions so as to set in motion specific processes of change (Brown *et al.* 2003). The premise is that a number of **system innovations** are capable of generating a transition, either in parallel or sequentially (Butter and Slob 2002).

This chapter aims to:

- Outline a new picture of possible innovations towards a sustainable society based on the concept of SSI

- Outline the seven main characteristics of SSI and present a proposal for the design of the innovation process

- Draw conclusions on the importance and applicability of the concept of SSI and the seven characteristics described, especially for sustainable mobility

The main conclusion is that SSI will only be successful where there is close collaboration between government and business, where government develops a vision (see Box 10.3) and where business coalitions explore short-term options that fit this vision. This certainly applies to sustainable transportation.

In the past decade, the Dutch Organisation for Applied Scientific Research (TNO) has gained a lot of SSI experience in a wide variety of joint ventures. This chapter refers to a few cases from this period, stating the years in which they took place. Although a lot can be learned from these cases, only a few of the aspects are discussed (for further analyses of the cases, see Brown *et al.* 2003 and Brezet *et al.* 2001).

Sustainable system innovation

A few empirical facts

The concept of SSI is based on the fact that environmental gain achieved by redesigning existing products and processes is limited. For example, once an office chair has been redesigned for the third time to meet environmental requirements, there will be no more environmental gain.

A significant environmental breakthrough (to a factor of four or higher) requires more drastic innovation (van der Horst *et al.* 1999). In the example of the office chair, the notion of a chair as a physical object should be abandoned; its function (providing a comfortable seat) and need (supporting the body to do office work) become the key aspects. This may produce the idea of introducing the concept of interchangeable workstations, in which one workstation is used by several employees, so reducing the environmental impact per function unit.

These drastic innovations, termed system innovations from now on, result in interdependences between several system elements. In order to be successful at this level, simultaneous innovation covering several aspects is required—technological, cultural and organisational. This increases the complexity of both the innovation itself and the innovation process. The introduction of interchangeable workstations at the office not only requires an ICT system that makes it possible for all employees to work anywhere, but also a change in organisational culture and adoption of a new management style.

Because of their versatility and complexity, system innovations must be achieved by coalitions of actors rather than by individual parties. Innovation in itself is usually expensive and may be risky; for system innovations this is even more pertinent. Meaningful innovation is possible only through synergistic combination of the specific roles of all players in the system that is to be renewed.

Innovations aimed at sustainability call for a clever and new interaction between national governments, as representatives of societal sustainability, and societal players with a clear interest (e.g. the business community, intermediary organisations).

Characteristics of sustainable system innovations

SSIs can thus be described as innovations that affect the components of the system and the system as a whole, leading to radically more sustainable performance or function fulfilment. From this definition, and based both on the broad literature and on experience, the following characteristics of SSI can be formulated:

- **Inherently sustainable.** SSIs encompass broad societal change towards sustainability, which means a substantive increase in ecological, economic and social sustainability or a deliberate acceleration of the processes of change that may lead to this. SSIs also aim to separate economic growth from increasing environmental impact (de-linking). The essence lies in finding solutions in which the individual economic interests of companies and organisations coexist with the societal sustainability objective (a win–win situation). Companies are enabled to develop economically, while ecological and social sustainability gains are achieved at the same time. This, in short, is inherent sustainability

- **Focus on the user.** Because SSI involves enlargement of the room for innovation (which consequently becomes more complex) and targets a fundamentally new way of function fulfilment, it is important to find new and meaningful methods of system definition and delineation. The developing user's needs are taken as the starting point of system innovation. Continuous interaction with (potential) end users and consumers during the innovation process appears to be crucial. Taking user needs as the starting point, the main dimensions of the system can be clearly defined and delineated

- **Balance short term and long term.** The far-reaching and complex character of SSI addresses both the short and the long term. After all, large-scale social changes cannot be enforced in the short term. On the other hand, progress is needed in the short term to create a basis of support for innovation. Finding the balance between long-term and short-term ambitions is, therefore, a key aspect of sustainable system innovations

- **Integral and multidisciplinary approach.** SSIs involve a combination of changes in technological, cultural (including behavioural) and structural (i.e. organisational, economic and administrative) aspects, necessitating an integral and multidisciplinary approach. In past and present practice, most innovations are implicitly or explicitly based on a technology-push approach, so they are ultimately doomed to failure

- **Multi-stakeholder.** System innovations exceed the boundaries of individual companies and can only be achieved with the involvement of multiple stakeholders. This means that versatile joint ventures (both private and public–private) must be developed and that the basis of support among the different stakeholders must be constructed step by step

- **Multi-level.** SSIs involve different levels of scale: micro, meso and macro (Rotmans and Kemp 2000). The macro level (i.e. that of national or, in the US, state governments), is of importance because system innovations can make a contribution to large-scale social change only if there is a basis of support at this level. The micro level comprises individual players, each with their own specific interests. Success also depends on their willingness to develop a system innovation or create a basis of support for it. The meso level describes regional governments, major cities and also lines of business and industry conglomerates. It is assumed that the meso level includes the strongest connected interests and therefore is the hardest to change

- **Multi-pliable.** Finally, SSIs are multi-pliable, meaning that they have the potentiality to lead to a broad social innovation towards sustainability. This is a prerequisite given the previously formulated starting point that a number of system innovations must be capable of generating a transition, either in parallel or sequentially

These seven characteristics of SSI reflect the main elements that system innovations have to fulfil in order to be successful, based on the experiences of TNO (in conjunction with Delft University of Technology) over the past decade. At the same time, they outline an ambition: is it possible to organise an innovation process with these characteristics and, if so, what will it look like? The next sections illustrate how this ambition can be achieved based on the experiences of TNO and Delft University of Technology. Recommendations for improvement and further research are provided.

The SSI method

This section summarises the approach toward SSIs developed by TNO. This SSI method emerges from TNO's experiences with innovative practical experiments over the past 15 years. The method is still under development. The SSI method comprises five phases (see Fig. 10.1).

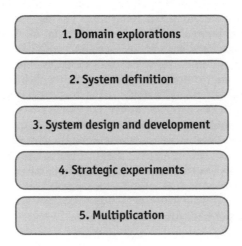

1. Domain explorations

2. System definition

3. System design and development

4. Strategic experiments

5. Multiplication

FIGURE 10.1 The five phases of the SSI method

Thus, the SSI method:

- Progresses from a macro perspective and macro analyses to strategic experiments at micro level which are, in turn, multiplied back to macro level

- Progresses from a sturdy basis of support for system innovation among a small group of players to general public support

- Advances from minor to major impacts on sustainable development

Phase 1: domain explorations

In this phase, a limited group of players (the initiators) map out a domain (e.g. short-distance transport) from a macro perspective. This includes the following trends:

- **User.** Expected demand development, demographic, cultural-anthropological

- **Ecological.** Identification of sustainability bottlenecks based on user trends

- **Economic.** Market developments

- **Technological.** What technology developments are under way and do they offer chances of solving the sustainability bottlenecks in an economically attractive manner?

In order to stand a chance of success, SSIs must be based on relevant social and technological developments. Sustainability as such is only rarely the exclusive driver of major breakthrough innovations.

An important question in domain explorations concerns the players that can influence the completion of a certain system innovation, and when and how they can best be involved—this is the players' analysis. As a minimum, a group of players always comprises users and end users, such as: the business community; local, regional and national governments; and intermediary organisations. It is not possible to indicate standard criteria for identification of key players, although it is thought that social aspects (such as networks of friends) and mix of personalities (enterprising versus risk-averse) are two key factors for success (Brown *et al.* 2003).

This results in opportunities for innovating the domain in question, formulated as **open system concepts**. These concepts are sufficiently concrete and challenging to interest the various players, while being sufficiently open to leave room for specific customisation (Weterings and van der Horst 2002). In combination with an analysis of the playing field, this provides information on which parties should be involved in the process.

The approach of phase 1 is illustrated by Box 10.1.

Conclusions from the case

An interesting and challenging open system concept has been defined in this case, with the players deserving special attention. With reference to later experiences, an important and fundamental issue during this first phase of innovation relates to the role of government, notably:

- Is the government (as representative of the common interest) also the primary problem owner for sustainable development?

- If government takes a proactive stand and wants to work with the business community on the development of SSIs, how far should its commitment go?

- Do SSIs and transitions entail government initiatives aimed at sustainable innovations that are then gradually adopted by the market, or do they work in a different way?

Although the answers to these questions are not unequivocal, the dominant impression is that government should take the lead in sustainable development because of its broad social nature. Ways will then have to be found for government to bracket this objective together with current interests and trends in society.

This explains why domain explorations on the one hand should look closely at autonomous developments (initiated by the market) that could make a major positive contribution to sustainability. On the other hand, it explains why, within domain explorations, the commitment of government must be ensured.

User trends and ecological trends

Studies conducted by TNO and Delft University of Technology in 1996 showed that 80% of transport movements in the Netherlands covered distances of between 0 and 20 km. For trips between 0 and 5 km, there was a certain level of competition between car and bicycle. The car was the main means of transport for trips between 5 and 20 km. Cars obviously consume more energy than bicycles, and commuter traffic contributes significantly to congestion on the roads (traffic jams).

Player analyses

The research team's ambition was to involve the field of players from a market perspective. Consumers and companies were chosen as the main driving force for innovation. In other words, the team's starting point was that the lack of sustainability in the Dutch mobility system could be solved primarily by market consortia.

Open system concepts

As a result of this domain exploration study, the following open system concept was defined: 'a new, environment-friendly mobility system, especially for distances between 5 and 20 km that combines the comfort and advantages of the car with the environmental advantages of the bicycle'.

Box 10.1 A new mobility system? (1996–98)

Phase 2: system definition

Based on the results of the domain explorations, a limited number of market parties are approached, known as the **initial partners**. Together with these initial partners and other relevant players, trends and developments are re-examined, this time interactively and aimed more specifically at these parties' interests. This results in scenarios (ranging from five to ten years), a scenario analysis, system delineation and analyses; these are then used to identify specific innovation chances and potential new partners.

There are many potential methods that may result in a useful definition and delineation of a system that eventually facilitates sustainable innovations. A proposal is given below for one new and useful approach: business models for inherently sustainable systems (BISS). This is followed by a brief description of an essential aspect of system innovation: system structure change.

Business models for inherently sustainable systems

As described for the first characteristic, an important issue of SSI is to find win–win solutions for ecological, economic and social sustainability. This has prompted TNO to initiate the BISS study. One of the main instruments used in this study is the BISS method for the analysis of this business model. The analysis takes as a focal point the combined services provided by the business community and government authorities aimed at fulfilling the specific needs of consumers. The concept of BISS differs from the concept of material chain or manufacturing chain in that it centres on the incentive structure of the players involved. This could be a combination of an economic value chain combined with the non-economic interests of relevant players (e.g. local government regulators) which could be completely independent of the material or manufacturing chain. One of the main hypotheses of the approach is that a system innovation can be created only if the business models within the system are capable of change. Box 10.2 outlines the case of Mitka, an innovation that emerged from phase 1.

During the system analysis phase, the development team of TNO and Delft University of Technology explored different need areas. The main question was to find parts of the mobility system in which a new sustainable mobility concept, for distances from 5 to 20 kilometres, could potentially fit. There was a breakthrough in the project when Nike-Europe, in the role of launching customer, decided to join the project.

A lack of parking space at the Nike-Europe headquarters in Hilversum had prompted the company to ask its employees to use public transport to commute to work. The idea of a new mobility concept was a challenging alternative solution to the parking problem. Nike was also interested in the sustainability ambitions of the project. For the project's part, Nike was an attractive high-profile brand with which to identify.

Mitka is the Dutch abbreviation for Mobility Concept for Individual Short-Distance Transport.

The Mitka is a three-wheeled, soft-top 'superbike' driven by muscle power but aided by an electric motor when headwinds and hilly terrain require. The concept was developed in close collaboration between the TNO Institute of Industrial Technology and Delft University of Technology. The bicycle manufacturer Gazelle and Nike-Europe were part of the project team, as were renowned Dutch companies such as the Peter van der Veer design studio and the specialist vehicle manufacturer Freewiel Techniek.

The sustainability strategy of the project was to make Mitka so attractive that car drivers would switch to it.

Box 10.2 Mitka, a new mobility system (1999–2000)

Conclusions on the Mitka case in the system definition phase

The following conclusions can be drawn regarding the characteristics of SSI and the approach during the system definition phase in the Mitka project.

Nike, as launching customer for the Mitka project, was a strong driver for its development. The big opportunity in this phase of the project could have been to develop new sustainable business models in which companies such as Nike delivered their employees' mobility services in a different way. For example, the government, together with some of the major Dutch employers, could have reached the conclusion that commuter traffic in the Netherlands needed to be more environmentally friendly and healthy. Based on that conclusion, they could have jointly decided on the need for new mobility services, of which Mitka could have been a part. However, there are several reasons why the Mitka project already has all the characteristics of a technology-push project in this phase, relegating attention for the necessary organisational and cultural modifications as described in the fourth characteristic to the background.

System structure

The system definition phase involves a key issue of the fourth characteristic: namely, integrated innovation at technological, cultural and organisational levels.

Depending on the system definition, several different levels of innovation are conceivable: incremental or radical innovation of the system itself and/or incremental or radical innovation of individual system elements. SSIs focus on radical innovations of the structure of the system, entailing all material and non-material system characteristics and including the driving forces (the incentives structure) that keep the system going. By definition, therefore, this concerns technological, cultural and organisational aspects.

A technology push of a fundamentally new technology is but one way of changing the structure of the system (and, accordingly, the system's sustainability impact); it can also be changed on the basis of organisational or cultural modifications. An example of this, albeit relating to a different context, is given in Box 10.3.

A striking example of transition-scope impact, from the field of civil engineering, was the Dutch government's decision to implement the Delta Plan following the 1952 floods. Because of the large number of victims, a broad basis of support had been created for a large-scale dike-heightening programme, including the development and construction of 10–15 permanent and semi-permanent flood barriers. This decision was made in the knowledge that the infrastructure of roads, waterways and fishing amenities would change drastically, with all its economic and ecological consequences. But this was widely accepted because of the scope of the disaster.

The subsequent demand for semi-permanent (because of ecological reasons) flood barriers boosted the Dutch civil engineering and industrial sectors and led to a range of system innovations. In other words, specific organisational or cultural modifications to the structure of a system may create a demand for sustainable technology. In the remainder of this chapter, decisions of this scope and magnitude will be called **Delta Plan statements.**

Box 10.3 Delta Plan

Conclusions on the Delta Plan regarding the structure of the system

It can be concluded that the Dutch government made the unique decision to carry out the Delta Plan (see Box 10.3) and, as a result, changed the structure of the system as a whole. The outcome of that decision was both impressive and positive. Apparently, a choice at this level has great implications for the success of SSIs.

In contrast to the single technology-push strategy, a prerequisite for the introduction of SSIs is a change in the structure of the system itself, in order to automatically create the logical need for new sustainable products, services, processes and technologies.

Conclusions on a Delta Plan statement in the Mitka case

A number of conclusions can be drawn from the Dutch government's decision to implement the Delta Plan and its very different response to Mitka. First, there was no conscious choice to change the structure of the system—no Delta Plan statement—in this project phase of Mitka. For example, no action was taken by the Dutch government, in conjunction with major employers, to make commuter traffic more environmentally friendly and healthy.

A second conclusion concerns the government's involvement in the project. If we assume that the government is the problem owner of the sustainability issue, its involvement is essential. In the Mitka case, however, involvement was insignificant, although the government did fund the project to a limited degree. In this phase, the government did not support or recognise the need for a Delta Plan statement or something similar. Traffic emissions and congestion issues always play a role in discussions at macro level in the Netherlands, but the link with the solution offered by Mitka was not made in this case. From the point of view of the fifth characteristic (basis of support among stakeholders), this represented a missed opportunity. Perhaps even more importantly, however, was the lesson that not all macro-level considerations (the sixth characteristic) had been fully recognised. The sustainability analysis was made at macro level during the domain explorations, and the traffic jam discussions were also held at macro level. From the point of view of the initiators, the lack of willingness to issue a Delta Plan statement at this level could have warranted more attention.

Phase 3 and phase 4: system design and strategic experiments

The third and fourth phases of the SSI method are discussed together in this section.

System design

Based on the system definition, a new system design is developed by the partners. The vision of the system is made more concrete (with a 5–10 year scope), thus illustrating the ultimate result the partners seek to achieve with the innovation process and the characteristics of the system. For the system design, the following criteria should be followed:

- It creates added value for the end user in all respects

- It is sufficiently concrete and applicable at the micro level in the short term, but fits in with the roadmap and has potential at macro level and in the long term

- It is sufficiently innovative in terms of technological, cultural and organisational aspects, but does not contain an overdose of high-risk innovations in one and the same concept

- It responds adequately to the interests of the players involved

Backcasting (Jansen and Vergragt 1999; Vergragt 2003) and sustainable roadmapping (van der Horst *et al.* 1999) are used to translate this vision into concrete and realistic innovation measures that can be implemented to achieve the system. The consortium (now consisting of initial and potential partners who are committed to the process) jointly designs and develops a new sustainable system design which is to be tested in a strategic experiment, to be carried out at the micro level.

Strategic experiments

Strategic, realistic, practical experiments, with clear learning objectives for all parties involved, are key elements of the SSI method. Although not primarily a practical test of the innovation, the strategic experiment is at the heart of research into system innovation in terms of all seven SSI characteristics. The parties determine in advance how all the relevant aspects of system innovation will be studied in the strategic experiment.

The following research questions are addressed:

- Can the lofty ambitions for sustainability and unlinking be achieved or are there any positive indications that they will be?

- Does the test group appreciate the value of the new products and services, and does their behaviour change?

- Do the long-term ambitions remain intact under the pressure of short-term interests?

- What does the interaction between technological, cultural and structural aspects look like in practice?

- How can lessons be learned at a micro level from the macro perspective of an experiment?

- How can the system innovation be scaled up to the level of transitions?

- What organisational and policy changes are needed to actually achieve a new system structure (at a large scale, as well)?

Conclusions on the Mitka case in the system design and strategic experiment phases

Based on the mixed successes achieved by this project to date, it can be concluded that the system design has elements in it that appeal to many people (see Box 10.4). The

The system design phase (2001)

In 2001, the Mitka made its debut as a model on the Gazelle stand at the Fiets-RAI bicycle show. It was only a wooden mock-up and could not be ridden. The Mitka team were able to assess initial public response at the show. People were so enthusiastic that development work was continued at full speed.

The mock-up was shown to Queen Beatrix at the opening of the new TNO Institute for Industrial Technology building in the Dutch city of Eindhoven. Her enthusiastic response prompted TNO to show the Mitka to Prince Willem-Alexander and Princess Maxima during their official visit to the province of Noord-Brabant (see Fig. 10.4). Both were very impressed.

A first version of the 'rideable show model' was presented to the partners.

FIGURE 10.3 Mitka

Business development expertise has been added to the team to define a business plan (the first business developer). Based on the show model, cost price estimations to manufacture the first 100 Mitkas were updated. Based on these cost price estimations, the bicycle producer Gazelle decided that the Mitka did not fit in its product portfolio. Gazelle decided to develop a two-wheel version based on the Mitka concept, the Easy Rider (see Fig. 10.5).

FIGURE 10.5 The Mitka spin-off, the Easy Rider

FIGURE 10.4 Prince Willem-Alexander and Princess Maxima with the Mitka

Strategic experiment (2002)

The first rideable show model was ready at the end of 2002. At Nike-Europe headquarters the Mitka was presented and tested by Nike employees. The employees used the Mitka for commuter traffic and were interviewed intensively afterwards. Although the show model had some teething problems the tests were nevertheless successful, leading to the business developer exploring different options for selling and distributing the Mitka.

Box 10.4 Mitka, a new mobility system (2001–02)

high level of involvement of the end users in the project—that is, the employees of Nike-Europe—contributed to this. Carrying out a practical test at Nike-Europe gave direction to the innovation project and created a broad basis of support. This, in turn, gave the project team great enthusiasm and momentum. The project also created its first commercial spin-off for Gazelle—the two-wheeled version of Mitka called Easy Rider. And a competitor of Gazelle, Giant, introduced the 'Easybike' (EZB) at the same time on the market, inspired by the Mitka project.

However, the development of the three-wheeled Mitka changed, mainly due to different business expectations between the partners. Gazelle decided to invest in a two-wheeled version, without cabriolet. The main reason for this decision seemed to be the perceived high price of a three-wheeled bicycle compared with the more usual two-wheeled variety. Gazelle's view was that customers would not pay the higher price. From an innovation point of view the Mitka was 'a bridge too far' for Gazelle. As a result, a business proposition 'from Gazelle' for Nike was not made.

The importance of managing the business expectations of partners in the right way appeared to be the dominant success factor in the Mitka project. Moreover, it seems possible and, indeed, necessary to imagine many different business models for this mobility concept. Greater creativity around the business models used at an earlier stage in the project could have changed views and expectations for the Mitka.

Phase 5: multiplication of system innovation

This phase encompasses the entire development of the new system concept in such a way that it results in large-scale changes at macro level. This phase naturally comprises various sub-phases.

The starting point is that the system design, tested at micro level, receives a positive evaluation. This evaluation needs to be in economic terms (i.e. will the product be bought and do companies want to invest capital in it?) and in consumer acceptance terms (i.e. will the consumer buy the product or use the system, is the consumer inclined to pay for it, can the consumer fit it into his/her lifestyle and will the product have a reduced environmental impact?).

The second sub-phase requires dispersion experiments in conjunction with government policy that endorses the system innovation. Grin *et al.* (2003) have termed this **third-generation environmental policy**, in which the structural barriers to system innovation towards sustainability are addressed. They recommend the development of 'an infrastructure which connects innovative practices with each other, just what the road system did (for cars) but what for instance a dealer network could do (for innovative transport systems)' (Grin *et al.* 2003).

So the government should provide the infrastructure for connecting experiments (such as Mitka) that do not fit in the present mobility paradigm. Just as Germany in the 1930s constructed a road system that boosted car transportation for the masses, so should a new infrastructure endorse experiments that are successful at the micro level. In this sense, infrastructure is more than physical infrastructure—it encompasses knowledge, regulations, economic incentives, communication and information, linkages between actors in strategic alliances, etc. It is important that there is continuous higher-order learning both within the micro experiments and in the structural connections between them (Brown *et al.* 2003). In these learning processes, social actors learn not only about the problems and new solution directions but also about the business aspects of implementation in practice, as well as about the other partners in the implementation process.

Multiplication is potentially conditioned by the space left by the dominant players in the dominant paradigm for experimentation and infrastructure building. The other condition is the extent to which governments (local, national and multinational [i.e. the EU]) can be convinced to change the rules in order to create the incentives for successful innovation.

In 2003, TNO, together with a government investment group, founded a formal company (BV) in which all rights of Mitka (three-wheeled) were laid down. A second business developer started an initiative to get funding for the production of the first series of 100 units.

Spin-off products such as Easy Rider and EZB realise a market penetration of thousands per year.

Today, there are many different initiatives inspired by the Mitka project, alive and seeking the opportunity to break through.

Box 10.5 Mitka, a new mobility system (2003–04)

Conclusions on the Mitka in the multiplication phase

The Mitka project has resulted in commercially feasible market products with a market penetration numbering thousands per year. These products were spin-offs from the original concept, promoted by the commercial partners (see Box 10.5). The conclusion has to be drawn that the spin-off products do not seem to share the sustainability ambition of the original Mitka concept (i.e. to tempt drivers away from their cars). The spin-offs are innovative products that will probably compete with other bikes rather then cars. In other words: they are not inherently sustainable.

This brings us to the following observations. First, it is not possible to manage system innovation based on blueprints and steer them by command and control. Innovation in a free market cannot be predicted. System innovation is complex, involving as it does different actors (the fourth characteristic) playing on different levels (the sixth characteristic). Second, the continuous involvement of a partner that is concerned about sustainability is necessary. As explained before, this should be government. Third, commercial companies and government should co-operate more intensively and share learning experiences in order to achieve sustainable innovations. Government could learn more from companies trying to realise sustainable innovations in practice and choose a different role to support the innovation. For example, it could be the launching customer for a new concept. Companies could share their innovation ambitions and problems with government and could interact in terms of new business models. Based on this, an infrastructure for system innovation could be identified. This infrastructure should help to change the structure of the system, as mentioned in phase

2, and create the need for new sustainable technology. Obviously, any change to the system structure for concepts such as Mitka should be totally different from the Delta Plan. But their similarities are inspiring and deserve further research.

Conclusions and recommendations

This chapter has attempted to describe systematically the concept of SSIs and to illustrate how it can lead to promising innovation projects. The deliberate and specific initiation of SSIs in society is a new phenomenon. As such it creates new possibilities and will, therefore, produce new results. It represents a learning process for all those involved.

The chapter describes the seven characteristics of SSIs and presents a five-phase approach. Examples of SSIs past and present have been provided. From the past it may be concluded that a strong commitment (e.g. a Delta Plan statement) is a prerequisite for success. From the present it becomes clear that this new concept is no panacea for quick and easy success. Several elements need to be in place in order to create a successful SSI:

- A strong vision of the future that is shared among the stakeholders

- A shared notion that stakeholders need each other in order to realise SSI

- Alignment between short-term business interests and long-term sustainability aims, discussed in terms of inherently sustainable business models

- An open approach to learning about both technological and sociocultural aspects

- A connection between experiments (which may be innovative and non-mainstream) and deeper societal trends

- An infrastructure for system innovation

These conditions are not easily fulfilled and a lot of experimentation and learning, together with monitoring processes are necessary for the realisation of SSIs.

The SSI approach seeks to combine bottom-up sustainable innovation initiatives with business drivers and the high-level societal needs of government. On the one hand, this interactive approach provides an answer to outdated top-down policy development approaches (the designed society). On the other, it is an antidote to purely market-driven approaches that fail to solve problems beyond individual interests (the free market). Using interactive processes, the SSI approach aims to develop far-reaching and innovative sustainable solutions by focusing on real-life projects. It seems to offer a new innovation approach for achieving the ambition to become a 'solutioning' society.

It can be concluded that programmes initiated by the SSI approach will continue. This gives an indication of the growing support for these initiatives and offers a perspective on multiplication. It also indicates that the SSI approach, as a starting point, can assist new sustainable innovation initiatives in a successful way.

From this, the following recommendations may be formulated. Domain explorations may serve as a starting point for orientation meetings in which relevant players develop system visions aimed at transitions towards sustainable mobility. A vision of the future may be constructed as a point of orientation for the development of solution directions and for the development of an open system concept. A **strategic problem analysis** is needed which means that the actors more or less agree about the nature of the problem—for instance, a congestion-free and environmentally sound short- to medium-distance transportation system for commuters. The concepts of BISS and changing the system structure help to identify opportunities for breakthrough innovations. Techniques such as backcasting and other methods may be used as a point of departure for the development of the system design. Finally, an experiment can be set up and carried out in which the stakeholders test the system concept and learn about its potentiality. If the system concept is successful in its initial phase, its potential for diffusion and multiplication may then be explored.

More experiments need to be carried out and evaluated in order to validate the framework in this chapter. Our main recommendation is to use the structure described in this chapter as a framework for setting up and evaluating SSIs.

The dominant opinion is that government, because of its broad social remit, should take the lead when it comes to sustainable development. The SSI approach facilitates a multi-actor innovation process, including important potential roles for government (e.g. representing societal needs, fostering innovation, creating new policy conditions for sustainable solutions, being the customer for new solutions and initiating the societal transition process).

The major challenge of system innovation is to find mutually supporting connections between trends and developments on the three levels: micro, meso and macro. Governmental priorities at the macro and meso levels could influence the domains and subjects that become the focus of micro-experiments. Learning about how projects work at the micro level is then fed back to the macro level.

Finally, the starting point of any system innovation must be that it is inherently sustainable—good for business and good for society. Thus, both companies and governments are motivated to multiply and propagate the solution.

References

Brezet, J.C., P.J. Vergragt and T.J.J. van der Horst (2001) *Kathalys: Visie op Duurzame Productinnovatie* [*Kathalys: A Vision of Sustainable Product Innovation*] (Amsterdam: BIS Publishers).

Brown, H.S., P.J. Vergragt, K. Green and L. Berchicci (2003) 'Learning for sustainability transition through bounded sociotechnical experiments', *Personal Mobility, Technology Analysis and Strategic Management* 13.3: 298-315.

Butter, M., and A. Slob (2002) *Flexibel Anticiperen op een Onzekere Toekomst: Een Handreiking voor Transitiebeleid* [*Flexible Anticipation of an Uncertain Future: A Guideline for Transition Policy*] (report no. 02-35; Delft, Netherlands: TNO STB).

Grin, J., H. van de Graaf and P.J. Vergragt (2003) 'Naar een derde generatie milieubeleid: een mogelijk sturingsconcept voor transities' [Towards a third-generation environmental policy: a possible steering concept for transitions], *Beleidswetenschap* 1: 51-72.

Jansen, L., and P.J. Vergragt (1999), *DTO sleutels* [STD keys] 1997, DTO Visie (STD Vision) and five other STD Keys on the subjects of mobility, food, water, chemicals and housing.

Kemp, R., J. Schot and R. Hoogma (1998) 'Regime shifts to sustainability through processes of niche formation: the approach of strategic niche management', *Technology Analysis and Strategic Management* 10.2: 175-95.

Rotmans, J., and R. Kemp (2000) *Transities en Transitiemanagement: De Casus van de Energiearme Energievoorziening* [*Transitions and Transition Management: The Case of Low-energy Energy Supply*] (Maastricht, Netherlands: ICES BV).

Van der Horst, T.J.J., P.J. Vergragt and S. Silvester (1999) 'Sustainable roadmapping', paper presented at *The Greening of Industry Conference*, Chapel Hill, NC, USA.

Vergragt, P.J (2003) 'Backcasting for environmental sustainability: from STD and SusHouse towards implementation', in J. Hemmelskamp and M. Weber (eds.), *Innovation Systems towards Sustainability* (Berlin/Heidelberg: Springer).

Weterings, R., and T. van der Horst (2002) Programmaplan Duurzame Systeem Innovatie [Programme plan for sustainable system innovation], confidential internal TNO memo.

11
Government behind the wheel and backseat driving
CO-ORDINATION AND INFORMATIONAL CHALLENGES OF VOLUNTARY PARTNERSHIPS AS PROGRAMMES FOR STIMULATING SUSTAINABLE TECHNOLOGY

Charles David White

University of California, Berkeley, USA

The US is facing enormous sustainable mobility and housing challenges. Transportation infrastructure and use patterns developed over decades have considerable inertia and already (or will) suffer from a mixture of woes—climate-destabilising greenhouse gas emissions, roadway congestion, depressed urban air quality, sprawling land-use patterns and social injustice related to transit access. Residential housing has analogous problems—increasing energy usage, toxic interior air, durability conundrums, etc. Ameliorating the bulk of these problems involves far-ranging, diffuse changes in infrastructure and markets. For example, an energy system shift to alternative transportation fuels depends on installation of non-petrol fuel-dispensing stations. Similarly, improved diffusion of advanced housing technologies and construction practices requires development of more communicative supply chain relationships.

To stimulate institutional transformation toward sustainable mobility and housing, over the past decade state governments in the US, as well as in other industrial countries, have experimented with **voluntary technology partnership** as an alternative style of policy implementation (de Bruijn and Norberg-Bohm 2005). Voluntary technology partnerships have two characteristics that distinguish them, in theory, from other types of state programming or public–private initiatives. The first is shared governance, which implies a greater ability to distribute authority and responsibility across stakeholders through voluntary participation. Partnership approaches imply more decentralised, co-operative decision-making and oversight than top-down administrative programmes which tend to concentrate authority and responsibility in a small set of actors. The second characteristic is an emphasis on technology innovation. Technology partnerships strive to bridge between sectors by employing technology as an organising concept. That is, technology functions not only as an instrument for public policy, but also integrates public discourse about the common good and business discourse about economic growth, competitive advantage and marketplace differentiation. In this regard, the ambiguity and malleability of technology (e.g. its nature as both a means and an ends) extends its usefulness beyond the mere physical to provide a co-ordinating mechanism through which actors express themselves, impact the choices and behaviour of others, and lay a foundation for institutional change (Bijker *et al.* 2001; Star and Griesemer 1989; Bowker and Star 1999; see especially Chapter 18).

The allure of technology partnership as a vehicle for progress rests on a democratic hope that decentralised authority and mutual consent, in combination with flexible mechanisms for pooling resources, can improve goal setting and co-ordinate action among stakeholders. The union of shared governance and technology innovation offers various advantages over more didactic modes of change (e.g. product regulations, supply-side initiatives or technology buy-down programmes). First, decentralised decision processes can make it easier to include diverse perspectives, such as those of technology users, whose insights may be necessary for identifying key issues. Second, shared ownership can spread the reach and appeal of a programme by leveraging the resources of multiple partners instead of just a principal actor (e.g. a government agency or other primary funding agent). Additionally, a partnership can have powerful effects if it is able to extend its influence beyond a specific technology target. By facilitating dynamic learning, the hope is that a partnership can encourage new technology interests and means of co-ordination, rather than merely one particular problem-solving orientation.

In light of these potentialities, partnerships can look promising, particularly when centralised governance appears to obstruct progress. However, partnerships present a variety of challenges. Their complex, amorphous nature can make it difficult for any one party to steer them. Consequently, progress towards a particular target (and certainly along a particular trajectory) requires more resources and active co-ordination among participants. Further, because of their relative youth as a mechanism of technologically based social progress, little is understood about how partnerships perform or about how to manage their development towards a particular goal.[1] Studies are needed to assess how partnerships perform, particularly in light of recent efforts to increase accountability in public administration.[2]

---

1 The contrast between Long and Arnold 1994 and Knaap and Kim 1998 demonstrates this gap in understanding.
2 Commentators and critics of public administration have recently placed great importance on building reflexive and responsive capability in public programming (Ayres and Braithwaite 1992) or performance-based environmental policy (Metzenbaum 1998; E4E 1997; NAPA 1995). In the US, the 1993 Government Performance and Results Act (5 USC 306) is particularly noteworthy because of its emphasis on outcome reporting and accountability for public programmes.

To advance understanding of partnerships in action, this chapter draws lessons from two US government programmes, each implemented as public–private, technology-oriented partnerships. The chapter discusses challenges that emerge, particularly for public managers, in setting, communicating and tracking sustainable technology goals and progress in voluntary partnerships. I pay particular attention to ways that goals are made visible and tractable in a partnership, and to how they create (or fail to create) a foundation for evaluation.

Methodology

The motivation for the research and findings described in this chapter is a current leitmotif in public administration—the pursuit of social objectives through co-operative and voluntary styles of programming (de Bruijn and Norberg-Bohm 2005). Because enthusiasm for these alternatives dwarfs knowledge about their usage and effects, we studied their functioning as social programmes.[3] As cases, we chose two non-regulatory, technology-change initiatives implemented by government as public–private partnerships (Norberg-Bohm and White 2004; Hart et al. 2003). Both are programmes chartered by the US Department of Energy (DOE) with the purpose of stimulating alternative, more energy-efficient technology and associated infrastructure.

The first case, and the main focus of this chapter, is the Clean Cities programme. This programme is a partnership between a broad collection of stakeholders interested in the development of infrastructure and markets to deploy alternative fuel vehicles. The second case, used here primarily to compare and validate inferences, is the Building America programme. This programme sponsors collaborative applied research between builders, scientists and others in the US residential housing sector to demonstrate and diffuse advanced building technologies.

To study the process and progress of these programme partnerships, we organised our research around a **programme evaluation** framework. Common in applied policy analysis, programme evaluation is an established approach for systematically assessing operations and outcomes. As the literature notes (Knaap and Kim 1998; Bartlett 1994), programme evaluation is a methodological umbrella spanning assessment techniques and, typically, three principal modes of analysis: outcome; process; and efficiency. In our study, we combined aspects of process and outcomes analyses. Our purpose was to analyse programme implementation and partnership-related technology changes with a two-part guiding question: what kind(s) of successes are being achieved through these partnership-based programmes; and what kind(s) of new challenges emerge from using this approach? To collect data we reviewed documents from programme archives and conducted qualitative interviews with programme managers and key participants. We first studied experiences in both programmes since their inception in the mid-1990s and then concentrated our examination on progress between 1998 and 2001, by which time the partnerships were more fully formed. When delving into this greater

---

3   A research group at the Kennedy School of Government at Harvard University.

degree of detail, we focused our inquiry on four of the 80 Clean Cities coalitions and all five of Building America's constituent teams.

Discussion of findings

This section begins by describing the mission and design of the two case partnerships. Then, drawing on their similarities and differences, the discussion turns to their function and structure, and to measuring their progress in stimulating technology innovation.

Clean Cities programme overview

The Clean Cities programme[4] refers to a large, voluntary public–private partnership that DOE launched in 1993 after years of upswing in legislation and R&D funding on alternative fuel vehicles (AFVs). The programme is intended to assist organisations required to meet vehicle fleet AFV requirements under section 505 of the 1992 Energy Policy Act[5] (42 USC 13255) and to support AFV deployment co-operation among voluntary partners. As interpreted by DOE, the term AFV refers to passenger, light-duty and heavy-duty vehicles that rely solely on natural gas, methanol, ethanol (E85), electricity, biologically derived fuels (e.g. bio-diesel), coal-derived fuels, liquefied petroleum gas (LPG) and/or hydrogen. As the flagship federal AFV deployment effort, Clean Cities encourages the deployment of all classes of non-gasoline, non-diesel vehicle technologies (e.g. personal automobiles, taxis, school buses, lorries, etc.) in the US. Since many market actors do not have the means or the motivation to share information and co-ordinate AFV deployment decisions, the purpose of Clean Cities is to synergise AFV deployment efforts.

The fundamental operating unit in the programme is a **Clean City**, a geographically based public–private partnership called a **coalition**. Each Clean City coalition is a collection of stakeholders interested in AFV deployment; its mission is to provide stakeholders with networking and co-operation opportunities about AFV purchase, infrastructure installation and usage. To enter the programme, each coalition must apply for DOE designation as a Clean City. Designation requires that each coalition chooses a co-ordinator who may be a representative from any stakeholder organisation and who serves as the primary contact with DOE. DOE's role is to assist the work of these coalitions by facilitating their development and, with time, their ongoing, independent operation. Its primary means of encouraging fledgling AFV technology is not via regulations or direct subsidies, but rather by facilitating stakeholder networks. Analogous to the networking opportunities that coalitions provide, the programme serves as a meta-coalition forum for collaboration and strategising. With about ten DOE staff mem-

---

4 See www.eere.energy.gov/cleancities.
5 Executive Orders 12844 (1993), 13031 (1997) and 13149 (2000) expand the federal fleet requirements of section 505, and a DOE regulatory decision in 2004 exempts private and local government fleet owners from its requirements (69 Fed. Reg. 4219).

bers and two annual partnership events in spring, Clean Cities guides coalitions through partnership fiscal planning, marketing and organising. In addition to this shepherding role, DOE makes general technical resources and case-specific technology research available to coalitions through its national laboratory-based Tiger Teams. As a federal agency, DOE cannot engage in political lobbying about AFVs, and many coalitions face the same restriction when their co-ordinator is a government employee. For this reason, DOE has supported the founding of a national non-profit organisation called Clean Cities Inc. to serve as a lobbyist for the coalitions; many coalitions have chosen a non-government co-ordinator to engage in this lobbying more freely.

Since the late 1990s, there have been roughly 80 coalitions and over 4,000 participating organisations. Early on, stated interest in AFV deployment and a list of stakeholders was sufficient to gain Clean City designation. Over the tenure of the programme, DOE has strengthened designation criteria to help coalitions develop. Before accepting a coalition into the partnership, DOE now requires substantial upfront planning and explicit delineation of coalition goals and action plans. With a total annual support budget of around US$44 million each year, and a cost-sharing requirement, the programme works to teach coalitions how to locate and secure funding more than it helps them financially. Coalitions have responded to the limited programme funding with several strategies. Some have limited their scope by serving primarily as a communications hub for broadcasting financial incentives and sharing technical resources about AFVs. With moderate support from other stakeholders, a coalition leader operating an email listserv and occasional meetings can maintain this mode of partnership. Other coalitions take more active roles to develop niche markets. For example, several members (e.g. transit agencies, taxi and shuttle companies, ground support vehicles, fuel providers and fuelling station operators) may collaborate on deployment of AFVs at an airport.

Building America programme overview

The Building America programme,[6] a case that helps validate the findings of the Clean Cities programme, is a residential housing technology partnership that DOE formed in 1995. Like the Clean Cities programme, Building America seeks to overcome market barriers and institutional gaps that obstruct technology learning. The programme focuses on the high-volume production housing industry[7] which is responsible for the vast majority of new dwellings constructed annually in the US and whose fragmented structure creates a variety of learning obstacles. These obstacles include a tendency to think of housing in terms of its individual components rather than as a dynamic system, weak market channels that fail to support dialogue about product performance and consequent difficulty co-ordinating innovations across organisations. Programme materials argue that: '[I]ndustry groups have traditionally worked independently of one another, slowing development and adoption of new technologies.' The concern is that, although many higher-performance technologies could improve housing, the

---

6   See www.buildingamerica.gov.
7   'Production housing' refers to the on-site construction and systematic replication of a set of housing designs. In everyday terms, this construction style is used to build housing subdivisions, townhouses and apartment communities.

industry is not systematically adopting them because their combined usage remains undemonstrated technologically or economically. The strategy is, therefore, to bring together all segments of the building industry (designers, builders, developers, financial institutions, material suppliers and equipment manufacturers) to demonstrate advanced technologies that can enhance housing performance. In doing so, the programme's ultimate goal is to infuse current practice with higher-performance technology and to improve housing industry learning capacity.

Like Clean Cities, the Building America programme is structured as a partnership managed by a core of government staff and based on the work of **stakeholder teams**. The purpose of these teams, each of which operates relatively autonomously and effectively functions as its own partnership (i.e. similar to a Clean Cities coalition), is to draw together industry members in learning projects about housing technology. In contrast to the dozens of Clean Cities coalitions, only five cross-industry teams comprise the Building America programme. Half of team funds come from multi-year, cost-sharing contracts with DOE which provide around US$1 million annually to each of them.

The programme affords teams considerable freedom to develop and carry out housing projects on their own and exhorts collaboration across teams only when necessity or economy dictates. Although teams can vary in composition, strategic focus and management style as befits their projects, their funding contracts with DOE require them to have the same general structure. Each team has a **team leader** who is a technical expert in building science. As the contracted agent, the team leader is responsible for partnering with housing industry actors to carry out and report on systems integration and advanced housing performance projects. The programme refers to the participating builders, suppliers and others as **team members**, but, reflective of a looser conception of the programme, team leaders usually call them **partners**. The business enterprise and construction practice of these industry partners provides the co-operative, practical workspace for learning among team leaders and practitioner team members. The R&D agendas for the teams are derivative of DOE programme goals, building scientist technology concepts and practitioner interests, and the projects that teams implement can take different forms—housing redesign and prototype construction, advanced design replication studies, performance monitoring, component technology R&D, and technology barrier identification studies.

Findings about partnership structure and function

In comparison to didactic or top-down programmes, a distinguishing characteristic of the partnerships studied is their emphasis on distributing decision-making authority among their members. To explore this characteristic, we used goals and goal accountability as a lens for examining authority structure (or participant agency) and the degree of co-ordination among participant agendas and the overall partnership. Albeit in different and revealing ways, we observed each programme struggling to achieve consistent traction toward their chartered goals. We found that an ongoing process of gaining and retaining partners, learning what they can contribute and developing co-ordinating mechanisms that enable productive co-operation underlay these struggles, and that this effort to enact participation created a continual learning loop that generally softened the constitution of the goals, if not in name, then at least in spirit. Based on the evidence presented here, we argue that this ongoing learning is a particularly important component of partnership-based programme management, since it complexifies the purpose of goals, their tractability, and their role in evaluation.

Beginning with the sustainable transportation programme, examining the cases in more detail helps to explain these findings. DOE sponsors the Clean Cities programme for the purpose of encouraging and co-ordinating deployment of AFVs and AFV infrastructure.[8] For the first few years of its existence, a lack of goal salience impeded the partnership's identity and ability to evaluate progress. Despite a positive report to Congress (DOE 1999), the programme and its coalitions floundered in evaluating progress and rationalising agendas. These circumstances changed when a veteran manager returned to the programme in late 1999 and introduced numerical goals not only to benchmark progress for direct AFV deployment, but also for the complementary technology and programme infrastructure needed to achieve it. Based on feedback from coalitions, DOE promulgated the following three partnership goals:

● To deploy one million vehicles operating exclusively on alternative fuels by 2010

● To stimulate AFV usage of one billion gasoline gallon equivalents per year by 2010

● To make 75% of Clean Cities coalitions self-sustaining by 2005

The first goal targets the main purpose of the programme to put into use passenger, light-duty and heavy-duty vehicles that DOE considers relevant AFVs. This distinction relies on the somewhat controversial (but tolerated) DOE definition of AFVs as vehicles that use one or any combination of programme-recognised alternative fuels. The second goal provides assurance that AFV numbers represent true deployment and petroleum replacement, not simply vehicle purchases. Fuel tallies also help to indicate the availability of alternative fuel infrastructure.[9] As opposed to these technology objectives, the third goal focuses on programmatic concerns about the management capacity of coalitions. Viewing Clean Cities as the glue that holds AFV deployment together, DOE targeted stable, self-sustaining coalitions as critical to the viability and growth of AFV technology deployment.

Mirroring the programme, early coalitions often did not have specific goals. To grow the partnership, programme managers were initially welcoming to all Clean Cities applications, with designated coalitions based primarily on expressed interest in AFV deployment. Many coalitions applied for participation with general goals (e.g. to

---

8   In 2004 DOE expanded the mission of Clean Cities and began to refer to the programme as a **portfolio**. Still in pursuit of its three numerical goals, the programme broadened its focus. The portfolio now includes efforts to: '[i] increase the use of fuel blends, [ii] accelerate sales of hybrid vehicles, [iii] promote informed consumer choice on fuel economy, and [iv] encourage the use of idle reduction technologies for heavy-duty lorries and other vehicles'; see www.eere.energy.gov/cleancities/pdfs/roadmap.pdf.

9   Unlike the fuel goal, a count of the number of alternative fuel-dispensing stations cannot indicate use. However, this measure is able to communicate the relative availability of stations, a critical and harder to measure aspect of AFV deployment. This tension between useful measures of AFV deployment and the untenable challenge of collecting adequate data from the partnership to measure it may explain why, despite the lack of a goal specific to it, DOE still tracks the number of AFV stations.

improve consumer education and public awareness about AFVs) but no specific strategy. Over time, coalitions dissolved or merged to stay afloat, and it became clear that intangible or incoherent coalition plans contributed to this failure. In response, DOE developed a comprehensive programme roadmap with clearer goals and a more rigorous designation process (DOE 2001). To help coherence, DOE obliged coalitions to move beyond their general statements of interest and adopt numerical targets for AFV deployment. This roadmapping encouraged coalitions to target stakeholders more specifically and to define participant responsibilities in a **memorandum of understanding**. Contemporaneous with this change, programme managers emphasised more targeted deployment. Most notably, DOE started encouraging coalitions to adopt a **niche market strategy** (i.e. to encourage stakeholders to co-ordinate around a common milieu, such as an airport). Both of these activities—the development of specific targets and the niche market strategy—have proven useful in orienting coalitions.

Like Clean Cities, the Building America programme is based on a broad purpose—to overcome the relatively slow speed of technical learning in the housing industry and to stimulate the construction of better housing. However, translating this purpose into specific programme goals has proven more difficult than for Clean Cities. Early programme pamphlets state that: 'The goal of the programme is to produce energy-efficient, environmentally sensitive, affordable and adaptable residences on a community scale.' In the contracts DOE issued to teams in 1998, this broad mission appeared in terms of specific, numerical objectives: 'To deliver 50% reduction in energy consumption (on average, depending on climate), 50% reduction in construction site waste, 25% increase in use of recycled materials, increase productivity and reduce construction cycle time.' The adoption of quantitative goals reflects an effort to rationalise the programme's agenda by resolving team project objectives. In reviewing team reports, we were not surprised to find that, when early partnership goals were vague, team project goals and reporting of results were similarly indistinct. What we found somewhat surprising was that the later, quantitative targets did not translate into comparable increased specificity in project goals. In fact, notwithstanding the numerical goals, over time the annual funding plans written between DOE and the teams have become less specific to allow teams more flexibility in their project development.

The reason for this divergence, it turns out, lies in the nature of the partnership and the technology. Unlike the coalition co-ordinators in the Clean Cities programmes, Building America team leaders operate under contracts. Although these contracts provide DOE principal input into team technology agendas, team leaders face the challenge not only of responding to DOE demands but also of blending this technology agenda with that of their partners. It is the responsibility of each individual team, not the programme, to recruit industry members to design, build and test projects. Team leaders work on projects at the pleasure of participating house builders and material suppliers, with industry members free to enter, leave or become inactive as individual projects begin and end. As a result, participation is temporary, intermittent and often not obvious for many of the industry members.[10] This ephemerality makes it hard for team leaders to plan or carry out technology research *ex ante*. Instead, every project involves a

10 Between 1995 and 2002, roughly 140 builders and developers and around 30 suppliers have participated as partners on the various teams. At any given time, however, only three to eight builders are actively involved in projects with a given team.

process of negotiation as team leaders learn what partners can and will contribute, and make adjustments accordingly.

The shifting population of partners helps to explain why creating a technology agenda based on the Building America goals has not proven straightforward or easy. The attempts to change goals exposed differences in opinion, both within and across teams, about measuring housing improvements and tracking progress. Despite the programme definitions, teams have conceptualised and prioritised housing improvements along several dimensions: energy efficiency; durability; economic value; occupant comfort; productivity; and environmental impact. Thus, despite the quantification of goals, the rather autonomous Building America teams have not adopted consistent measures of progress, and project plans remain fuzzy about their contribution to the overall technology agenda. Although DOE has tried to improve the alignment by holding teams to the programme goals, doing so has proven elusive because of the need for team adaptability to bring industry members into the partnership. The irony is that contract relationships between the funding public agency and the programme participants in Building America has not resulted in superior goal alignment to that of the Clean Cities programme.

These goal management experiences are instructive for both public administration and programme evaluation. Translating and scaling programme goals for individual projects exposes a trade-off that is common in programming but is especially relevant for partnership-based technology change initiatives such as Clean Cities and Building America—indefinite goals create a broad and flexible direction for co-operative learning but do not create the tractable basis for project co-ordination that precise goals offer. As discussed in the next section, the degree of co-ordination among partners has consequences not only for the way the programme operates but also for the data management and progress measurability that enable programme evaluation as well.

Findings about technology progress

As the discussion of the Clean Cities programme here demonstrates, the extent of data infrastructure affects the nature of technology claims and reveals challenges for developing representative measures and verifying results. Although many programmes have trouble assessing and attributing progress during their early phases of development, voluntary partnerships, particularly those with shifting participants, seem remarkably and continually susceptible.

Based on data collected from its partners, Clean Cities reports steady growth both in AFVs and in the number of alternative fuel-dispensing stations installed over the ten-year life of the programme (see Fig. 11.1). In 2004, the programme attributed 200,000 deployments and nearly 6,000 refuelling stations to the work of its coalitions. DOE estimated that operation of this infrastructure displaced approximately 200 million gallons per year of gasoline. Additionally, DOE considered 41% of coalitions to be self-sustaining.[11] Based on these results, DOE stood one-fifth of the way towards its first two goals and halfway to its third.

Clean Cities' tracking of technology progress has been based on voluntary participant reporting, an approach that has demonstrated limitations. To compile data about

11   See www.eere.energy.gov/cleancities/pdfs/roadmap.pdf.

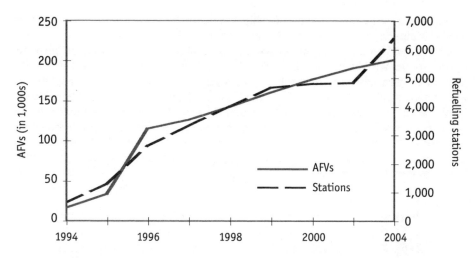

FIGURE 11.1 AFV and AFV deployment

Source: Clean Cities programme data, from annual coalition surveys

AFV technology, Clean Cities programme managers send co-ordinators an annual survey which asks them to self-report deployment information for their coalitions. Generally speaking, co-ordinators cannot compel their members to provide information and, since many lack expertise in data collection, tend not to verify the data they receive. As a result, the quality of AFV data received from coalitions has been uncertain. The discrepancy between DOE estimates of the AFV population and the reports received from coalitions highlights this problem. The Energy Information Administration (EIA) estimated that the 2004 population of AFVs in the US at 500,000;[12] however, even though DOE has assumed that Clean Cities coalitions have connections to almost all AFV usage and deployment, they account for only 40% of this total. Programme managers have interpreted this difference as a sign of significant under-reporting but, without deeper pockets or a stronger mandate, have had little ability to lean on coalitions to improve data collection. One might suppose that, as an alternative, DOE could develop data collection channels that do not rely on co-ordinators, such as a direct data request from coalition members. However, it is individual coalitions, not the overall programme, that govern membership, and they accept participation at the pleasure of the stakeholder. Coalition co-ordinators generally have not kept careful partner records and have resisted DOE data collection initiatives that sap resources for their projects. Reluctant to step on toes, DOE has had no database of participants and only general information about participant demographics.[13]

Even with perfect AFV statistics, the larger challenge for programme evaluation is relating the AFV population to the work of the programme. A first step in this process is

---

12   See www.eia.doe.gov/cneaf/alternate/page/datatables/aft1-13_03.html *or* www.eia.doe.gov →
      'Renewable & Alternative Fuels' → 'Inventory Stocks'.
13   We briefly explored another alternative—querying State departments' databases of motor vehicles. Unfortunately, these databases do not distinguish AFVs from other petrol-fuelled vehicles adequately enough to improve AFV population estimates.

explaining the structure of the partnership and the processes that underlie it or can be used to claim credit for AFV deployment. To their credit, DOE programme staff recognised this need and, in 1999, undertook an informal review of coalitions to correlate characteristics with higher AFV deployment rates. Based on this study, they concluded that coalition success (i.e. higher deployment rates, based on available data; see Fig. 11.2) depends on the effectiveness of the co-ordinator, the amount of utility company involvement (for infrastructure support), and the level of local and state incentive for AFV use. However, the DOE review neither pinpointed specific activities or strategies (e.g. consumer education, development of niche markets and lobbying) nor explained differences in coalition outcomes across geographies. In short, data poverty and attribution presented an impasse.

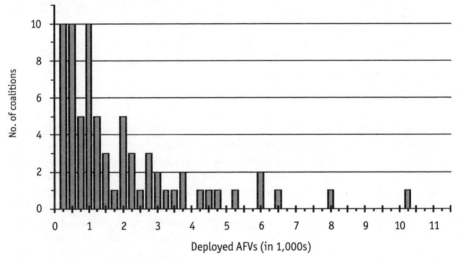

mean = 2,000; median = 1,000; SD = 2,000

FIGURE 11.2 AFV deployment statistics

Source: Clean Cities programme data

To delve deeper into the partnership and its effects, we tried to sidestep this impasse (i.e. incomplete data about the entire AFV population) by studying a representative sample of coalitions. We believed that dissecting purposively selected representative coalitions would allow us to identify and generalise causal factors that contribute to individual coalition and overall programme success in deploying technology. However, we found sampling an insurmountable task. Since the programme's inception, the number of participating coalitions has grown steadily, from 34 in 1993 to more than 85 in 2004, and the number of stakeholders has reached just under 5,000 participating organisations (see Fig. 11.3). These coalitions and stakeholders vary along several, quite likely significant dimensions: geography (from mid-sized towns to large metropolitan regions to transportation corridors); partner size (from small to large corporations); number of members (from a dozen to over 100); and co-ordinator and membership demographics. Our in-depth interviews with four coalitions also revealed

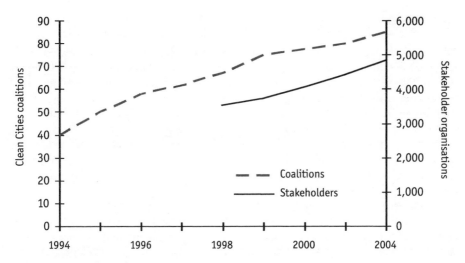

Figure 11.3 Clean Cities participation

Source: Clean Cities programme data

considerable differences in the way they operate. Some have leaders whose initiative and centrality become defining factors in the coalition's purpose; others have part-time co-ordinators who generally facilitate the coalition but do not set an overarching agenda. Co-ordinators told us that participant continuity and funding stability affect coalition-related AFV deployment, while the mode of participation—as defined by the type and range of coalition activities—is likely to play an important role too. Data about these characteristics of coalitions and the overall population were not available nor easily collectible.

The implication of these findings is twofold. First, partnership-based programmes require data infrastructure, both for their goals and their constitution, that is consonant with the nature of the partnership and the technology. Second, this requirement puts partnership-based programmes in a relatively weaker position in order to satisfy the strictures of administrative accountability and responsiveness.[14]

---

14 As validation of this claim, progress tracking in the Building America programme is more multi-dimensional and has proven even more elusive than Clean Cities. Between 1993 and 2001, teams and their partners constructed 10,000 houses that met a minimum 30% energy use reduction criterion. During this same period, teams demonstrated housing designs that cost-neutrally (or near-neutrally) reduced energy use by up to 70%, abated moisture-related failures and improved thermal distribution and air quality. However, progress tracking suffered notably in two respects. First, housing performance data along dimensions other than energy efficiency (e.g. durability, habitability, environmental burden, etc.) were not systematically measured. Second, despite the programme's commendable work in combining the findings into deployable building systems packages and encouraging team communication of findings through conference reports and journal articles, disseminating the knowledge generated through the teams has been uneven.

Conclusions

This chapter reflects on two voluntary technology partnerships, both of which function as energy and environmental policy implementation mechanisms for the US Department of Energy. To tackle fragmented markets and vertically disintegrated industrial sectors that constrain technology innovation, the Clean Cities and Building America programmes (re)connect stakeholders and (re)integrate supply chains through extra-market, extra-institutional fora called, respectively, coalitions and teams. Because their progress depends on collaboration among stakeholders to innovate technology practice and to stimulate networks that can diffuse technologies and catalyse infrastructural change, these programmes are interesting cases, both from public administration and sustainability perspectives.

In comparison to traditional, didactic programme designs, partnerships are more decentralised, administratively looser confederations of actors. The overarching challenge in the use of partnership-based programmes is an evaluation of their effectiveness in stimulating more sustainable technology. We found that collaborative programmes require considerable effort to make objectives tractable across levels of the partnership, to synchronise data collection and to make outcomes visible. Low goal specificity and high participant discretion in the programmes seemed initially attractive because they permitted independent adjustment among partners and between partners and their environments. However, in order to improve partnership coherency, both programmes needed to increase the specificity of their goals after flexible, vague missions proved insufficient to make progress tractable and outcomes measurable.

We observed commendable programmatic adjustments that improved a particular, lagging aspect of partnership: goal resolution to improve visibility and tractability (in the Clean Cities case), and innovative bundling and communicating results that otherwise would lay dormant within the partnership (in the Building America case). To bolster the Clean Cities programme, DOE resolved and externalised programme goals to improve the tractability of the overarching mission, enable progress tracking and galvanise the partnership. DOE's promotion of a niche market strategy was a clever choice that helped struggling coalitions to structure their otherwise weakly co-ordinated efforts to develop AFV market and infrastructure. To disseminate lessons from the Building America partnership, the programme cleverly chose to create deployment-ready technology systems systems to enable better diffusion of lesson learned. DOE and teams also shifted team reporting from contract deliverables to technical reports prepared for public consumption.

At the conclusion of our study, we did not doubt that each of these programmes had made significant contributions to the development and diffusion of fledgling alternative technologies. Nonetheless, there was no way to gauge the effectiveness of these partnerships. Since analysis depends on partner data collection, and partners had insufficient motivation to collect data diligently, outcome assessment had remained ambiguous. Despite anecdotal evidence and strong belief in their partnerships' achievements, both programmes demonstrated trouble marshalling systematic proof of their progress when programme managers lacked incentives or social capital to demand rigorous data management

To aid management and study of partnership-based programmes, the following recommendations are offered in response to these findings:

- **View voluntary, partnership-based programmes as fluid arrangements.** As partners exit and enter, they change the constituent matrix of ideas and wills that compose the partnership. Even though government may initially design a voluntary programme, as only one actor in the process, a public agency cannot control a partnership the way a principal directs the work of a contracted agent. Over time, partner ebb and flow changes the tenor of the process, the texture of the discussion and the process of decision-making. This transience requires renegotiation and, from the standpoint of programme evaluation and administrative accountability, makes it much more difficult to track progress and attribute responsibility for outcomes

- **Choose goals that increase tractability.** Goals provide an important basis for continuity, as well as a guidepost for co-operative innovation. When used to co-ordinate a partnership, goals should be visible to partners, translatable into objectives for different subunits in the partnership and scalable to allow data aggregation and assessment. However, because choices about coherency and cohesion are embedded in goal structures, programme managers must pay careful attention to trade-offs between encouraging convergence and impeding innovation

- **Develop robust data infrastructure.** Accountability depends on assessment, and programme evaluation requires data collection. Programmes should develop procedures and channels to collect data not only about technology progress but also about participants and modes of participation. Because partnerships depend on partners to collect and verify information, voluntary programmes must devote special attention to incentives that encourage consistent and thorough data management

- **Recognise that programme evaluation for partnerships introduce new challenges.** Theoretical discussions about more reflexive and responsive governments are missing an important point if they overlook the impact of programme design on systematic and useful progress assessment. Partial and temporary participation make it difficult to draw a clear boundary about what occurs 'inside' and 'outside' the partnership. Programme evaluation requires more intermediate technology outcomes measures, as well as attention to the functional role(s) that partners and the partnership play in creating change

The larger obstacles to achieving sustainable mobility and housing through technology change programmes should not be underestimated. Alternative technologies such as AFVs are not fully mature and require further innovations (e.g. cost reductions) to enable their widespread adoption. The experiences of Clean Cities and Building America reinforce the perception that voluntary partnership can contribute to technological transitions. However, a better foundation for their evaluation will enhance their ability to do so.

References

Ayres, I., and J. Braithwaite (1992) *Responsive Regulation: Transcending the Deregulation Debate* (New York: Oxford University Press).

Bartlett, R.V. (1994) 'Evaluating environmental policy success and failure', in N. Vig and M. Kraft (eds.), *Environmental Policy in the 1990s* (Washington, DC: CQ Press).

Bijker, W.E., T.P. Hughes and T. Pinch (eds.) (2001) *The Social Construction of Technological Systems* (Cambridge, MA: MIT Press).

Bowker, G., and S.L. Star (1999) *Sorting Things Out: Classification and Its Consequences* (Cambridge, MA: MIT Press).

De Bruijn, T., and V. Norberg-Bohm (2005) *Industrial Transformation: Environmental Policy Innovation in the United States and Europe* (Cambridge, MA: MIT Press).

DOE (Department of Energy) (1999) *Report on Voluntary Commitments for the Replacement Fuel Supply and Demand Programme*, Energy Policy Act 1992, Section 505, second report to Congress.

—— (2001) *Clean Cities Roadmap: A Resource for Developing, Implementing, and Sustaining Your Clean Cities Programme*, Report BK-540-26021, www.ccities.doe.gov/roadmap.shtml, accessed August 2001; the most recent roadmap is accessible at www.eere.energy.gov/cleancities/roadmap.html.

E4E (Enterprise for the Environment) (1997) *The Environmental Protection System in Transition: Toward a More Desirable Future* (Washington, DC: Centre for Strategic and International Studies).

EIA (Energy Information Administration) (2004) 'Table 1: Estimated Number of Alternative-Fueled Vehicles in Use in the United States, by Fuel, 1995–2004', www.eia.doe.gov/cneaf/alternate/page/datatables/atf1-13_03.html, accessed February 2005.

Hart, D., D. Rutu and C.D. White (2003) *Clean Cities Programme Evaluation*, Report to the US Department of Energy, Kennedy School of Government, Harvard University.

Knaap, G.J., and T.J. Kim (eds.) (1998) *Environmental Programme Evaluation: A Primer* (Urbana, IL: University of Illinois Press).

Lindblom, C. (1965) *The Intelligence of Democracy* (New York: Free Press).

Long, F.J., and M.B. Arnold (1994) *The Power of Environmental Partnerships* (Fort Worth, TX: Dryden Press).

Metzenbaum, S. (1998) *Making Measurement Matter: The Challenge and Promise of Building a Performance-focused Environmental Protection System* (Washington, DC: The Brookings Institution).

NAPA (National Academy of Public Administration) (1995) *Setting Priorities, Getting Results: A New Direction for the US Environmental Protection Agency* (Washington, DC: NAPA).

Norberg-Bohm, V., and C.D. White (2004) *Building America Programme Evaluation*, Report to the US Department of Energy, Kennedy School of Government, Harvard University.

Star, S.L., and J. Griesemer (1989) 'Institutional ecology, translations, and boundary objects: amateurs and professionals in Berkeley's Museum of Vertebrate Zoology, 1907–39', *Social Studies of Science* 19: 387-420.

12

Process- and product-oriented environmental policy within the car chain
EXAMPLES FROM BMW AND GENERAL MOTORS

Carla K. Smink, Eskild Holm Nielsen and Tine Herreborg Jørgensen
Aalborg University, Denmark

With revenue of well over US$1 trillion and ten million employees worldwide, the automotive industry is the world's largest manufacturing industry (Klein and Selz 2000). It is also one of the most resource-intensive of all major industrial systems (Mildenberger and Khare 2000). Through its lifetime, a car has serious environmental impacts. Many environmentalists even suggest that the car is the most polluting product on earth (Gouldson 1993).

The lifetime for an average car in a typical industrialised country is 10–12 years. That is, it takes a car 10–12 years to go from vehicle assembly to dismantling, recycling and landfill. The raw materials extraction and processing phase adds one year to this. In addition, car manufacturers typically require three to five years in order to develop new models, which may then remain in production for anything between four and 15 years. Thus, any initiatives implemented in vehicle designs will carry environmental implications for at least the next 20 years (Nieuwenhuis and Wells 1997).

For decades, different legal instruments have been used to regulate the environmental and societal impacts of the car. In this chapter, we will analyse how BMW and General Motors (GM) have responded to environmental regulations and which activities they have initiated to improve their environmental performance. Empirically, this study is based on interviews with environmental managers at BMW's production facility in Rosslyn (near Pretoria, South Africa) and GM's assembly facilities in Port Elizabeth in South Africa. We will analyse how the environmental performance of these facilities relates to the environmental strategies of the parent companies within the whole product chain.

The focus of the first part of this chapter is on the environmental activities in the product chain and on developments in environmental regulation over the past 30 years. This is followed by a more detailed analysis of the corporate responses of BMW and GM to environmental issues. Can their responses be regarded as a process-oriented strategy or a product-oriented one? And what are the consequences for the environmental performance of their facilities in South Africa? Conclusions are provided at the end.

Environmental activities in the product chain

Environmental activities in the product chain are increasingly based on co-operation throughout the chain with the goal of making environmental improvements at each stage of the production process. The product chain includes the following (Danish EPA 2003):

- A flow of materials from acquisition of raw materials to production, to use, to disposal

- A value and cash flow from the consumer to the producer

- Communication and co-operation in the form of mutual exchange of knowledge and experience

The different flows are illustrated in Figure 12.1. So far, attention has been paid mainly towards the flow of materials (e.g. life-cycle assessment [LCA]). However, the value and cash flow is important as well. For example, it is important to know what expectations consumers have about a product's environmental characteristics, and how consumers rate environmental considerations related to other aspects such as price, quality, functionality, design, etc. (Danish EPA 2003). For a long time, 'green' cars have not been marketed by car retailers; instead, they have been largely promoted via government subsidies and EU policies. In general, consumers do not (and are not triggered to) establish a link between the end-of-life vehicle (ELV) policies adopted by chain actors in the automotive industry and the environmental performance of the automotive industry in general (Smink et al. 2003). However, more recently, Toyota and Honda have introduced hybrid electric cars in order to gain competitive advantage in the market, without prompting from government.

For companies, the challenge is to connect the links in the product chain in order to focus on both environmental optimisation of the material flow in the supplier chain; and on the customer's expectations regarding environmental considerations in the value chain. Communication and co-operation between all actors involved will build connections between the supplier chain and the value chain (Danish EPA 2003).

As with all models, co-operation and communication in the product chain is more complex than presented in Figure 12.1. For example, the linkages between the different phases in the life-cycle of a product are different; some linkages are weaker and some

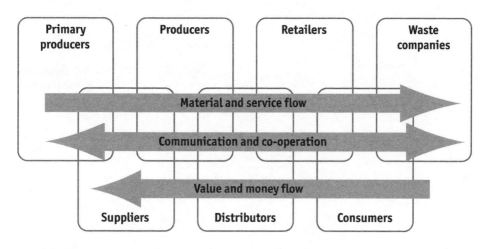

FIGURE 12.1 Co-operation and communication in the product chain

Source: Remmen and Münster 2002: 44

are stronger than others. Furthermore, Figure 12.1 does not show that a global product chain exists in many environmental contexts. The environmental context is deeply rooted in the local situation which can make huge differences within a product chain, especially when focus is on products, such as cars, that are produced in many countries around the world. Finally, emissions and waste from each of the phases in the product chain are missing from Figure 12.1.

Figure 12.1 serves as a point of departure for our empirical study in terms of investigating environmental communication and co-operation in the car chain. However, as focus here is on the automotive industry, we cannot pass over the complexity of car chain (see Fig. 12.2).

The car chain consists of two, more or less independent, networks: a production network; and a use, recycling and disposal network. Especially in Europe, contacts between actors in these two networks are limited. According to den Hond and Groenewegen (1993: 351), a reason for this weak link is that car manufacturers have had no specific interest in connecting with car-dismantling companies. In fact, they may even have tried to avoid association with dismantling activities which are often dispersed, sometimes semi-legal or illegal, and often directly competitive with dealers for the spare-parts market. Most interactions are incidental, focused on specific activities, or informal, based on personal relations. Co-operation and communication between the two networks are not institutionalised (Smink 2002). The predominant situation has been that environmental regulations have developed independently in both networks (Smink *et al.* 2003).

Figure 12.2 shows that the relationships between actors in the car chain are complex and cannot be represented in a linear way, as in Figure 12.1. However, Figure 12.2 also indicates that some relationships are stronger than others. In the next section, environmental policies and regulations in the car chain will be described in order to pro-

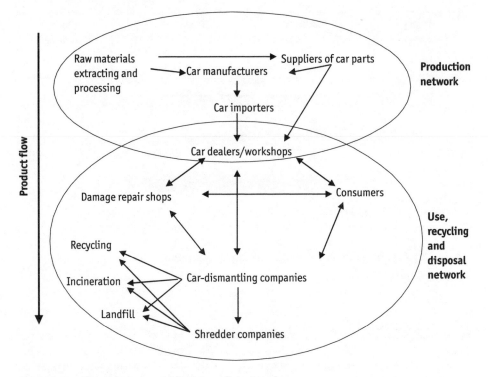

FIGURE 12.2 The car chain and its two sub-networks

Source: Smink 2002: 163

vide an overview for our analysis of the environmental performance of BMW and GM in the product chain.

Modernisation of environmental regulation

In this part, we will briefly summarise modernisation of environmental regulation in industrialised countries over the last 35 years. This description will be used as a framework for analysing developments in environmental regulations in the automotive industry.

Since the 1970s, command-and-control regulations have been the dominant form of public environmental regulations. For many years, command-and-control regulation was aimed primarily at emissions from material production, product manufacturing and disposal, but not at the product life-cycle. With regard to waste management, regulations focused on the efficient removal of waste rather than waste prevention. Continuity of production was the basis of the major guidelines for practical policy (van der Woerd 1997). In other words, the focus was on single companies who, often individually, developed solutions to meet the emission standards set by the government. In this approach, a company is regarded as a 'black box'. That is, governments do not have an interest in the activities within the company (e.g. resource consumption) (Remmen and Nielsen 1994).

Reflection over the possibilities and limitations of command-and-control regulation started in the mid-1980s, causing a shift in the regulatory approach of many industrialised countries (Smink 2002) from a media-specific approach to a process-oriented one. In a process-oriented strategy, the emphasis is on individual companies in the product chain and on how they can reduce their environmental impacts. An environmental management system (EMS) is an example of a process-oriented strategy. Individual companies who want to improve their environmental performance have taken this step towards a process-oriented approach, but governments have also encouraged an increased focus on the production process. That is, government regulation has been an incentive for companies to look further into their production processes. In regulatory terms, it can be stated that public environmental regulations have been supplemented with self-regulation.

During the 1990s, the process-oriented strategy has increasingly been supplemented with a product-oriented strategy in a number of industrialised countries. Limitations of the process-oriented strategy are that environmental efforts are limited to single companies. Sooner or later, therefore, the possibilities for environmental improvements will be exhausted. In a product-oriented strategy, companies make demands on other companies in the product chain in order to improve their environmental performance. Hence, next to the government, the market will make demands on companies as well (i.e. business-to-business demands).

Figure 12.3 illustrates the development from 'pure' public environmental regulations via a process-oriented strategy to a product-oriented strategy.

Examples of product regulations are various. A well-known example in the automotive industry is the EU ELV Directive (2000/53/EC) which was adopted in 2000. One of the main objectives of the Directive is to prevent waste from ELVs (European Commission 2001). By 2015, 95% of an ELV must be recycled. Car-dismantling companies cannot achieve this target alone. The Directive also requires car manufacturers and material and equipment manufacturers to reduce the use of hazardous substances in new cars. Furthermore, they have to design and produce cars to facilitate the dismantling, re-use, recovery and recycling of ELVs, and they also have to increase the use of recycled materials in car manufacturing. These initiatives will influence all the actors in the car chain.

The next section focuses on environmental policies and regulation in the car chain.

Environmental regulation in the car chain

In this part, we will briefly pay attention to environmental regulations in the car chain. Focus will be on how BMW and GM have responded to changes in environmental regulations.

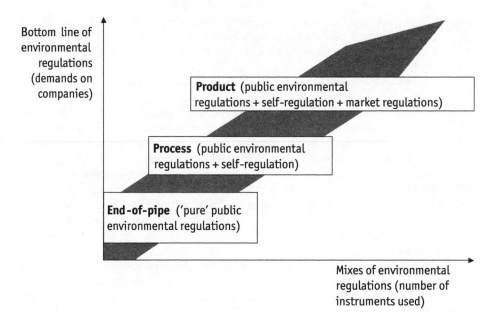

FIGURE 12.3 Bottom-line of environmental regulations

Source: Smink 2002: 247

All actors in the car chain are subject to public environmental regulations. Often, these are aimed at single life-cycle phases, such as the raw materials extracting and processing phase, the manufacturing phase, the use phase and, finally, the dismantling phase (see Table 12.1). Even though the regulations mainly reflect the local environmental context, they may nevertheless have global implications. If the EU implements regulations on carbon dioxide emissions for cars, for example, US and Japanese car manufacturers will also have to meet the specified criteria if they want to access to European markets. The same is true for the ELV regulations.

Primary producers	Car manufacturers	Use	Disposal
● IPPC permit ● Depletion quotas on extraction and import of virgin materials ● Taxes on the use of virgin materials ● Recycled materials quotas ● Emission limit values based on best available techniques (BAT)	● Taxes on the use of virgin materials ● Emission standards ● Emission limit values based on BAT	● Speed limits ● Car care products ● Fuel price ● Tax	● Waste regulations ● Recycling quotas

TABLE 12.1 Examples of public environmental regulations in the life-cycle of a car

Source: adapted from Mildenberger and Khare 2000

Environmental regulation in South Africa

The apartheid regime has fostered an environmental regulation in Roman–Dutch legal tradition, and has continued into the new political era of the African National Congress. So far, environmental law-making and enforcement is fragmented both horizontally and vertically. At the national level, a number of ministries, such as the Department of Environmental Affairs and Tourism, and the Department of Water Affairs and Forestry, are involved in different pieces of environmental regulation. At regional and local level, a number of institutions are also involved in regulating industries (Jeppesen 2004; Glazewski 2000). At the national level in 1998, the National Environmental Management Act (NEMA) was implemented in order to establish a new structure of co-operative governance between national, regional and local spheres (Jeppesen 2004). The environmental regulations of industries are based on different media-oriented acts, such as the Water Act (1998) and the Atmospheric Pollution Prevention Act (1965). Environmental regulations in South Africa have suffered from lack of enforcement which is related to insufficient human and financial resources (Jeppesen 2004).

The environmental justice movement in South Africa has also shown that both the regulation of treatment plants and the application of technical standards are insufficient. Solid and hazardous wastes are a major problem in South Africa. The black population tends to suffer disproportionately from the environmental burden arising from outdated technology and solutions (Peeks 2002): due to apartheid planning they live close to industrial areas.

So far, the South African government has not launched a product-oriented policy. The situation in South Africa is dominated by the need for capacity building in terms of human and technical resources. One of the fundamental problems in South Africa is that regulations are not enforced and environmental standards do not meet the public's expectations. Transnational companies with proactive environmental strategies are challenged by the inadequate enforcement combined with the use of outdated technology in South Africa. Many transnational companies have implemented an EMS in order to ensure that emissions from a specific plant are handled in an environmentally sound manner. In the South African context, the challenge for the EMS is to include a life-cycle perspective, in order to take local environmental problems, the stage of applied technology in South African and poor enforcement into account. In other words, in a developing context, transnational companies must take responsibility for the lack of environmental governance if their plants are to reflect modern environmental standards.

Corporate responses: a process- or product-oriented strategy?

Our empirical work is aimed at analysing how BMW and GM have responded to changes in environmental regulations in the car chain. To be more precise, the analysis will look at the extent to which these two transnational companies have implemented a product-oriented strategy to improve their environmental performance, and to what extent this strategy is applied at their facilities in South Africa. In order to answer these questions, we took the corporate environmental policies of BMW and GM as a reference point. We then conducted interviews with environmental managers at BMW's production facility in Rosslyn and GM's assembly plants in Port Elizabeth, South Africa. But first we will briefly describe the automobile industry in South Africa.

The South African automobile industry incorporates the manufacturing, distribution, servicing and maintenance of cars and components. The industry's total contribution to the country's GDP in 2003 was around 6.6% (DTI 2004a) which makes it the third largest sector in the South African economy, after mining and financial services (DTI 2004a). The EU was South Africa's main export destination in 2003 in value terms with 69.6% of the industry's automotive components, 19.5% of light vehicles and 22.8% of medium and heavy commercial vehicles (DTI 2004b).

Ford was the first original equipment manufacturer (OEM) to establish a subsidiary company in 1924 in Port Elizabeth in the Eastern Cape. Currently, all the major OEMs in the world are represented in South Africa with seven plants producing 13 brands (DTI 2004a).

Environmental regulations in Europe, Japan, the US and other major markets will also impact on the South African automotive industry, but we will not be addressing the extent to which South Africa is able to take advantage of global trends.

BMW: Group and South Africa environmental strategy

In a speech at the World Summit on Sustainable Development (WSSD) in Johannesburg in 2002, BMW director Dr Norbert Reithofer stated: 'the issue [of sustainable development] is not environment versus development, or ecology against the economy. Contrary to popular belief, we can integrate the two'. BMW is firmly convinced that sustainability is not a distant vision. According to Dr Reithofer: 'It is the core of our current company strategy and it establishes the foundation for the future of the BMW Group as a global provider of premium cars and motorcycles.' Dr Reithofer went on to state that environmental protection is an important aspect of BMW's environmental policy. BMW has opted for two instruments, design for recycling (DfR) and LCA, to integrate environmental and recycling standards. Already in the developmental stage, a recycling-oriented design process takes the dismantling aspects of vehicles into account. As a result, Dr Reithofer explains: 'All our vehicles are almost completely economically recyclable'. Furthermore, all BMW production facilities have a certified EMS according to the international EMS standard ISO 14001 and/or the EU Eco-Management and Audit Scheme (EMAS).

As mentioned above, BMW has adopted a number of product-oriented initiatives, such as DfR and LCA. These are not, however, incorporated in all the Group's divisions and sites. Different initiatives are taken at each production facility. For example, so far, DfR has only been applied within the research department. As a result, BMW has not implemented a Group-wide product-oriented strategy as such.

We will now focus on BMW's environmental strategy at its South African production plant in Rosslyn in order to analyse the extent to which product-oriented initiatives have been implemented there.

BMW South Africa is owned by the BMW Group and is covered by the corporate management of BMW. The Rosslyn plant was the Group's first foreign location. At this plant, more than 40,000 BMW 3 Series are produced a year, many being exported to the US, Japan, Australia, Africa and the Middle East.[1]

In 1999, the Rosslyn plant received certification for its integrated management system for quality, work safety and environmental protection in compliance with ISO 9001, ISO 14001 and BS 8800.[2] The main reason for the Rosslyn plant to implement ISO 14001 was the requirement from the parent company, but in an interview Mrs Boscho, an environmental advisor, observed: 'the demand from the parent company is also the demand from the customer . . . It took approximately six months to implement the EMS'.

During implementation of the EMS the three staff in the Rosslyn plant's environment department were assisted by an environmental manager from the parent company, BMW Germany. Once the system was implemented, the environmental manager returned to Germany and the system stagnated. Mrs Boscho explained: 'there was no momentum to keep it going . . . It took approximately a year before the Rosslyn plant started working within the EMS again' as it took time to become familiar with the system and start working with continuous improvement.

The company has reduced environmental impacts, risks and accidents considerably. From 1998 to 2001, it reduced water and electricity consumption per manufactured vehicle by approximately 90% and 45% (BMW 2002). However, the environmental policies of the Rosslyn plant do not reflect the local South African context, although they do reflect the environmental focus of the BMW Group. As mentioned above, South African environmental regulation is not well developed and it is difficult for South African companies to identify and address environmental problems. From the interview with Mrs Boscho, it became clear that the most difficult part of complying with ISO 14001 was determining relevant South African environmental legislation which is extensive but inconsistent and sometimes incomprehensible. Where local regulations and standards were lacking, US Environmental Protection Agency (EPA) guidelines were used: for example, on atmospheric emissions. Dutch guidelines on, for example, water pollution, were also referred to. BMW staff attended a number of courses in order to achieve improve their knowledge and understanding of environmental regulation. As stated previously, limited government resources in South Africa have resulted in poor enforcement. This has implications for industry. For example, companies have to contact the authorities themselves in order to ask for specific pollution permits, and they must also take their own water samples. Adopting ISO 14001 ensures that companies in these situations do comply with regulations.

In 2000, the Rosslyn plant integrated a supply chain management programme into its EMS. The initial target was that all suppliers were to have a certified EMS according to ISO 14001 in order to improve the supplier's environmental performance. Most suppliers to the Rosslyn plant are local: for example, in the steel and plastics industries. The few overseas suppliers are mainly BMW's own component manufacturing plants. The latter are already certified to ISO 14001 due to BMW's corporate environmental strategy.

---

1   'BMW plants: where the ultimate machines are made', www.bmwworld.com/bmw/plants.htm, accessed 26 November 2004; BMW South Africa: Export, www.bmwplant.co.za/Content/frame_ content.jsp@content=http-3a-2f-2fhafogau02~6.htm, accessed 28 April 2006.

2   *Ibid.*

The supply chain management programme was designed to provide the company's 48 key suppliers with support to help them implement an EMS. In July 2002, 28 suppliers were certified to ISO 14001. By the end of 2002, the Rosslyn plant expected 70% of its suppliers to be ISO 14001-certified (BMW 2002). In the course of implementing this programme, however, BMW realised that aiming at an EMS for all suppliers was too high an ambition as it was too complicated and expensive for some of its small suppliers. It was therefore decided that small suppliers should be subject to regular environmental audits to ensure that their environmental performance was in line with BMW's aims. Suppliers failing the audit are excluded from the supplier list. However, some suppliers are the only ones for the entire industry in South Africa. As Mrs Boscho observed: 'So our hands are kind of tied if [our suppliers] are not performing, because they know we need them . . . At the moment, the only stick BMW has to encourage these suppliers to improve their environmental performance is by giving a lower price for the product.'

BMW has taken a new role in relation to the local community with a waste club initiative involving other major industries in the area. The next step is to get a government representative and local environmental authorities to participate. BMW wants to provide guidance to companies to help them improve their environmental performance. For instance, it is difficult for individual companies to keep up with new environmental laws and developments, so BMW is willing to share its knowledge in this area in order to deter 'free-riders'. As a transnational corporation, BMW has put its own resources into organising the waste group due to the lack of enforcement and resources from the local and national authorities.

GM: Group and South Africa environmental strategy

According to its corporate responsibility and sustainability report for 2001–02, GM is dedicated to protecting human health, natural resources and the global environment:[3]

> At GM, sustainability drives us to be systematic and proactive in seeking continuous improvement in our operations and products in a way that integrates economic, environmental and social objectives into our business decisions.

In 1994, GM was among the first manufacturing companies to formally endorse the Ceres Principles.[4] This was seen as a step in affirming GM's commitment to environmentally responsible business activities. The company's original expectations from its endorsement of Ceres were continuous improvement in terms of public accountability and corporate disclosure, plant environmental performance and product performance.

In relation to sustainable development, GM has been actively involved in the World Business Council for Sustainable Development (WBCSD) and it also participated in the 2002 WSSD in Johannesburg. GM's environmental policy and strategy have evolved in accordance with its degree of involvement with such environmental forums. In practice, the environmental strategy is directed towards the company's products as well as its manufacturing processes, with the adoption of a number of programmes on, for

---

3   See www.gm.com/company/gmability/sustainability/reports/02/home.html, accessed 13 May 2003.

4   See www.ceres.org/coalitionandcompanies/principles.php.

example, recycling, resource management, product design and supply chain management.

GM requires an EMS for all its manufacturing facilities, and it also requires tier-one suppliers to conform to ISO 14001. With the advent of ISO 14001, GM redesigned its global environmental management framework. This includes several additional requirements that place increased emphasis on environmental performance and cost reduction activities. These elements provide a global and common framework plus a specification to help understand how individual plants interact with the environment, and to improve management of these plants in an ongoing cycle.

GM first penetrated the South African market in 1913 by importing Chevrolet vehicles to the country. Until 1987, when GM withdrew from South Africa as result of the anti-apartheid movement, GM assembled the Cadillac, La Salle, Oldsmobile, Buick, Opel and Vauxhall ranges.[5] In 1987, the name GM South Africa (GMSA) was changed to Delta Motors South Africa. Delta Motor Corporation is the Southern African manufacturer and distributor of Opel and Isuzu. In 1997, GM acquired 49% in Delta Motors and, in January 2004, GM announced that it had acquired a 100% shareholding in Delta Motors and would return to South Africa as GMSA. Delta Motor Corporation has two manufacturing plants in Port Elizabeth: the first manufactures the Opel Corsa and the Opel Astra; the second manufactures Isuzu vehicles. GMSA is an exporter of fully assembled vehicles to Zimbabwe, Zambia, Mozambique, Malawi, Kenya and Mauritius.[6]

In 1997, Delta Motors began to discuss the possibility of implementing ISO 14001. However, the firm's senior management was reluctant to implement an EMS because of uncertainty regarding return on investment. In 2000, when the environment function moved from human resources to the manufacturing department, Delta Motors started working on ISO 14001 implementation. By mid-2002, Delta Motors had implemented an EMS according to ISO 14001, although this has not been certified. According to an interview with the company's environmental managers in November 2002, this was due to the perceived high costs of maintaining a certified EMS.

Delta Motors viewed its EMS mainly as a condition for retaining future access to the export market. In this regard, it is under increasing pressure to comply with the principles of its parent company. If GM fully realises its corporate strategy over the coming years, Delta Motors will be forced to respond. In 2002, GM conducted an environmental audit at Delta Motors. This highlighted a number of deficiencies that needed addressing. As a result, Delta Motors formulated a series of environmental targets and improved its environmental performance: for example, by reducing spills significantly and introducing robotic spraying to reduce the amount of paint and solvents used. The environmental manager at Delta sees ISO 14001 as the solution to dealing with the deficiencies highlighted by the GM audit. All in all, however, the attitude of Delta Motors towards environmental performance does not match the principles outlined by GM. Evidently, there is a gap between GM's vision and environmental practice at Delta Motors.

5   GM South Africa, 'Vehicle Exports', www.gmsa.com/content_data/LAAM/ZA/en/GBPZA/999/ vehicle_exports.html, accessed 28 April 2006.

6   GM South Africa, 'Historical Milestones', www.gmsa.com/content_data/LAAM/ZA/en/GBPZA/999/ historicalmilestones.html, accessed 28 April 2006.

Conclusions

In this chapter, we have analysed to what extent BMW and GM have implemented a product-oriented strategy and what consequences this has had for the environmental performance of their production and assembly facilities in South Africa, respectively.

During the last 35 years or so, environmental regulations have developed from 'pure' command-and-control regulations, supplemented in the 1980s with a process-oriented strategy and, in the 1990s, with a product-oriented strategy in most industrialised countries. The South African government has not yet launched a product-oriented environmental policy. Moreover, one of the fundamental problems in South Africa is that regulations are not enforced and the environmental standards in industries and facilities do not meet the expectations of the public or 'green' consumers. This is context is important when analysing to what extent BMW and GM have implemented a product-oriented strategy and what consequences this has had for their environmental performance.

The environmental policy of BMW's production facility at Rosslyn is not fully integrated into the South African context. The nature of the company's environmental efforts reflects the policies and culture of BMW headquarters rather than the local situation. In other words, the environmental focus of the Rosslyn plant is primarily directed towards issues that emerge from the targets of the parent company. The process of adopting the company's EMS framework has therefore been primarily one-way, from the headquarters to the production facilities.

Some of the activities at the Rosslyn plant can be described as product-oriented: for example, the supply chain management programme. Furthermore, the plant has been flexible in relation to small companies, introducing environmental auditing rather than insisting on a certified EMS as a condition of continuing collaboration. It is our impression that the Rosslyn plant has been able to improve the environmental performance of its suppliers. By doing so, it has been able to implement the vision of the parent company with respect to better environmental management and performance in the product chain.

One way of considering the local context is by formulating environmental targets that reflect both the environmental situation in South Africa and, at the same time, comply with the environmental policy and strategy of the BMW Group in Germany. National environmental regulations are not well developed in South Africa. This means that it is more difficult for South African companies to identify significant environmental problems. The authorities do not play a role in identifying problems or suggesting solutions. Weak enforcement means that companies find it difficult to determine whether or not they are in compliance with the regulations. Although it is our impression that the Rosslyn plant is operating beyond compliance, it should nevertheless be noted that a focus on EMS does not particularly reflect national or local environmental needs.

Common problems in many developing countries are weak administrative and institutional capacities, poor regulatory enforcement and centralised systems. In countries with weak enforcement of environmental standards, ISO 14001 and the environmental requirements of the parent company play a role in securing compliance with the environmental regulations, as is the case with BMW.

The situation at Delta Motors is different from that at the BMW Rosslyn plant. On cost grounds, Delta Motors has not yet implemented a certified EMS. However, the company is under increasing pressure to comply with GM's environmental principles, which means that its EMS will have to be certified. As with BMW, it is the parent company that determines corporate environmental standards and practice. So far, Delta Motors considers an EMS primarily as a condition for continuing as an agent in the export market.

If product orientation is to have a global impact, then parent companies must develop environmental policies in a way that is relevant in other countries' contexts. For example, the top-down ELV policies of BMW Group and GM cannot be integrated into the production plants' EMS. It is our impression that this can, in fact, only be achieved if communication and co-operation is intensified and becomes genuinely two-way. However, the BMW Group has implemented a number of product-oriented initiatives in certain departments. In order to achieve a product-oriented policy at corporate level, the Group needs to transform these initiatives into corporate strategies.

The companies need to implement an integrated product policy as their dominant environmental strategy. In order to do this, the Rosslyn plant must improve its approach to product orientation so that it can comply with the environmental policies of its parent company. One way of dealing with environmental aspects in the entire product chain is for the parent company to establish a closer and more intensive interaction with all the actors in the product chain. The benefits of a closer and more intensive interaction are that policies can be adjusted in line with the local context and the experiences of subsidiary companies. Active use of dialogues will also help to ensure that EMS frameworks and policies can be more easily adapted for use in the subsidiaries.

References

BMW (2002) *2001–02 Sustainability Report: Making a Decision for the Future* (Pretoria: BMW).

Danish EPA (Environmental Protection Agency) (2003) *An Introduction to Life-cycle Thinking and Management* (Copenhagen: Danish EPA, www.mst.dk/udgiv/Publications/2003/87-7972-458-2/html/kap09_eng.htm, accessed 29 November 2004).

Den Hond, F., and P. Groenewegen (1993) 'Solving the automobile shredder waste problem: co-operation among firms in the automotive industry', in K. Fischer and J. Schot (eds.), *Environmental Strategies for Industry: International Perspectives on Research Needs and Policy Implications* (Washington, DC: Island Press): 243-368.

DTI (Department of Trade and Industry South Africa) (2004a) *Current Developments in the Automotive Industry 2004: General Information* (Pretoria: DTI South Africa, www.thedti.gov.za/publications/AUTOMOTIVE/GeneralInformation.pdf, accessed 16 December 2004).

—— (2004a) (2004b) *Current Developments in the Automotive Industry 2004: Exports* (Pretoria: DTI South Africa, www.thedti.gov.za/publications/AUTOMOTIVE/Exports.pdf, accessed 16 December 2004).

European Commission (2001) *Waste Management: Management of End-of-life Vehicles* (Brussels: European Commission, www.europa.eu.int/scadplus/leg/en/lvb/l21225.htm, accessed 12 September 2001).

Glazewski, J. (2000) *Environmental Law in South Africa* (Durban, South Africa: Butterworth).

GM (General Motors) (2003) *Corporate Responsibility and Sustainability Report 2001–02* (Detroit, MI: GM, www.gm.com/company/gmability/sustainability/reports/02/home.html, accessed 13 May 2003).

Gouldson, A. (1993) 'Fine-tuning the dinosaur? Environmental product innovation and strategic threat in the automotive industry: a case study of the Volkswagen Audi Group', *Business Strategy and the Environment* 2: 12-21.

Jeppesen, S. (2004) *Environmental Practices and Greening Strategies in Small Manufacturing Enterprises in South Africa: A Critical Realist Approach* (PhD series 11; Copenhagen: Copenhagen Business School).

Klein, S., and D. Selz (2000) 'Cyber mediation in auto distribution: channel dynamics and conflicts', *Journal of Computer-mediated Communication* 5.3, www.ascusc.org/jcmc/vol5/issue3/kleinselz.htm, accessed 26 November 2004.

Mildenberger, U., and A. Khare (2000) 'Planning for an environment-friendly car', *Technovation* 20: 205-14.

Nieuwenhuis, P., and P. Wells (1997) *The Death of Motoring? Car Making and Automobility in the 21st Century* (Chichester, UK: John Wiley).

Peeks, S. (2002) 'From colonial to community-based conservation: environmental justice and the transformation of national parks', in D.A. McDonald (ed.), *Environmental Justice in South Africa* (Cape Town, South Africa: University of Cape Town Press).

Remmen, A., and E.H. Nielsen (1994) *New Incentives for Pollution Prevention, Environmental Strategies for Companies and Public Regulation* (Aalborg, Denmark: Aalborg University).

—— and M. Münster (2002) *An Introduction to Life-Cycle Thinking and Management* (Copenhagen: Ministry of the Environment).

Smink, C.K. (2002) 'Modernisation of environmental regulations: end-of-life vehicle regulations in the Netherlands and Denmark', PhD thesis, Department of Development and Planning, Aalborg University, Denmark.

——, C.S.A. van Koppen and G. Spaargaren (2003) 'Ecological modernisation theory and the changing dynamics of the European automotive industry: the case of Dutch end-of-life vehicle policies', *International Journal of Environment and Sustainable Development* 2.3: 284-304.

Van der Woerd, F. (1997) *Self-regulation in Corporate Environmental Management: Changing Interactions between Companies and Authorities* (Amsterdam: Free University of Amsterdam Press).

13
The switch to CNG in two urban areas in India
HOW WAS THIS ACHIEVED?

Mahesh Patankar and Anand Patwardhan

SJM School of Management, Mumbai, India

After China, India is the second largest contributor to greenhouse gas emissions in the developing world (ADB 1998). Carbon emissions are a function of gross domestic product (GDP), population, energy intensity and carbon intensity. Several sectors have shown remarkable increases in energy use, especially electricity generation and transport. Electricity generation and use is a function of level of usage and end-use efficiency. This chapter concentrates on the urban public road transport system. It analyses the technology transitions that can potentially reduce the carbon intensity of the transport sector.

Important questions that this chapter attempts to answer are:

- Can a technology regime framework be used to characterise individual and company-level changes?

- In what way, and to what extent, can large-scale changes in the energy or carbon intensities result from the aggregation of micro-level changes?

The second part of this chapter elaborates on the definitions of technology and regimes, and the transitions needed to achieve a sustainable change. Based on the literature review and the discussion on technology regimes and transitions theory, the chapter then develops a specific framework for transport-sector transitions in the domain of alternative fuel use. Two case studies illustrate the use of alternative fuel technologies in Mumbai and Delhi, followed by analysis and conclusions.

Technology regimes and transitions theory: evidence from the literature

In the context of this chapter, we analyse two perspectives of technological change and innovations. The first perspective examines change and improvement in technological characteristics while the second examines the adoption and diffusion of technology. Technology diffusion and substitution models (Fisher and Pry 1971; Stier 1983) reflect on annual increases in percentage share of new technologies in the available technology mix or substitution of a type of technology with other competing new technologies. Such models map advances in the use of individual technologies which can be used to examine impacts on energy use and carbon emissions. However, it has been recognised that there are several other factors such as technology advances, innovations and policies which impact the diffusion but are not considered in the modelling (Stier 1983; Fisher and Pry 1971).

A more holistic way of explaining the technological, economic and social perspectives has been addressed by Kemp (1997), Kash and Rycroft (2002), Geels (2002) and Rotmans and Kemp (2002). Transitions are defined as a set of interconnected changes that reinforce each other but take place in different areas, such as technology, the economy, institutions, ecology, culture, behaviour and belief systems. Transitions are long-term (25 years and beyond) changes that occur in the economy. In relation to the transport sector, transitions are explained as changes in the mode of transport: for example, from sailing ships to steamships (Geels 2002). At the same time, several changes taking place in smaller geographical regions and end-use applications are important, too: for example, changes in fuel mix. These changes can result in large-scale changes over a period of time. Rotmans and Kemp (2002) describe the need for the micro-, meso-, and macro-level changes to happen simultaneously in order to gain large-scale change; fuel change options can be termed as micro-level changes. An important question raised by several researchers on how changes occur in the economy, and how to characterise them, is addressed in this research, by evolving a framework theory behind technology hierarchy. This hierarchy differentiates the technology, technology systems and regimes.

Technology changes can happen at one or more levels, with varying outputs. Changes in individual technologies, systems and regimes are illustrated in Figure 13.1.

Rogers (1995), Kemp (1997), Dijk (2000), Geels (2002) and Jacobsson and Johnson (2000) have defined technologies and regimes. Kemp (1997) defines a technological regime as the overall complex of scientific knowledge, engineering practices, production process technologies, product characteristics, skills and procedures, institutions and infrastructures that make up the totality of a technology. Dijk (2000) defines the technological regime as a particular combination of opportunity, appropriateness, cumulativeness conditions and properties of the knowledge base, common to specific activities of innovation and production and shared by the population of companies undertaking those activities. Kathuria (1989), Stier (1983) and Kemp (1997) have used examples from product/process and system diffusion to describe changes in technologies and technology systems. Figure 13.1 emphasises that a technology product or process forms part of technology systems which in turn make up technology regimes. Table 13.1 highlights the constituents of a framework that can describe this change.

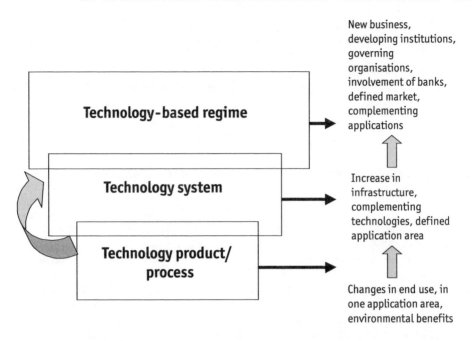

FIGURE 13.1 Hierarchical explanation of technology

Theoretical description	Technology change	Technology system change	Technology system change	Technology regime change
Authors	Stier 1983	Rotmans and Kemp 2002	Kathuria 1999	Geels 2002
Level of describing change	Micro (single production process)	Macro (long-range societal changes)	Micro (single process—CNC machines)	Macro (long-range technology change)
Constituents of framework	Increasing share of the technology in the pulp and paper industry	Technology, economy, institutions, ecology, culture, behaviour, belief system	Component supplier, user, competition in the export and domestic market, participation in fairs, exhibitions, patents disclosure	Financial network, suppliers, user and producer groups, research network, societal groups, public authorities

CNC = computer numerically controlled

TABLE 13.1 Features of frameworks explaining technology change

In addition to the sources listed in Table 13.1, several others, including Jacobson and Johnson 2000, have presented an analytical framework to represent a technology system and the interdependence of players. A framework explaining the changes in the technological paradigm related to the transport sector is not found in the literature. The proposed framework in this research will explain the relevant determinants and draw from the literature referred to above.

Framework describing technology transitions in alternative fuel use

Based on the literature review, we propose a framework applicable to alternative fuel options in the transport sector. This framework (Figure 13.2) is a screening tool to assess past changes in the transport sector which will be used for future changes in alternative fuel options. The framework illustrates a distinct two-stage process that leads to the desired outcomes. The outcomes can be environmental gains (local air quality and greenhouse gas emissions or carbon intensity), market outcomes (market share, cost and penetration) and technology outcomes (new technology, innovations).

The response to policy interventions is constructed around two stages. The first is the enabling stage to act as the policy push and the second is the use stage to act as market pull. The objective of introducing a two-stage model to analyse the response to policy interventions is to enable a link with the technology change framework. The enabling policy environment is expected to come into force by a variety of factors, including public perceptions and technology supplier readiness. These give a policy push to the transition. The use stage is driven by the infrastructure made available by the evolving technology regimes. Loiter and Norberg-Bohm (1999) discuss supply push and demand pull as two important aspects of environmental policy-driven market transformation. The importance of the framework needs explanation. Successful implementation of a changed technology regime is also expected to come from one or the other, or from a combination of policy push and market pull. Some changes in technology regimes are attributed to policy push alone, while others need the presence of market pull as well.

The use stage is supported by the technology regime and system to bring about the desired change in the use pattern. Technology regime frameworks define the presence of a technology-driven system and other determinants characterising the change. Four broad determinants, as illustrated in Figure 13.3, are identified: technology and technology systems; policy and standardisation; developing institutions and markets; and societal benefits. These features are drawn from the literature, as discussed above (Kash and Rycroft 2002; Geels 2002; Loiter and Norberg-Bohm 1999; Kathuria 1999), and encompass an existing technological regime around a specific transportation fuel. Figure 13.3 describes this framework with particular reference to the regimes designed around fuel use in urban public road transport systems. Kathuria (1999) developed a similar framework to explain advances in CNC (computer numerically controlled) technologies in India. Kash and Rycroft (2002) postulate that technologies are innovated by self-organising networks that are made of linked organisations that create, acquire and integrate the diverse knowledge and skills to innovate complex technologies. Kash

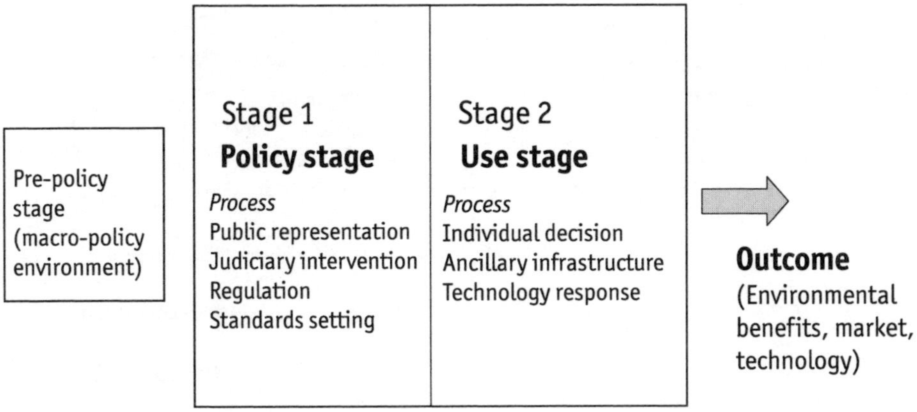

FIGURE 13.2 Framework describing technology transitions

and Rycroft (2002) also stipulate that innovation patterns are of three types—incremental, major and fundamental. The authors categorise the changes in transport fuel use and the evolving infrastructure as major innovations. Rotmans and Kemp (2002) define societal changes at three levels—micro, meso and macro. Parallel to transition management theory, these authors define the proposed framework as meso (regime) changes in the fuel mix. As the transport fuel infrastructure and the policy environment evolves as a result of the changing regimes defined under this research, these can have long-term effects on the energy intensity of the transport sector in India.

These features are explained in greater detail below. As this research strives to build a bottom-up approach to transition management theory, measurement and description of the features or the change agents are essential. Table 13.2 describes the attributes in the above framework.

Interdependence of determinants and causal relationships

A strong causal relationship is identified among the determinants of change listed in Table 13.2. A causal relationship between the determinants is expected to drive the technological transitions to take place at a faster pace than expected. In the framework explained in the previous section, pressure to develop the required fuel infrastructure is induced by specific policy interventions suggested by policy-makers. Pressure by public-interest groups to improve local air quality is expected to trigger development of institutions involved in clean technologies in the transport sector. Markets, comprising technology producers, fleet owners and financing institutions, are expected to react positively to the business opportunity and deliver the required services.

Linking transitions theory (macro-) and micro-transitions

Transitions and changes in technological regimes explained so far can still relate to micro-transitions based on the geographical and application areas. Intention of long-

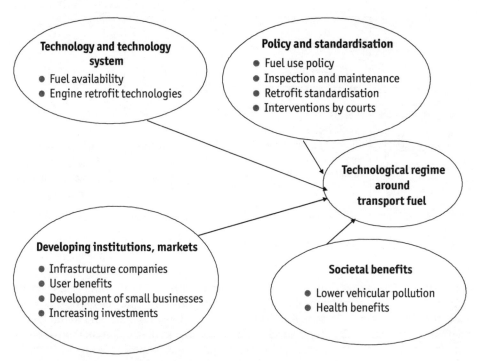

FIGURE 13.3 Determinants of transport sector technology regime

Variable	What is represented
Technology and technological changes	● Clear, identified individual technologies, evolving complementarity in the technologies ● Increase in compressed natural gas (CNG) network developed, average queuing time in a month (relative queuing time—compared to conventional fuel)
Policy changes and standardisation	● Captures the legislative directives in the proposed fuel-switching options ● Evolving standards in the existing products and systems
Developing markets and institutions	● Share of indigenously manufactured components in CNG supply and use ● Share (cost) of indigenously manufactured components in product chain ● Return on investment (ROI) changes over time or rate of change of net disposable income for individual operators ● ROI for infrastructure developers
Societal benefits	● Identified and measured environmental benefits, reduced health impacts ● Representation by public-interest groups and the resulting changes in policy, infrastructure

TABLE 13.2 Framework variables and quantification criteria

range change in technology use is explained by macro-changes that span more than a decade. A link between these two levels is established below. Transitions are defined as long-term changes in technology and economy. Examples of transitions from the literature include:

● Horse-drawn carriages to automobiles (Grubler 1998)

● Sailing ships to steamships (Geels 2002)

● Emergence of radiotherapy, GE (General Electric) turbine blades (Kash and Rycroft 2002)

● Evolution of the electricity society, shift in computing towards digital (Rotmans and Kemp 2002)

● Changes in the energy source mix (Grubler 1998)

An important link between the micro-changes, as in the case of fuel switching options in the transport sector, and the large-scale economy-wide macro-changes rests in the use of alternative fuel in a hybrid system. The use of compressed natural gas (CNG) in the transport sector which then triggers its use in the industrial sector illustrates this hybridisation effect.

Examples reflecting long-range changes, which are brought about over 25 years and beyond (Rotmans and Kemp 2002), show significant changes in technology, sometimes driven by breakthrough innovations. Another feature of these changes is the scale of use. Transitions can be identified as a change in scale and scope. The shaded region in Figure 13.4 shows an aggregate effect of simultaneous changes in the scale and scope of the evolving transitions.

The micro-changes that are non-marginal in nature evolve out of current state-of-the-art technology; with a change in packaging the technologies are represented by changes in individual sectors. Changes in the supporting policy, societal concerns and benefits, and economy (markets, institutions) lead to non-marginality.

Research questions

A major contribution of this study is a framework (developed in the previous section) and its validation with alternative fuel use examples. Three important questions are studied as a part of the analysis:

● Can the framework map the transitions from a technology/process to an established technological regime?

● Can the analysis establish a link between the policy interventions and the success of alternative fuel policy resulting in reduced energy intensity in the long term?

● Can the micro-level changes in a particular domain of study (such as the transport sector) pave the way to large-scale transitions with a potential to expand the applications?

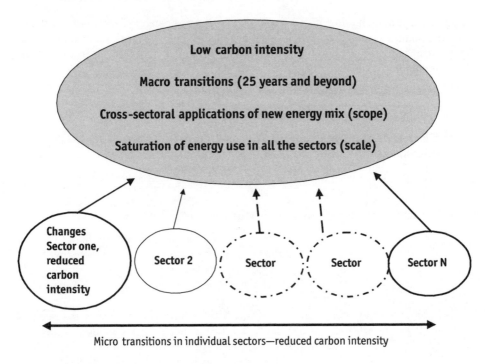

FIGURE 13.4 Aggregating effect of transitions

Case studies: Mumbai and New Delhi

In this section, we present two case studies relating to alternative fuel use in the urban public road transport sector. The studies are structured in order to give the background, data from the field and, lastly, applicability to the theories of technology regimes and transitions.

Use of CNG as an alternative fuel in public transport in New Delhi

As New Delhi is located inland, there has been a lateral growth in the city limits which are connected primarily through a network of roads. Each day, close to 500,000 commuters travel using a combination of private and public transport. As of October 2004, 10,199 buses, 16,098 taxicabs and 59,027 three-wheelers used CNG as transport fuel.[1] The total number of CNG filling stations as of 1 September 2004 was 56 mother stations, 31 online stations, four daughter stations and 33 daughter booster stations; totalling 124 stations supplying 772,000 kg of CNG per day.[2] These numbers show a remarkable

---

1   Personal communication with Mr V.S. Prabhakar, General Manager (Co-ordination), Indraprastha Gas Ltd, 4 October 2004.
2   *Ibid.*

increase in comparison to 2000, when 8,000 kg/day of CNG was supplied by just 30 CNG filling stations.[3] This is close to 100% of the entire fleet converted to CNG, including buses, taxicabs and three-wheelers. This conversion was achieved between 1997 and 2004 in a bid to improve local air quality. Several stakeholders were responsible for this conversion.

Macro-policy environment

The Department of Transportation, National Capital Region (NCR), New Delhi is responsible for issuing permits and regulating inspection and maintenance through roadworthiness tests for in-use vehicles.[4] Landmark changes in fuel use in New Delhi came about as a response to a citizens' petition.[5] The courts intervened by suggesting the creation of a special committee (EPCA) to comment on the feasibility of changing to alternative fuels. The courts considered the committee's recommendations and special orders were passed to shift public transport vehicles to CNG as an alternative fuel.[6] The Environmental Protection and Control Association (EPCA) followed an elaborate process of stakeholder consultation, involving automobile manufacturers, petroleum product suppliers, the government of NCR, and research and policy advocacy groups.[7] Different stakeholders realised the importance of the weaker links in the implementation process which resulted in specific recommendations by the courts and EPCA to improve the inspection and maintenance infrastructure.[8] During the course of implementation, availability of fuel and the allocation of CNG to the transport sector were recognised as concerns and were addressed by court orders.[9]

Policy advocacy by non-governmental organisations

Realising the health impacts of bad ambient air quality, some non-governmental organisations (NGOs), advocacy groups and civil-society groups became involved in the evolving policies and implementation process.[10] Civil-society groups assisted the courts in finding solutions that were fuel-neutral and met the wider policy goals, primarily targeted at improving the local air quality in New Delhi.

Developing markets

The development of an alternative fuel market is complex. In this case, it included enterprise development in the area of fuel supply, manufacture and running of vehicles

---

3 www.indraprashthagas.com, accessed 13 June 2003 (now www.iglonline.net).
4 Personal communication with Mr V. Jain, Pollution Control Officer, Department of Transportation, NCR, 16 September 2004.
5 *Ibid.*
6 Personal communication with Ms Bhure Lal, EPCA, 4 October 2004.
7 *Ibid.*
8 *Ibid.*
9 *Ibid.*; communication with V. Jain.
10 Personal communication with Ms Anumita Roychowdhary, Director (Research and Advocacy), CSE, 10 September 2004.

on alternative fuel and benefits to user groups. In the case of CNG use in New Delhi, the incorporation of Indraprastha Gas Ltd (IGL) in 2000 resulted in a large gas-supplying agency. IGL operates in a monopoly market and was formed as a joint venture between the government of NCR, New Delhi, the Gas Authority of India Ltd and the Bharat Petroleum Corporation Ltd. IGL has shown successful growth in the past few years, with increased profits carried forward from 611.58 million rupees in the financial year 2002–03 to 1,354.55 million rupees in 2003–04. Dividends offered to IGL shareholders also rose, from 5% in 2002–03 to 15% in 2003–04.[11] The higher level of turnover for IGL was achieved not only by demand but also by the creation of additional infrastructure to increase CNG compression capacity.[12] These changes were brought in at IGL through a series of efforts to overhaul the technology in order to respond to market forces. However, IGL was directed from time-to-time by the judiciary to increase the supply position to cater to the growing needs of the transport sector.[13]

The vehicle population in New Delhi has also shown considerable growth in the past five years, with several new licences given to bus owners.[14] When the court orders to switch to CNG buses were passed by the judiciary, old licences were cancelled and new licences were issued by the Department of Transportation on the basis of the purchase of new buses operating on CNG or on the production of proof stating that the fleet owners had placed orders for CNG vehicles with the bus manufacturers. Compared with the engine retrofit option possible in the case of petrol engines, diesel engine retrofits were found to be a bit more complex, so, as a logical positive step towards ensuring compliance, the Delhi Transport Corporation (DTC) and the private fleet owners purchased factory-fitted CNG buses.[15] In Delhi, DTC owns only 30% of the city buses (around 3,500 buses). The remainder of the permits to operate buses on routes specified by DTC, and for contract buses plying as point-to-point private services, are issued by the Department of Transportation under a competitive licence distribution system. This was a sudden change in the business opportunity for the two largest bus manufacturers in India—Tata Motors and Ashok Leyland—who supplied close to 9,000 buses over a two-year period in Delhi alone. As regards the profitability of the bus services, DTC traditionally operated as a loss-making undertaking, but profits made per trip have now increased to 20%. With the new investments made in the purchase of buses, DTC is still operating at a sub-optimal level, especially as it now has more employees.[16] With a ratio of government-owned to private fleets of 30:70, the maintenance of vehicles in New Delhi is a concern, as private bus owners are expected to maintain the safety standards of their vehicles with minimal enforcement. Visual inspections are only provided at a facility operated by the Department of Transportation. This is inadequate. Standards of vehicle maintenance and, in particular, the efficacy of the catalytic converters required to keep emissions of nitrogen oxides under control, are questioned by several groups who want to see stricter compliance controls.

Taxicabs used in the city of New Delhi show a very distinct operating feature. In New Delhi, close to 16,000 taxicabs operate from airports and taxicab stands at hotels, resi-

---

11   www.indraprashthagas.com, accessed 2004 (now www.iglonline.net).
12   Communication with V.S Prabhakar.
13   Communication with Ms Lal; communication with A. Roychowdhary.
14   Communication with V. Jain.
15   *Ibid.*; communication with Ms Lal; communication with A. Roychowdhary.
16   Communication with V. Jain; communication with A. Roychowdhary.

dential areas and major commercial hubs. During the course of this research, a structured questionnaire was used to capture the operating parameters for the taxicab owners.[17] One of the distinct features of taxicab owners operating in Delhi is that most of the drivers work very long hours and live at the taxicab stands, as they come to Delhi to work without their families. At the domestic airport alone, around 200 taxicab owners operate their vehicles with an average of two daily trips earning between 400 and 600 rupees. Net disposable income of taxicab owners using CNG is higher than when they used petrol or diesel. In Delhi, most of the fleet comprises Hindustan Ambassadors. Hindustan Motors responded to the business opportunity of selling company-fitted taxicabs in New Delhi by introducing higher-capacity engines backed up by a specific servicing programme with trained mechanics operating out of its dealer network.[18] As regards the three-wheelers, daily-wage drivers who pay the owners a fixed sum of 100–150 rupees a day as rent, drive most of the three-wheelers. With a daily income of 250–300 rupees, after paying for the CNG, the individual daily-wage driver takes home around 50–100 rupees. Maintenance of the three-wheelers is the responsibility of the owner, but most owners pay little attention to this. Several organisations interviewed during the course of this research raised concerns over increasing emissions and white smoke, especially from the old two-stroke three-wheelers.[19] The largest manufacturer of three-wheelers in India, Bajaj Auto Ltd, introduced new four-stroke models with company-fitted CNG kits on the vehicles. Due to lower fuel costs, this was beneficial to owners and, interestingly, several buyers of new three-wheelers opted for CNG-fitted three-wheelers on this account. However, the inspection and maintenance of vehicles still remains a challenge and needs to be addressed, with a better infrastructure for vehicle testing.[20]

The network that evolved with the introduction of CNG as a green fuel in New Delhi is explained in Figure 13.5.

Use of CNG as an alternative fuel in public transport in Mumbai

As Mumbai is an island city and a commercial hub, its roads and rail links act as important feeder modes in the city road transport system. More than 600,000 commuters depend on the public road transport system in the city. As of October 2004, 35 out of a total fleet of 3,386 buses, 55,000 taxicabs (100% of the registered non-air-conditioned) and 96,000 three-wheelers use CNG as the transportation fuel.[21]

---

17 Targeted at taxicab/three-wheeler owners, the questionnaire captured information on: the capital investment; operating expenses incurred, including any debt servicing if applicable; and technology-related issues, including the mileage with CNG as a fuel and views on engine performance.

18 Personal communication with Mr M. Ali, Business Head (North), Hindustan Motors, 29 September 2004.

19 Communication with V. Jain; communication with Ms Lal; communication with A. Roychowdhary.

20 Communication with Ms Lal; communication with A. Roychowdhary.

21 Personal communication with Mr M.S. Kadam, Assistant Engineer, Transportation, Engineering Department, Bombay Electricity and Suburban Transport, 31 August 2004; personal communication with Mr D. Goenka, Bombay Environmental Action Group, 1 September 2004; personal communication with Mr Quadros, General Secretary, Bombay Taximen's Association, 31 August 2004.

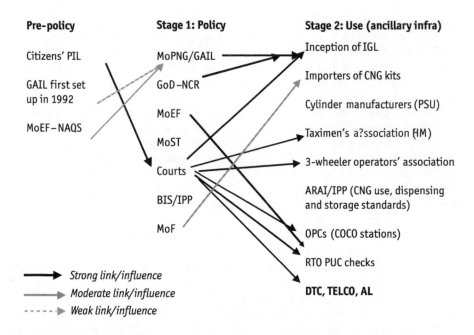

Pre-policy	Stage 1: Policy	Stage 2: Use (ancillary infra)
Citizens' PIL	MoPNG/GAIL	Inception of IGL
GAIL first set up in 1992	GoD–NCR	Importers of CNG kits
	MoEF	Cylinder manufacturers (PSU)
MoEF–NAQS	MoST	Taximen's a?ssociation (HM)
	Courts	3-wheeler operators' association
	BIS/IPP	ARAI/IPP (CNG use, dispensing and storage standards)
	MoF	OPCs (COCO stations)
		RTO PUC checks
		DTC, TELCO, AL

➤ *Strong link/influence*
➤ *Moderate link/influence*
▷ *Weak link/influence*

AL = Ashok Leyland; ARAI = Automobile Research Association of India; BIS = Bureau of Indian Standards; COCO = company-owned-company-operated (gas stations); DTC = Delhi Transport Corporation; GAIL = Gas Authority of India Ltd; GoD–NCR = Government of Delhi, National Capital Region; HM = Hindustan Motors; IGL = Indraprastha Gas Ltd; IPP = Institute of Petroleum Products; MoEF = Ministry of Environment and Forests; MoF = Ministry of Finance; MoPNG = Ministry of Petroleum and Natural Gas; MoST = Ministry of Surface Transport; NAQS = national air quality standards; OPC = oil-producing companies; PIL = public-interest litigation; PSU = public-sector undertaking; PUC = pollution under control (test); RTO = Regional Transport Office; TELCO = Tata Engineering and Locomotive Company

FIGURE 13.5 New Delhi sociotechnical network diagram

Macro-policy environment

The Department of Transportation, Government of Maharashtra and the Regional Transport Office (RTO) are responsible for setting policies and implementing these in the city.[22] Like New Delhi, in Mumbai the decision to switch fuel came about primarily through the intervention of the courts.[23] However, a pilot scheme by the Gas Authority of India Ltd (GAIL) in 1992 introduced taxicabs running on CNG[24] in the southern part of the city. In response to court rulings, the Department of Transportation, in co-ordination with the RTO, issued specific directives to ban vehicles older than eight years from operating within the city limits.

22   Communication with D. Goenka.
23   Communication with M.S. Kadam; communication with D. Goenka; communication with Mr Quadros.
24   Communication with Mr Quadros.

Policy advocacy by NGOs

An important thrust to the debate on air quality issues in Mumbai came from the Smoke Affected Citizens' Group and, in turn, the Bombay Environmental Action Group (BEAG) which filed petitions in the Bombay High Court during the period 1995–97.[25] Among other sectors, transport was identified as the primary source of particulates and sulphur and nitrogen oxides emissions. Realising that, despite the court orders, the representatives of the taxicab and three-wheeler drivers were not complying, and also the fact that the gas supply companies were not meeting the targets to create adequate infrastructure in the city, the petitioners prevailed in the court hearings to drive the implementation process.[26] NGOs also raised important points relating to fuel-neutral policies. During the court hearing process, the NGOs made important recommendations in favour of CNG, as other types of clean fuel were import-dependent and not available in the required quantities. CNG, however, was abundantly available from the nearby offshore well owned by GAIL. These policy–advocacy groups played an important role in pushing the transport policies.

Developing markets

In a similar way to New Delhi, the market development process in Mumbai evolved from two drivers—one starting at the supply side and the other at the demand side. Most importantly, the supply-side efforts resulted in the creation of a unique public–private partnership in the form of Mahanagar Gas Ltd (MGL), a joint venture between the Government of Maharashtra, GAIL and British Gas (BG).[27] With the formation of this joint venture, and with BG providing the important technology base, a unique business proposition was developed. MGL has been showing increases in profits and has also been instrumental in the development of new sectors in the city targeted at supplying piped natural gas to households. However, the lack of an adequate fuel infrastructure within the city limits was identified as one of the barriers to implementation.

The number of vehicles converted to CNG showed a higher diffusion rate in Mumbai than in Delhi, which was possible also with the involvement of the Bombay Taximen's Association (BTA) which represents the majority of taxicab owners in the city. Technologically, the stock of taxicabs used in Mumbai is from Premier Automobiles Ltd (PAL), a company that has now withdrawn from the taxi market.[28] This resulted in the development of CNG retrofit technologies, with several roadside retrofit shops catering to the market and provided by well-known players such as Bharat Cylinders Ltd and importers of conversion kits such as Transenergy which is a brand name of kits sold by the TVS Group from India.[27] The RTO, which was given the responsibility of ensuring periodic testing of the converted kits, uses visual inspection as the tool to certify the vehicles on

---

25 Communication with D. Goenka.
26 *Ibid.*
27 Personal communication with Mr Gary Morgan, Technical Director, MGL, 18 June 2004; see www.mahanagargas.com, accessed 13 June 2003.
28 Communication with Mr Quadros.
29 Communication with D. Goenka; communication with Mr Quadros.

an annual basis.[30] One of the barriers identified in the Mumbai case study was the limited effort by PAL and other four-wheeler manufacturers in raising the technology standard. In response to the court orders, and to meet the deadlines, most of the taxicab owners ended up bringing scrap engines from other cities in India, some of which were two-stroke engines which did not comply with the new standards.[31] Based on interviews conducted in Mumbai, the average estimated net income of taxicab owners, after paying for CNG, is 200–250 rupees, from an average daily gross income of 400–600 rupees.

Three-wheeler purchasers in Mumbai, on the other hand, benefited from the introduction by original equipment manufacturer (OEM) Bajaj Auto Ltd of factory-fitted CNG vehicles.[32] Similarly, bus purchasers such as Bombay Electricity and Suburban Transport (BEST) benefited from the efforts of Tata Motors and Ashok Leyland, the two largest manufacturers of buses in India.[33]

The network that evolved in the case of Mumbai is explained in Figure 13.6.

Analysis

Both case studies demonstrate the presence of a technology hierarchy beginning with individual technologies such as CNG conversion kits, CNG transport techniques for bulk as well as small quantities and dispensing technology at filling stations. The technology response to policies formulated as a result of public pressure is an indication that the interplay between policy and ancillary infrastructure is important for the use of alternative fuel. Some of the individual technologies traditionally used in other sectors have found applications in this new end use. With the new application, individual technologies such as dispensing units, bulk storage and transport have evolved as systems. Several new businesses and regulatory processes (inspection and maintenance) have evolved which complement the new applications. Most importantly, there have been increased investments by the public and private entities, thus boosting the market. In both cities, government and private entities have come together to form large infrastructure companies (MGL and IGL). Societal groups have been actively involved in bringing about this change in the transport sector, as some of the landmark decisions in favour of alternative fuel by the courts in India were in response to public-interest litigations. Policy-makers (state governments in both the cities, transport authorities) and the standardisation agency BIS have also responded to set norms for standardisation and certification. Thus, there is an established technology regime that is supported by infrastructure, finance and user interest, with clearly defined roles for policy-makers and regulators.

---

30   Communication with Mr Quadros.
31   Communication with D. Goenka; communication with Mr Quadros.
32   *Ibid.*
33   Communication with M.S. Kadam.

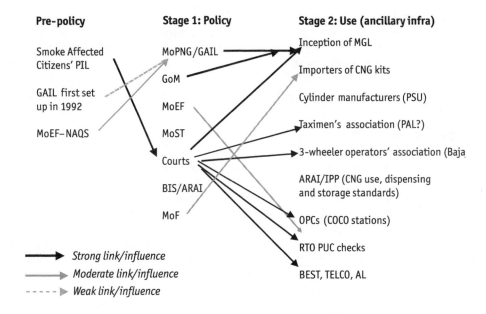

AL = Ashok Leyland; ARAI = Automobile Research Association of India; BEST = Bombay Electricity and Suburban Transport; BIS = Bureau of Indian Standards; COCO = company-owned-company-operated (gas stations); GAIL = Gas Authority of India Ltd; GoM = Government of Maharashta; HM = Hindustan Motors; IGL = Indraprastha Gas Ltd; IPP = Institute of Petroleum Products; MoEF = Ministry of Environment and Forests; MoF = Ministry of Finance; MoPNG = Ministry of Petroleum and Natural Gas; MoST = Ministry of Surface Transport; NAQS = national air quality standards; OPC = oil-producing companies; PAL = Premier Automobiles Ltd; PIL = public-interest litigation; PSU = public-sector undertaking; RTO = Regional Transport Office; TELCO = Tata Engineering and Locomotive Company

FIGURE 13.6 Mumbai sociotechnical network diagram

Importance of policy interventions

There are clearly defined policies on the use of CNG as an alternative fuel in both cities. These policies are set by the courts which also direct infrastructure development. There are two important decisions that fleet owners have to make: the first is to convert vehicles to CNG and the second is to actually use the fuel. In the case of converted taxicabs and three-wheelers, owners have the option to run the vehicle in dual-fuel mode. The first decision is prompted by the need to meet legal requirements. It is the second decision, to run the vehicle in CNG mode, that is key to meeting environmental goals. However, this decision is determined by the adequacy or otherwise of the fuel infrastructure. The relationship between these two decision stages is evident here as availability and provision of ancillary infrastructure is dependent on the evolving technology regimes.

The new infrastructure, developed as part of the transport sector in the two cities, has also paved the way to other uses and applications of natural gas. In both cities, the use of natural gas in power, steam generation in power plants, end uses such as boilers and even for domestic purposes have increased. This hybridisation effect of the new technology product and process is expected to result in environmental benefits going well beyond the transport sector.

Conclusions

The technology domain covered by the case studies is of alternative fuel use in urban public road transport. In the context of Indian urban transport sectors, changes proposed by the government were supported by a variety of factors, including societal pressures, technology packaging, presence of markets and setting of policies. Case studies, and the causal relationships established in the discussions here, support this change as one being represented by a technological regime that complements these policies by providing the necessary conditions for large-scale implementation. Micro-changes represented in such examples also support the path towards a long-range transition to a more beneficial energy mix. Understanding these changes at a micro level is also beneficial in understanding long-range technology transitions.

References

ADB (Asian Development Bank) (1998) *Asia Least-cost Greenhouse Gas Abatement Strategy* (Manila: ADB).

Dijk, M.V. (2000) 'Technological regimes and industrial dynamics: the evidence from the Dutch manufacturing', *Industrial and Corporate Change* 9.2: 173-94.

Fisher, J.C., and R.H. Pry (1971) 'A simple substitution model of technological change', *Technological Forecasting and Social Change* 3: 75-88.

Geels, F.W. (2002) 'Technological transitions as evolutionary reconfiguration processes: a multi-level perspective and a case study', *Energy Policy* 31: 1,257-74.

Grubler, A. (1998) *Technology and Global Change* (Cambridge, UK: Cambridge University Press).

Jacobsson, S., and A. Johnson (2000) 'The diffusion of renewable energy technology: an analytical framework and key issues for research', *Energy Policy* 28: 625-40.

Kash, D., and R. Rycroft (2002) 'Emerging patterns of complex technological innovations', *Technological Forecasting and Social Change* 69: 581-606.

Kathuria, V. (1999) 'Role of externalities in inducing technical change: a case study of the Indian machine tools industry', *Technological Forecasting and Social Change* 61: 25-44.

Kemp, R. (1997) *Environmental Policy and Technical Change: A Comparison of the Technological Impacts of Policy Instruments* (London: Edward Elgar Publishing).

Loiter, J.M., and V. Norberg-Bohm (1999) 'Technology policy and renewable energy: public roles in the development of new energy technologies', *Energy Policy* 27: 85-97.

Rogers, E.M. (1995) *Diffusion of Innovations* (New York: The Free Press).

Rotmans, J., and R. Kemp (2002) 'Managing societal transitions: dilemmas and uncertainties. The Dutch Energy case study', paper presented at the OECD *Workshop on the Benefits of Climate Policy: Improving Information for Policy-makers*, Paris, France, 12–13 December 2002.

Stier, J.C. (1983) 'Technological substitution in the United States pulp and paper industry: the sulphate pulping process', *Technological Forecasting and Social Change* 23: 237-45.

14
Local needs in urban transport

Merih Kunur

Royal College of Art, London, UK

In 2004, a £2 million advertising campaign was launched by Transport for London to persuade car users to use the bus instead of their car during off-peak hours. One of the adverts portrayed a young couple with children leaving their car in the drive of their house and catching a bus to the city centre from a bus stop almost in front of their home. The clip ended with the message: 'My other car is a bus'.

For many years, London was closely associated with the red double-decker Routemaster bus.[1] Today, there are new buses on the capital's streets. Some are articulated, with more space but reduced seating allocation to cater for more standing passengers. More bus lanes are being introduced to make journeys faster. Yet, for many people, catching a bus is fraught with difficulties. Most do not live next to a bus stop and so may have to walk a fair distance to get to one and, once they get there, they often face a long wait for the service they want. One thing is very clear: the Transport for London advert did not accurately portray most people's experience of using bus transport in the capital.

Improved public transport services are often regarded as the most effective way of encouraging people to leave their cars for urban travel, but such an approach has, so far, had little success. As the patterns of urban mobility in Britain show, measures to encourage people to walk and cycle are far more efficient and cost-effective than those aimed at getting them to make greater use of public transport (Hillman and Cleary 1992).

---

1 The last Routemaster was withdrawn from service on 9 December 2005.

However, the importance of door-to-door journeys should not be underestimated. Personal transport is still the most frequently used mode of transport, as most of us prefer to start our journeys literally from our doorsteps and travel directly to our destination. Public transport in many urban areas is not easily accessible. Many people encounter difficulties when travelling by public transport due to their age, health or disability. When the weather is wet or cold, the experience of using bus transport can be thoroughly miserable. Parents with buggies, people carrying heavy shopping, wheelchair users and others with limited mobility, all find it hard to travel if there is no easy access to public transport from where they live. This is partly because, as yet, there are no other viable public transport alternatives that replace the door-to-door convenience of personal transport, such as the car, the motorbike, the scooter or the bicycle.

There are specific reasons why people prefer cars to public transport for short trips. According to Mackett and Ahern (2000), the main factors when using a car for a short journey (less than five miles) were the need to transport heavy goods and convenience. These reasons differ between men and women, the young and the old, and time of day. The UK National Travel Survey and the Census for Population (National Statistics 1998) found that 78% of car trips could be made by alternative transport modes. Over 70% of trips were less than five miles, and half of these were by car. Mackett and Robertson (2000: 4) observe: 'In order to reduce car use, it is important that the alternatives match the combination of qualities that the car has.'

The public transport dilemma

Mobility is not just about making better connections between various modes of city transport; it is also about the quality of urban travel. In terms of mass transit systems, people should be able to sit if they want to, and there should be sufficient space for bags, briefcases, shopping, buggies, etc.

So far, transport policies have been largely unsuccessful in enticing drivers out of their cars; the answer is not simply to increase capacity or range. In order to encourage more public transport use, several issues need to be addressed. These include cleanliness, security (particularly at night) and the provision of accurate travel information so that journeys can be planned with confidence. Urban travel in the cities of the 21st century will be different to that in the 20th century. Changes will be driven not just by government policies and legislation, but also by new technologies, social trends and the market.

Public transport performs well when it has a good flow of movement within dense urban areas. The benefits of collective mass transport abate when densities decrease. A string of empty buses on a busy street will exacerbate the problems of congestion and pollution rather than solving them (see Fig. 14.1). There is no single solution to achieving sustainable urban mobility; instead, different types of transportation are needed for different city zones.

FIGURE 14.1 Bus congestion on Wigmore Street, London

An increasingly urban world

Most cities in the world are becoming ever more densely populated. A century ago, only 10% of people lived in urban areas. Today, more than half the world's population are city-dwellers. Suburbs grow and commuters travel further as trains and cars become faster and transport networks expand. But what price are we paying for becoming an increasingly urbanised society? As urban populations continue to grow, such a massive scale of movement becomes increasingly unsustainable, both socially and environmentally.

The majority of transport experts argue that investing in public transport, rather than building more roads, will improve mobility and alleviate the adverse effects of car travel such as accidents, congestion and pollution. This investment will need to be substantial if public transport is to match the comfort, convenience and speed of the car.

Bovy and Wee (2002) argue that congestion is a sign of a fluent and abundant network, with many access points and high population densities. Nor should cars be blamed entirely for causing congestion. In London, for example, the contribution of car use to urban travel during the morning 'rush hour' fell from 15.11% in 1992 to 13.5% in 1999 according to the Department for Transport (DETR 1999). In other words, fewer motorists drive into London during morning peak hours than in they past.

An alternative approach is to build better roads, redesign and regulate access points and junctions, conceptualise other car types (featuring smaller size, user adaptability and flexibility, alternative and cheaper fuel use and intelligent vehicle systems) and promote initiatives such as car-sharing. Thus, according to Gerondeau (1997): 'Only the road can save the road.' Such a viewpoint considers that public transport will never replace car use to any great degree. Building new motorways will never solve traffic congestion nor avoid gridlocks; therefore, new forms of political and strategic approach are needed in order to keep traffic flowing. It is challenge to find the correct innovative and alternative solutions for the efficient use of existing road systems. The introduction of electronic speed controls to eliminate bottlenecks, electronic tolling, car-sharing, intelligent vehicle systems and variable pricing may all contribute.

Infrastructure needs

Large metropolitan areas that are polycentric[2] in nature require constant updating of their mobility network structures and transport systems. Land use, demography and patterns of movement need to be reassessed within the urban nodes and compared with existing modes of transport in terms of their capacity, efficiency, performance and quality of journey.

In 2002, an international forum and workshop for young architects was held in Rotterdam. *Five Minutes City: The Architecture of [Im]mobility* was organised by the Berlage Institute in collaboration with the Mies van der Rohe Foundation, Barcelona, and the Institut Français d'Architecture, Paris. Participants were asked to redesign Rotterdam and New York in such a way that all amenities were no more than five minutes' walk from a bus stop or metro station. The workshop concluded that not only were good connections vital but quality transport modes—that are accessible, cleaner, comfortable, emission-free, secure and safe—were also necessary in order to minimise walking distances. Consideration was given to travelling centre-to-centre or within-centre, as most cities are becoming polycentric.

Defining the problem

Establishing three-phase mobility scenarios for a specific city or a district can help clarify the present situation, predict future scenarios and identify possible solutions. A research matrix of three primary fields of investigation—spatial organisation of cities, social change and sustainability—can be supplemented by economic, technological and institutional factors in order to formulate the best possible combination of transport modes, including any substitute and complimentary vehicle systems of the future. Mass transit has long been the backbone of urban population movements. Nevertheless, any ideal future scenarios of urban mobility and transport will be informed by innovative transport systems and vehicles throughout the world.

The spatial organisation of an urban environment requires investigation of spatial integration, traffic management, interchange and urban zones. Land use or, more generally, an urban spatial structure, is the product of the interaction between land markets and regulations. Increasingly, urban transport is considered to be the major unresolved problem in large cities due to the pollution and congestion it generates. In

---

2   A polycentric city contains more than one developed centre. Polycentric cities have a range of high-density urban clusters, each of which can be defined as a centre.

Europe and the US there is an increasing demand for transit-oriented development (TOD), the partial administrative allocation of land through regulations. This is seen as particularly important for the generation of sustainable future urban transport concepts.

Traffic management arranges the best use of available road space and encompasses the management of all modes of transport and all travellers. Its main objective is to reduce vehicle delays and stops. The research and development of intelligent transport systems (ITSs) in urban areas is instrumental in achieving this.

Transport infrastructure and the passenger interchange points where modal transfers occur are essential to achieve well-connected, door-to-door trips using different modes. At EU level, the MIMIC, PIRATE and GUIDE projects[3] investigate the cost-effective and successful development of such public transport interchanges.

Sociopsychological factors also influence urban mobility. The success of future urban movement lies in changing travellers' perceptions and expectations of city travel. Socially inclusive solutions are needed in order to give better access to public transport for the ageing population and for disabled users.

The success, or otherwise, of a mass transit system will depend on cost. If fares are too expensive, people will choose cheaper options such as the car. Subsidising fares makes them affordable and encourages more people onto public transport. High parking costs, congestion charges and high fuel costs push car travellers to find other forms of cheaper transport. Schemes such as free travel cards for senior citizens and disabled users, concessionary fares and the abolition of bus and tram fares for under-18s in full-time education encourage more travellers to use public transport. For example, there are more public transport users in highly subsidised cities such as Achterhoek in The Netherlands, Barcelona in Spain, Graz in Austria and Stuttgart in Germany than there are in UK cities.

The third primary field of investigation, sustainability, looks at the long-term effects of energy use and industrial processes. Sustainable sources of energy, energy efficiency and affordability are important elements in the design of new urban transport systems.

In terms of fuel, technology hybrid electric vehicles (HEVs), fuel-cell buses, alternative-fuel vehicles (AFVs) and MagLev (magnetic levitation) technology should be considered in order to determine the types of transport most suitable for a specific urban environment. Zero-emission vehicles (ZEVs) will become widespread by the year 2020, and internal combustion engine (ICE) vehicles will be gradually phased out.

Designing solutions

These factors were considered for a recent research project that was part of the Helen Hamlyn Research Associates Programme 2004 in the Vehicle Design Department of the

---

3   MIMIC (Mobility, Intermodality and Interchanges) studies interchange-specific factors influencing travellers in their choice of single-mode options. PIRATE (Promoting Interchange Rationale, Accessibility and Transfer) tries to enable more efficient public transport interchanges through research, development and testing. GUIDE (Group of Urban Interchanges, Development and Evaluation) looks into existing European research on interface issues.

Royal College of Art. The project was commissioned by automotive design consultancy Capoco Design Limited which was interested in how these factors would affect the mass rapid transit systems of 2025. All key drivers of this research matrix were reviewed and expanded in an expert forum within which architects and urban planners, social researchers and sustainable technology and vehicle experts came together to debate a future in which world cities are more polycentric.

The research phase of the project led to the selection of three polycentric and diverse cities—Hong Kong, Istanbul and London—chosen for their disparate styles of transport and their geographical locations. Specific localities were examined and, at each locality, the focus was given to a particular route where journey patterns could be observed. Each route involved different types of urban journeys, typical to that location, that linked one type of urban node to another (e.g. town centre, international gateway, suburb, business district, etc.). Pedestrianised locations, residential areas and interchanges were all included in the chosen route.

In each city, a user was asked to travel by means of the city's public transport system on a specific route and at a certain time of the day. Each journey was filmed and time efficiencies and user discomforts analysed. The problems each user encountered were noted and a detailed film was made documenting their journey. The issues highlighted by this research fed into the design brief for a new vehicle system. These are summarised in Figure 14.2.

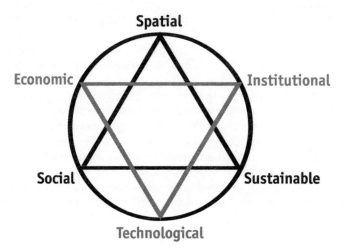

FIGURE 14.2 Research matrix

In London, a businessman made a midday journey from Covent Garden to City Airport; in Hong Kong a female senior citizen made a trip through a densely populated shopping district to the main train terminal; and in Istanbul a female office worker made a long evening commute home across the Bosphorus Bridge.

London

In London, the team looked at how international nodes and urban centres could be better connected. Using current public transport, the journey proved to be a long trip with many interchanges and staircases, and long walks and waiting times. Carrying luggage to the airport added to the difficulty and stress.

Hong Kong

In Hong Kong the question was: how can a rapid mass transit system intersect with more local modes of transport, from the point view of a senior citizen? There were several interchanges and long corridors between station platforms, despite the journey being off-peak. This proved fatiguing for the user. Hong Kong also has a very efficient walkway network supported by escalators and travelators above street level which links buildings, shopping malls and stations. These walkways significantly reduce road traffic. However, outside this web of walkways people still depend on buses or the metro system. A single train journey with one interchange may be time-efficient but, if there are more interchanges, it can take more time than road-based transport. For older and frailer travellers, the bus is a better option than the metro because of long walks down to metro station platforms. However, in local areas far from bus routes people still have a long walk to their nearest bus stop unless they use either special services—such as previously booked carrier-type vehicles for the disabled or taxis—or personal transport. The project found poor access to local districts from main routes and vice versa.

Istanbul

In Istanbul, the project looked at how to incorporate local and express services. A form of shared taxi or minibus called a dolmus runs either alongside bus routes or where there are no bus services. Because the dolmus is a much smaller vehicle, and more flexible, journey times are much shorter than the bus as there is less stopping and waiting throughout the entire route. The problem here was the 36-minute wait at the start of the journey to board the dolmus.

Research findings

Research into urban mobility raises a series of questions:

- What would a city look like if it could be accessed only by public transport or by walking or cycling?
- What happens if personal transport is the only mode of transport?
- How fast can we travel in the cities?
- How important does speed become in an urban environment?
- How sustainable are future forms of transport and city infrastructures?

Although there is a great diversity among world cities in terms of population, urban structure, economic conditions, social trends and culture, an adaptable and flexible intelligent road-based vehicle system is needed for large metropolitan centres. Such a system must accommodate changing trip patterns and diverse routes. The urban spatial structure is path-dependent rather than linear. It requires accessibility within the routes into local streets. Therefore, for any proposed solution, modularity and variable size would give more flexibility to the urban transport system.

Within inner city areas, vehicles should have zero emissions. Outside these areas, they could switch to alternative fuels such as liquefied natural gas (LNG). They could operate using hydrogen fuel cells when travelling on corridors between the urban nodes. In the shorter term a diesel electric hybrid solution may be viable. In terms of reduced operating costs it is advantageous to use an autonomous vehicle system, as driver costs are high. This is especially true in Western cities.

The design concept

The latest vehicle system that emerged from the design criteria addressed the difficulties of each scenario. Battery-intensive hybrid vehicle modules form the basis of this system. They have the ability to form a single roadtrain of up to six units for express journeys or split apart into smaller modules for local access (see Fig. 14.3). These easy-access, low-floor and high-visibility modules or 'pods' could be made available in different sizes for up to 24 passengers, with different interior design arrangements according to service needs. When they are linked together, about 150 passengers can be carried. This is the equivalent of two to three buses or a single tram. As it uses global satellite guidance sensors, the system does not require a fixed track thus allowing a flexible network according to changing traffic conditions throughout the day and night. Using the modules separately, people can be delivered to within five minutes' walking distance of their destination.

FIGURE 14.3 Driverless modular vehicle system

In London, for example, the pods collect travellers from around the streets of the West End before joining up as a single roadtrain at a given point to head out to City Airport. In Istanbul, the opposite occurs: an express roadtrain heading out of the city divides into smaller local services, combining express and local services in a single vehicle journey. The system thus combines the efficiency of a tram in areas of high demand while featuring the advantages of much smaller minibus-type vehicles in areas of lower public transport demand.

Conclusion

Although there are variations in polycentric city models, cost-effective and zero-emission vehicles combining centre-to-centre express services with very local, modular access will go a long way to improve the quality of urban travel.

By offering public transportation that directly meets the diverse needs of local residents, I believe we can deliver a transport system that is both socially and environmentally sustainable. The concept outlined in this chapter, and shown in Figure 14.3, could provide a significant contribution to such a transport system, by combining the characteristics of conventional mass transit with those of smaller vehicles in a modular, driverless system.

References

Bovy, P.H.L., and B. van Wee (2002) 'Infrastructures and congestion: can rail save the road? Can public transport replace the car?', in E. Stern, I. Salomon and P.H.L. Bovy (eds.), *Travel Behaviour: Spatial Patterns, Congestion and Modelling* (Cheltenham, UK: Edward Elgar): 123-42.

DETR (UK Department for Environment, Transport and the Regions) (1999) *Transport Statistics, 1999* (London: DETR).

Gerondeau, C. (1997) *Transport in Europe* (Norwood, MA: Artech House Inc.).

Hillman, M., and J. Cleary (1992) 'A prominent role for walking and cycling in future transport policy', in J. Roberts, J. Cleary, K. Hamilton and J. Hanna (eds.), *The Need for a Sustainable Transport Policy for Britain* (London: Lawrence & Wishart).

Mackett, R.L., and S.A. Robertson (2000) *Potential for the Mode Transfer of Short Trips: Review of Existing Data and Literature Sources* (London: Centre for Transport Studies, University College London).

National Statistics (1998) *National Travel Survey* (London: The Stationery Office)

15

Web-based environmental management systems for SMEs
ENHANCING THE DIFFUSION OF ENVIRONMENTAL MANAGEMENT IN THE TRANSPORTATION SECTOR

Adeline Maijala, Lassi Linnanen and Tuula Pohjola

Proventia Solutions, Lappeenranta University of Technology, and Helsinki University of Technology, Finland

The need of small and medium-sized enterprises (SMEs) for a reliable means of managing environmental issues has become increasingly important (Biondi *et al.* 2000). SMEs represent 99.8%[1] of all EU enterprises (Starkey *et al.* 1998) and 92.5% of these have fewer than ten employees. It is estimated that SMEs have a significant impact on ecological systems—around 50% of the EU total (ECOTEC 2000; Revell and Rutherfoord 2003). The problem is that SMEs often lack the time and resources to integrate environmental considerations into their management processes, so engaging SMEs in environmental improvements is viewed as a vital part of the drive towards sustainable development (European Commission 2002).

Transportation companies are a priority when it comes to mitigating the environmental impacts of SMEs. Transportation uses substantial amounts of energy and produces a lot of air emissions, the impact of which is visible in most life-cycle assessments (LCAs). Fortunately, the activities of transportation companies are broadly similar, so it

1   If one considers all the criteria included in the EU definition of an SME, in addition to the number of employees criteria, the turnover/balance sheet criteria (either a turnover not exceeding €40 million or an annual balance sheet total not exceeding €27 million) and the ownership criteria (capital or voting rights owned by a larger enterprise cannot exceed 25%), then the proportion of SMEs in the EU is about 80%–90% (Starkey *et al.* 1998; European Commission 1996).

is possible to identify the typical significant environmental aspects of transportation SMEs. This allows a standardised approach to environmental management in the sector.

The case study presented here concerns the development of a web-based tool aimed at integrating environmental considerations into the decision-making processes of companies to help them continuously and cost-effectively improve their environmental performance. The tool is specifically developed for transportation SMEs and should enable them to identify, analyse, manage and report environmental factors related to financial functions. It should help users to cost-effectively determine alternatives for improving the environmental performance of their business processes by simulating and considering the environmental benefits and economic efficiencies of alternative propositions. In effect, it is a decision-making tool for integrating environmental management into strategic business management.

Drivers and barriers to the adoption of EMSs by SMEs

Drivers

Gondran (2001) identifies five groups of drivers for the adoption of environmental management systems (EMSs) by SMEs: regulatory; economic; strategic; events; and managerial. Strategic drivers correspond to stakeholders' concern for environmental protection, public health issues and quality of life in general. The stakeholders identified as the main drivers for the adoption of a formal EMS are: the customer; local government; the local community; regulators; and employees (Hillary 2000). Customers were also cited as the key audience for EU Eco-Management and Audit Scheme (EMAS) statements of small firms and, to a lesser extent, of medium-sized firms in an EU-wide EMAS survey (Hillary 1998). Customers and supply chains are also prominent in driving SMEs' environmental improvements (Charlesworth 1998). Relationships with local communities, local authorities, and economic and financial partners all benefit from the improved image resulting from better environmental performance (Gondran 2001). Events drivers can force SMEs to consider environmental issues—these drivers can, for instance, be environmental accidents or complaints from stakeholders and shareholders (Biondi *et al.* 2000). However, regulatory and local authorities exert greater influence on the general environmental performance of SMEs (particularly medium-sized enterprises) than do customers (Hillary 2000). These constitute the regulatory drivers—SMEs seek to reduce the risks of fines and liabilities by ensuring legal compliance. This correlates with the main drivers identified by Association Orée (1997) (a French organisation promoting environmental management) for SMEs to implement an EMS. First, ensure legal compliance, then reduce costs and, finally, improve or create the image of a responsible enterprise. Economic drivers range from resource minimisation (water, energy, raw materials) to the minimisation of waste, tax and insurance costs. Managerial drivers result from the pressure of the other drivers on a company's management, so that it responds to the environmental awareness of its stakeholders and its own ethical values. Implementation of an EMS can improve the overall quality of the work environment, by creating safer and healthier working conditions, and so motivate employees.

Barriers

However, there are both internal and external barriers to the adoption of EMSs by SMEs, some of which are specific to SMEs.

Internally, SMEs often lack resources, both financial and (more importantly) human (Hillary 2000). This lack of resources is both quantitative and qualitative, and is particularly acute for micro-firms.[2] The availability of staff is limited because they are multifunctional and have little time to implement and maintain an EMS; this can be exacerbated by inconsistent management support. Internal environmental expertise is often lacking (Personne 1998; Hillary 1999), hindering the effective implementation of an EMS. The company's culture and management attitudes can also constitute barriers, with short-term economic difficulties often taking the place of medium- and long-term strategic perspectives. SMEs are largely ill informed about environmental issues and legislation, management's environmental responsibilities and EMSs in particular—how they work and what benefits can be derived from their implementation (Hillary 1999; Personne 1998). Environmental issues are seen as peripheral to the core business while a lack of staff resources leads to initiative fatigue (ECOTEC 2000). Moreover, EMSs are perceived as expensive and bureaucratic (Hillary 1999; Starkey et al. 1998).

On the other hand, in her study of the perception of the environment in SMEs of fewer than ten employees, Personne (1998) describes their pragmatic approach to environmental issues. The economic benefits of environmental management were identified immediately by the interviewed companies (reduction of energy and water consumption, waste cost minimisation, etc.). Although this constitutes a driver, it can mask the other benefits, and SMEs often fear that an EMS would fail to meet their expectations.

Information reaches a company in several ways, the most common being through oral communication. However, SMEs will often verify this information by cross-checking with a more formal source such as clients, specialist and trade magazines, and their employees. Their environmental perception is therefore mostly focused on their micro-environment (Gondran 2001).

Because of these internal barriers, implementing an EMS is often difficult for SMEs. The environmental review and the EMS elements are the aspects they find most difficult to understand and which require additional guidelines (Hillary 1998). Moreover, there are external barriers too, notably the certification system for ISO 14001 and the verification system for EMAS. SMEs have also found the cost of certification to be a problem (Hillary 2000). SMEs appear to need support and guidance for the environmental review, environmental aspects and significance evaluation (Hillary 2000). For instance, the legislative constraints are fragmented and their complexity makes it very difficult for SMEs to get an overall understanding of the relevant legislation for their sector in relation to working conditions, health and safety, and environment. Few have access to appropriate training and assistance (UNESC 1998). The lack of sector-specific guidance and material tailored to different-sized firms, especially micro-firms, is frequently identified as an external barrier (Poole et al. 1999).

2   Micro firms are defined as those with a head count below ten and a turnover below €2 million.

The vicious circle and how to break it

SMEs' lack of resources creates a vicious circle (see Fig. 15.1) that works against integrating the environment into business management (Gondran 2001). The lack of human, time and economic resources prevents SMEs from obtaining the environmental information and know-how that they need. Managers tend to be ill informed about the environment; consequently, they do not understand the benefits that could be gained from integrating environmental management. Combined with a focus on dealing with short-term issues, these aspects mean that managers in SMEs are not always aware of changing regulations and so tend to have a reactive rather than proactive approach.

There are two ways to break the circle presented in Figure 15.1. One is to provide information in a way that takes into account the reasons why it had not reached the manager earlier. The second is to provide a tool that is built on environmental and other knowledge that the manager lacks. These two approaches are compatible and are combined in the web-based tool EcoTra.

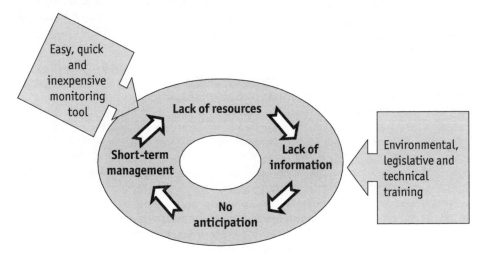

FIGURE 15.1 The vicious circle and how EcoTra breaks it

The environmental information is selected for its relevance to the transportation sector and is used in two ways. First, it is used as a calculation tool so that the manager can benefit from the information directly. Second, it is provided to the user through a training system adapted to non-expert readers. For instance, case studies are integrated in the tool to provide sector-specific examples (Personne 1998) and the tool's vocabulary is also adapted to increase its long-term benefits. Indeed, by raising the environmental awareness and skills of its users, the tool gives them the resources to recognise the value of environmental information. In turn, this raises the interest of managers in such issues and can lead them towards seeing environmental issues as an opportunity rather than a constraint.

Designing a web tool for transportation SMEs

In practice, EMSs require a tool to manage the gathering, use and follow-up of information on a regular basis (Personne 1998) and a high degree of confidentiality is needed because companies can be reluctant to provide data (Personne 1998). In Eco-Tra, the data for each user account is stored behind a firewall and is only accessible to that user. If the user agrees, figures and results can be used anonymously for benchmarking purposes. Because SMEs have limited resources in terms of time, personnel and money, the tool is computerised to provide a user-friendly interface and to facilitate information management such as updating and archiving. To some extent, data input can be automated to save time and increase the reliability of the data used in calculations. However, since SMEs cannot allocate much time and human resources to the implementation and maintenance of a formal EMS, the tool is not aimed at implementing a fully constructed EMS, but rather at integrating the principles and assumptions of an EMS. It can therefore be seen both as a simplified EMS and as a first step towards a fully implemented and standardised system. In the development phase of the tool, the requirements of the two formal EMSs in the market place (EMAS and ISO 14001) were taken into account.

As discussed earlier, the environmental review of an EMS is more of a challenge for SMEs because it is difficult for them to identify the significant environmental aspects of their activities. The activities of transportation companies vary little from one to another, and it was possible for EcoTra's developers to identify the significant environmental aspects, as defined by ISO 14001, of a typical transportation SME—vehicle emissions and fuel consumption. EcoTra also takes financial costs into account. Even though other activities (e.g. loading/unloading, washing, administration, office work, waste management, vehicle maintenance, etc.) have been modelled similarly, the tool includes only the maintenance and driving activities in cost accounting, and only the driving in the environmental loading calculations. This is because these are priorities for SMEs and the environmental impacts of these aspects are comparatively large in comparison to other activities such as office work. Equally, this simplification of the model makes it accessible to SMEs that have a limited time to measure and report environmental and financial factors.

Modelling the business processes of transportation SMEs

The calculation tool is based on the environmental modelling system discussed by Pohjola (1999). The transportation SME's activities are analysed from three points of view—operational, environmental and financial—and the environmental modelling system is developed to take into account the interactions between these factors.

From a generic environmental model, three basic models are defined—energy consumption, transportation and logistic chains. The transportation model was developed for road, rail, air and water transport, and several vehicles were modelled for each type of transport. EcoTra is based on the road transportation model. To develop a generic environmental model, the business processes of a given organisation must be described by representing the interrelationships between their process, environmental and financial components.

According to Pohjola (1999), business processes can belong to one of the following:

- **Business factors:** management, support and operational processes

- **Environmental factors:** energy consumption, material flows, packaging materials, transportation and waste management

- **Financial factors:** legislative and other variable costs

All these factors are usually considered separately for process management, financial management, management accounting, environmental business accounting, environmental management and total quality management (TQM). Even though they belong to different groups, these factors can be used to calculate indicators and new factors such as the ratio of fixed cost per finished product.

In EcoTra, financial factors include the cost of the vehicle and its maintenance, the fuel costs and the salary of the driver. The user provides all this data. Process and environmental factors correspond to the output factors of processes—the current environmental loads, risks and liabilities. For transportation SMEs, process and environmental factors are associated with each vehicle and include those technical characteristics of the vehicle that influence its emissions: namely, the type of engine and the model. They also include the operational variables used to evaluate the environmental load of the driving activity: namely, the type of fuel, the distance driven at a given speed and the number of cold starts. Analysing these factors enables SMEs to measure the environmental performance of their vehicles. By following the evolution of the environmental load, the fuel consumption or the costs, users can detect anomalies and benchmark their performance.

Parameters of the tool

The user is asked to input only a limited amount of data and does not need any specific training to do this; it is simply a matter of filling in forms and fields, and each field is described in the manual and in the help menu. EcoTra is built on the expertise and environmental skills of its developers to process data, calculate environmental indicators and costs, and display the results. Figure 15.2 describes the data managed by the tool and the relationship of one set of data to another.

The user inputs the technical description of the vehicle (as shown in the box in the top-left corner) only once. For each combination of engine and fuel type with driving speed there corresponds an emission factor for eight compounds emitted to the air (CO, CO_2, SO_2, NO_x, PM, VOC, CH_4 and N_2O) expressed in mass per distance driven (typically g/km). The user also inputs the vehicle purchase price and salary of the driver only once, although the latter needs to be updated as necessary. The data linked to operations (as shown in the box in the bottom-left corner and the box labelled 'distance driven') must be input each time the vehicle is used or when undergoing maintenance. Thanks to on-board devices that measure and send the data to a remote station, this data input can be automated. Each cost can be estimated and the user can prepare a budget for each vehicle, following the changing costs calculated by EcoTra and comparing them with the budget.

Environmental cost factors correspond to current legislative and internal environmental costs and to the costs of liabilities. Together with the environmental factors and

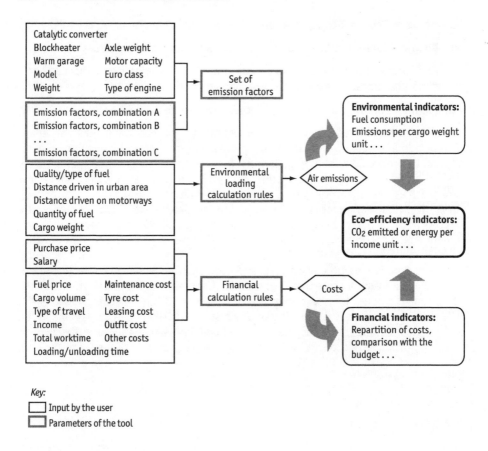

Key:
☐ Input by the user
☐ Parameters of the tool

FIGURE 15.2   Data handled by the tool and how one set of data interrelates with another

outputs of processes, they enable the user to measure the financial performance of environmental issues (Pohjola 1999).

Environmental and financial performance indicators

The user's environmental performance can be expressed by indicators that represent the relations between the environmental impact and outputs of operations (Pohjola 1999). Indicators can, for instance, be expressed as a ratio of annual emissions and distance driven (e.g. average amount of carbon dioxide emitted per kilometre driven) or of total energy consumed and load carried (e.g. average energy consumption per unit of freight delivered). These indicators are calculated by EcoTra and directly reflect the evolution in environmental performance. The financial performance of environmental aspects is determined as a ratio of environmental transport costs to the intensity of the

SME's operation, measured by total energy consumption, as well as the corresponding distances and freight transported.

These results and indicators can be used as an environmental decision-making aid only if the user thoroughly understands them. Decision-making processes consist of three phases (Pohjola 1999). During the first phase, the decision-maker analyses the situation and identifies the problems. This corresponds to the use of the environmental modelling system to analyse the performance of a transportation company with EcoTra reporting the result of calculations that estimate the environmental and financial performance of the user. The second phase is performed by the 'simulation' function of the tool which develops possible alternatives. Finally, the third phase identifies the best option.

When considering internal environmental costs, an environmental business accounting approach is used. Environmental business accounting is a combination of environmental performance evaluation and cost accounting in order to analyse the alternatives for environmental decision-making. If environmental business accounting is combined with environmental management, we achieve the goal of environmental decision-making.

As the environmental and financial performances of the company are modelled and analysed in the second phase of the decision-making process, the evaluation of possible alternatives for improvement can begin. EcoTra can help here by enabling comparison of the current situation (in terms of environmental performance or cost) and a simulated situation where, for instance, an old vehicle is replaced by a newer, more energy-efficient one. Thus, the user can decide whether replacing a vehicle is both environmentally and cost effective.

The user also gains a better general understanding of the company's activities. By simplifying accounting tasks, EcoTra indirectly allows the user to allocate more time to other tasks such as environmental performance monitoring. While using the tool's financial functions, users can recognise the links between costs, operations and environmental performance and, in the long term, integrate these concepts into their business management.

Meeting ISO 14001 and EMAS requirements

As mentioned previously, the requirements of ISO 14001 and EMAS were taken into account when developing EcoTra. Common to both initiatives is the need for an organisation to implement a number of management system stages to formalise the organisation's policies, procedures and practices that control environmental aspects (Hillary 2000). Several aspects of EcoTra satisfy these requirements.

By using EcoTra, organisations enter a cycle of continual improvement by considering their significant environmental aspects as defined in ISO 14001 and measuring their environmental performance. Consequently, once the situation has been analysed and possible improvements have been evaluated and compared, they review their environmental objectives and targets in order to improve their performance. This continual improvement cycle is characteristic of the ISO 14001 EMS. Indeed, all EMSs consist of a continual cycle of planning, implementing, reviewing and improving the processes and actions that an organisation undertakes to meet its environmental obligations (NSF International 2001). EMAS has the added requirement of an environmental statement which publicly reports the environmental performance of a company. The reports provided by EcoTra, and the guidelines available in the training system, help users prepare such documents if they wish. EcoTra can help SMEs meet EMAS requirements to: 'be able to demonstrate that they . . . provide for legal compliance with environmental legislation; and have procedures in place that enable the organisation to meet these requirements on an ongoing basis' (European Commission 2001).[3] EcoTra can be used to monitor environmental performance and analyse the improvements achieved or required.

Training

ISO 14001 (and EMAS) also require organisations to provide appropriate training to their employees (ISO 1996: 17):

> the organisation shall identify training needs. It shall require that all personnel whose work may create a significant impact upon the environment have received appropriate training. It shall establish and maintain procedures to make its employees or members at each relevant function and level aware of . . . the significant environmental impacts, actual or potential, of their work activities and the environmental benefits of improved personal performance; . . . personnel performing the tasks which can cause significant environmental impacts shall be competent on the basis of appropriate education, training and/or experience.

Thanks to the training system, the user can better understand the framework in which EcoTra has been developed, its aims and how to use the reported results for decision-making.

The content covers general environmental issues such as air emissions and their impact, but also offers suggestions for improvement by taking into account the environmental aspects that are not included in the tool. This general environmental knowledge serves two purposes: in the short term, it enables the user to understand, for instance, the impact of a particular emission; in the longer term, it raises the awareness of the user and should help SMEs consider the benefits of environmental management beyond simple economics. One of the barriers to SMEs getting environmental information and adopting EMSs is communication, so the training system aims to adapt general legislative text and standards to the transportation sector.

Concepts such as eco-efficiency and life-cycle are explained. Eco-efficiency is essential to understand the reports and work towards environmental performance improvement. Life-cycle approaches are used at several levels of the environmental model; both when considering the environmental aspects of the transportation activities (life-cycle inventory or LCA), and when modelling the processes and considering the environmental costs inherent in them (life-cycle cost assessment). The concept of the life-cycle is also behind the motivation of organisations that require a better environmental performance from their supplier. As transportation accounts for a relatively large part of the life-cycle impact of products, road freight companies would understand their role and the expectations of their clients better if they were familiar with the life-cycle concept.

---

3   This is an additional requirement specific to EMAS; it is not required by ISO 14001.

More specific knowledge of EMSs is provided so that environmental considerations can be slowly integrated into other aspects of the business. Guidance is also provided to facilitate EMS implementation without employing costly consultants or reading time-consuming documents. For instance, the tool helps users perform the environmental review through pre-selection of the main environmental aspects, while the training system provides concrete examples of their direct and indirect environmental aspects. In the same way, the Global Reporting Initiative (GRI) (2002) sustainability reporting guidelines (which attempt to fit all types of organisations) can be presented to transportation SMEs in a more tailored way.

Results

Until August 2004, the tool has been through an 18-month testing period, during which transportation SMEs have used it and given their feedback and suggestions for improvements. The main problems and limitations have been identified and positive results noted.

In general, the same barriers to the spread of EMSs hindered the spread of EcoTra. SMEs who were contacted to test the tool and participate in its development lacked the resources and environmental awareness to do so, and, because the benefits were not yet demonstrated, it was difficult to convince companies to take part in the test. Some of the managers did not perceive any need for environmental management or did not value it sufficiently to be willing to pay for the service offered.

One of the critical factors for SMEs testing the tool was the time required to use it. It was a necessary precondition that most of the data collection and data input would be automatic. However, although some existing technical solutions were tested (an on-board device measured fuel consumption, speed and driving duration, and sent the data automatically to the EcoTra database via GSM [global system for mobile communication] or GPS [global positioning system] communication), the cost of those solutions remains a barrier to some SMEs. One of the most promising evolutions is to use the built-in on-board computers that vehicle manufacturers now provide in new vehicles. Data can be collected automatically from them with the only minor extra costs being telecommunication fees. The relatively expensive on-board devices tested during the project will become obsolete as the fleet is renewed.

Among the factors affecting the diffusion of the tool are the timing of its entry onto the market and the number of SMEs who have already adopted the use of EcoTra. In Finland, the project was realised at an appropriate time as Finnish transportation companies already understand to some extent the need for environmental management. Some of them also recognise the potential competitive advantage from good environmental performance. In this context, an SME is familiar with the use of mobile technologies and the internet which are the only technical aspects of the tool. Although the market is demanding better environmental performance, these market pressures are still not strong enough to make SMEs adopt good environmental management practices. The tool was tested in seven SMEs in Finland. In the two other participating countries, Hungary and Portugal, the project seemed to come too early or at an inappropriate time. In Hungary, the accession to the EU diverted the SMEs' attention and receptivity to the dissemination efforts of the local partner participating in the development of the EcoTra tool. Internet and mobile technologies also have a shorter history and coverage in transportation SMEs in Hungary. However, the situation is changing quickly and in future it is expected that the only remaining barrier to the adoption of the tool should be the relatively low environmental awareness among SMEs in Hungary. In Portugal there were similar problems, with poor environmental awareness among transportation SMEs and low-level access to the internet and/or mobile technologies. These constituted barriers for the diffusion of the tool. Unfortunately, no SME could be convinced to test the tool or participate in its development in these countries, even though the interface was simplified to enable users unfamiliar with advanced structures to navigate the web pages and use the tool after a very short learning period. The tool was perceived by companies as a new technology that would require a long learning process and be difficult to use. They expressed mistrust in new technology and feared that electronic communications would not be secure. Only at the end of the project did two companies start testing the tool in Portugal.

As for the implementation of the tool, a certain level of adoption should be reached for the tool to be attractive. The number of users should constitute a critical mass so that each can benchmark their results against other users and represent together a movement towards integration of environmental management. With only a few users, the benefit is less because they will not be able to explain to their customers why the tool is a sign of sound environmental management and because they will not be able to benchmark their performance.

Compared to other software-based EMSs, the main advantage of EcoTra is its sector specificity. Other clear advantages are the automatic data collection system and its simplicity, as the main environmental aspects have already been identified for the transport sector. It is also possible with EcoTra to extend the environmental accounting scope to collect and report data on indirect environmental issues.

So far, it has been possible to analyse the costs/benefits in bigger organisations, but not in SMEs. The tool has been developed and implemented during this two-year project but during the pilot phase only minor improvements could be made as the data collection system did not generate sufficient data to enable comparisons to be made. However, those who have been involved with the pilot have learned about the environmental impacts of their activities and been motivated to manage environmental issues in a more integrated way.

EcoTra is a state-of-the-art tool for environmental data collection and is now being used to collect emission and energy use data from the transportation sector at national level in Finland.

Conclusions

A more systematic analysis of the results and feedback should be made in a few years to place the results in a longer time-span.

The information needed to consider environmental performance measurement and improvement is usually available in a format that is too general for SMEs. The degree of abstraction can be lowered and information selected to develop sector-specific tools and training systems so that the effort required is minimised and awareness increased through training and practical demonstration. In this way, environmental issues can become part of decision-making.

Sector-specific solutions seem to be the way to overcome barriers to the diffusion of environmental management in SMEs. The model of business processes and their environmental factors might not be as generally applicable in other industries, but a common framework can be defined for a flexible tool that would adapt to each user.

The tool constitutes only one element of the effort to encourage more firms to practise environmental management. As the environmental awareness of users increases so they become more receptive to other elements, such as updating information, networking and training through other media. As transportation SMEs collectively are major energy users and polluters, better environmental performance on their part should have far-reaching consequences. At a broader level, the tool is part of a process that makes consumers and the industry aware of their environmental responsibilities. Not only do the transportation SMEs become aware of their responsibilities, but their customers also are made more accountable for the indirect environmental impacts associated with purchasing transportation services.

References

Association Orée (1997) *Recueil des Expériences de Gestion Environnementale d'Entreprises Européennes.* [*Collection of Case Studies of Environmental Management in European Enterprises*] (Paris: Association Orée, www.oree.org/outils/collection_oree/recueil_experiences/recueil_exp.html): 150.

Biondi, V., M. Frey and F. Iraldo (2000) 'Environmental management systems and SMEs: motivations, opportunities and barriers related to EMAS and ISO 14001 implementation', *Greener Management International* 29: 55-69.

Charlesworth, K. (1998) *A Green and Pleasant Land? A Survey of Managers' Attitudes to and Experience of Environmental Management* (London: The Institute of Management).

ECOTEC (2000) *Report on SMEs and the Environment: Analysis of the Replies given by Six EU Member States to a European Commission Questionnaire on Small and Medium-Sized Enterprises (SMEs) and the Environment* (Brussels: European Commission, Directorate-General Environment).

European Commission (1996) 'Council Recommendation of 3 April 1996 concerning the definition of small and medium-sized enterprises', *Official Journal of the European Communities* L107.39, 30 May 1996.

—— (2001) 'Regulation No 761/2001 of the European Parliament and the Council of 19 March 2001, allowing voluntary participation by organisations in a Community eco-management and audit scheme (EMAS)', *Official Journal of the European Communities* L114/3, 24 April 2001, europa.eu.int/comm/environment/emas, accessed 30 April 2003.

—— (2002) 'Sixth Community environment action programme', *Official Journal of the European Communities* L242.45, 10 September 2002.

Gondran, N. (2001) *Système de Diffusion d'Information pour Encourager les PME-PMI à Améliorer leurs Performances Environnementales* [*Information Diffusion System to Encourage SMEs to Improve their Environmental Performance*], PhD thesis, Ecole Nationale Supérieure des Mines, Saint-Etienne, France, November 2001, emse.fr/site/themerecherche/systdiff.html, accessed 5 May 2006: 376.

GRI (Global Reporting Initiative) (2002) *Sustainability Reporting Guidelines* (Amsterdam: GRI, www. globalreporting.org): 104.

Hillary, R. (1998) *An Assessment of the Implementation Status of Council Regulation (No. 1836/93) Eco-management and Audit Scheme (EMAS) in the EU Member States (AIMS-EMAS)* (London: Imperial College, europa.eu.int/comm/environment/emas/pdf/general/aimsemas.pdf, accessed 30 April 2003).

—— (1999) *Evaluation of Study Reports on the Barriers, Opportunities and Drivers for Small and Medium-sized Enterprises in the Adoption of Environmental Management Systems* (London: DTI, www.inem. org/htdocs/iso/hillary.html).

—— (2000) 'Small and medium-sized enterprises and environmental management systems: experience from Europe', in J. Hamschmidt and T. Dyllick (eds.), *Nutzen Managementsysteme? Vom Umwelt-zum Sustainability-Managementsystem* (Berlin: IWÖ-Diskussionbeitrag 82): 16-28.

ISO (International Organisation for Standardisation) (1996) *ISO 14001: Environmental Management Systems: Specification with Guidance for Use* (Geneva: ISO).

Personne, M. (1998) *Contribution à la Méthodologie d'Intégration de l'Environnement dans les PME-PMI: Évaluation des Performances Environnementales* [*Contribution to the Methodology for Environmental Integration in SMEs: Evaluation of Environmental Performance*], PhD thesis, Ecole Nationale Supérieure des Mines, Saint-Etienne, France, January 1998: 294.

Pohjola, T. (1999) *Environmental Modelling System: A Framework for Cost-Effective Environmental Decision-Making Processes* (FEMDI Research Series No. 12; Helsinki: Finnish Employers' Management Development Institute): 258.

Poole, M., J. Coombs and K. Van Gool (1999) *The Environmental Needs of the Micro-company Sector and the Development of a Tool to Meet Those Needs* (Plymouth, UK: Payback Business Environmental Association for the Southwest).

Revell, A., and R. Rutherfoord (2003) 'Environmental policy and the small firm: broadening the focus', *Business Strategy and the Environment* 12: 26-35.

NSF International (2001) *Environmental Management Systems: An Implementation Guide for Small and Medium-sized Organisations* (ed. P.J. Stapleton, M.A. Glover and S.P. Davis; Washington, DC: US Environmental Protection Agency and NSF International, 2nd edn, www.epa.gov/owm/iso14001/ wm046200.htm).

Starkey, R., R. Welford, W. Young, M. Brophy, P. Rikhardsson and C. Johnson (1998) *Environmental Management Tools for SMEs: A Handbook* (Copenhagen: European Environment Agency).

UNESC (United Nations Economic and Social Council) (1998) *Industry and Sustainable Development, Report of the Secretary-General, Addendum: Industry and Environmental Protection* (Document E/CN.17/1998/4/Add.3; New York: Commission on Sustainable Development, 20 April–1 May 1998, www.un.org/esa/sustdev/csd/CSD6.htm): 7.

16
The reinvention of the automobile

Chris Borroni-Bird

General Motors Corporation, USA

Fuel cells are the most advanced powertrain under consideration by auto-makers. They appear uniquely able to offer vehicles very high fuel economy, zero tailpipe emissions and long range. Around ten years ago, fuel cells shrunk to the point where they could fit inside passenger vehicles and auto-makers have incorporated fuel cells into existing internal combustion engine vehicles (ICEVs).

If, however, the fuel cell replaces the ICE then auto-makers will design the vehicle around the fuel cell. This shift will offer benefits both to the consumer and the producer. The fuel cell's high-voltage (HV) electrical output makes it easier to integrate with advanced by-wire chassis systems (throttle or drive, brake, steer and suspension) and this will improve vehicle dynamics, interior layout and passenger comfort. Intriguingly, this combination of fuel cells and by-wire chassis systems also offers the possibility of interchangeable bodies and upgradable chassis with significant consequences for all stages of vehicle development. This is the reinvention of the automobile.

This chapter describes General Motors' (GM) thrust into reinventing the automobile around the emerging technologies of fuel cells and by-wire chassis systems. Up to now, this programme has comprised three vehicle phases, each of which will be discussed in turn. The first is a concept vision, called AUTOnomy. The second is a proof-of-concept called Hy-wire. The third, and most recent, is a truly credible and compelling prototype called Sequel.

GM AUTOnomy concept: vision statement for reinventing the automobile

The combination of fuel cells and by-wire chassis systems is very interesting from a vehicle design perspective. This is because the fuel cell propulsion system can be housed completely inside a skateboard-like chassis which creates more exterior styling freedom, particularly at the front of the vehicle where there is no longer an engine. This is mirrored by the design freedom offered in the interior by the elimination of mechanical links (steering column, foot pedals and hydraulic lines) that is made possible by by-wire chassis controls. The AUTOnomy concept vehicle, developed and introduced in the US in 2002, demonstrates this vision.

In short, the AUTOnomy concept takes the conventional pick-up truck body-on-frame architecture to a new level by offering greater front-end design variation, more freedom with interior arrangements and more flexible chassis tuning. In the AUTOnomy vision, a USB-type port could connect the chassis skateboard to the body in a similar way to how a docking station connects to a laptop, and software could allow chassis settings to be automatically adjusted to accommodate the different (branded) bodies that join with the chassis. A schematic representation of the skateboard is shown in Figure 16.1.

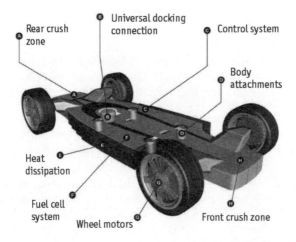

FIGURE 16.1 Schematic representation of GM AUTOnomy's skateboard

© General Motors 2002; reprinted with permission

AUTOnomy has a truly open interior since it may be possible for all the functionality embedded in today's instrument panel to be displaced into the floor, door, roof and steering pod. This is, admittedly, a long-term vision, but it would create an interior where all but the absolutely essential hardware is moved out of view so liberating space inside the vehicle to allow passengers greater comfort without compromising safety. All of this newly created open space can give the interior a much more 'living room-like' atmosphere.

In addition to creating interior space there is greater opportunity for personalisation. As an example, every vehicle today, whether it costs US$5,000 or US$500,000, has the same human–vehicle interface—a steering wheel and foot pedals. By-wire chassis systems offer the potential to provide much greater opportunity for blending this interface with the theme of the vehicle concept. For example, a sports car driver may prefer a different way to steer, brake and accelerate than the driver of a conservative, luxury vehicle.

By eliminating mechanical connections between driver and vehicle, by-wire chassis systems may also give the driver more freedom to relocate within the occupant cabin. For example, while commuting to work alone, a driver may prefer to sit more towards the centre-front seat position, whereas at weekends, the driver might move back to the conventional position to accommodate family members or friends. In Europe, travelling between the Continent and the UK would become easier since the driver could control the vehicle from both right and left seats. This left-hand drive and right-hand drive flexibility is also of value to auto-makers in allowing more commonality in vehicles that are sold worldwide.

Greater interior flexibility can also contribute to increased occupant comfort. For a given vehicle length, the elimination of the engine compartment can increase the usable length of the interior and enable greater couple distance between the front and rear seats. This would create more leg room and an evolution to business class rear seating for all classes of vehicles.

In addition to the substantial opportunity for redesigning the outside and inside of the vehicle, the AUTOnomy concept offers potential to improve manoeuvrability, ride and handling, and stability control. By placing all the 'running gear' inside the skateboard-like chassis, the vehicle's centre of gravity is lowered compared to a conventional vehicle of similar proportions; this translates into improved vehicle ride and handling and to greater vehicle stability. At the same time, it also provides the occupant with the 'command of the road' seat position for enhanced visibility and feeling of security.

The AUTOnomy vision is to place electric motors at all four wheels and this will enable sports car-like acceleration and greatly enhanced manoeuvrability; wheel motors will allow a vehicle to 'turn on a dime', making parking much easier. Since wheel motors will allow each wheel to be independently variable, vehicle stability control could be improved significantly beyond what is possible today.

Finally, the increased ability of the various by-wire chassis systems to talk to each other should allow far superior chassis performance than is possible today. Adding collision avoidance technologies can help active safety in a conventional vehicle, but the active safety benefits are increased when combined with by-wire chassis systems. The combination of wheel motors and by-wire chassis technology could enable the four corners of the vehicle to become interchangeable electronic modules with packaging and software-tuning flexibility adaptable to multiple vehicle types. In the long-term, braking and steering may blend to some extent since it may be possible to slow the vehicle down by turning the wheels in towards each other and to steer the vehicle by selectively applying brakes to one or more of the wheels.

A carefully designed AUTOnomy will not only be cleaner, but also safer, more stylish, more fun to drive and more comfortable. It will simplify life for the owner because it will no longer need oil changes, could be refuelled at home and could provide back-up electrical power at home. Travelling from left-hand drive regions to right-hand drive regions will become much easier as the driver and driving controls can slide over.

Outside of the vehicle performance and design benefits, the AUTOnomy 'plug-and-play' concept between interchangeable body and common skateboard can also catalyse a reinvention of the automobile industry, where all facets of the business are profoundly changed (design, engineering, manufacturing, marketing and servicing). The plug-and-play concept could create a manufacturing advantage because it may allow large manufacturing plants to eventually mass-produce a small number of skateboard chassis types (e.g. compact, mid-size and large) which would save costs. Local subsidiaries could then manufacture 'snap on' bodies designed to appeal to regional tastes. The bodies could even be replaced over time, and the by-wire controls could be upgraded with software. In affluent markets, the chassis might be all-new every four years and consumers could purchase new bodies as often as they want; seasonal or lifestyle changes might occur by installing different body pods. Hardware and software upgrades could be offered within the four-year period for consumers who desire a higher-performance chassis. This decoupling of body and chassis could allow consumers to upgrade independently. In less affluent markets, the chassis could be leased for 20 years. New body pods could be built locally and would use far less material and energy to produce than to replace complete vehicles. In this model, the chassis remains with the owner for life and, along with the bodies, can be continually upgraded. This chassis/body decoupling may also enable a faster response to market shifts and more ability to adjust manufacturing accordingly. Combined with the ease of shipping, the low-profile chassis and the economies of scale inherent in having three or four chassis platforms spanning the vehicle fleet, this model could dramatically lower the barriers to enter emerging markets (where most growth is expected).

In order to convey this message of the reinvention of the automobile, GM developed an AUTOnomy concept vision model (see Fig. 16.2) which was introduced in January 2002 at the North American International Auto Show.

FIGURE 16.2 GM AUTOnomy vision model

GM Hy-wire: proof-of-concept and world's first fuel-cell by-wire vehicle

To demonstrate GM's commitment to the AUTOnomy vision concept, a functioning proof-of-concept vehicle, Hy-wire, was developed and has been extensively driven by the media since its introduction in September 2002. Key elements of the AUTOnomy concept that were demonstrated by the Hy-wire were the world's first functioning combination of fuel cells and by-wire chassis technologies packaged inside a skateboard-like chassis. Although the AUTOnomy vision concept had a 6 inch (150 mm)-thick skateboard, the available fuel-cell hardware required an 11 inch (275 mm)-thick skateboard with a kick-up behind the backseat to accommodate the side-mounted fuel-cell stack (with this tilted on its side from its original orientation in the engine compartment of the HydroGen 3, a fuel-cell version of the Opel Zafira). For similar reasons, the Hy-wire has the same electric traction system (a single front electric motor) that was previously

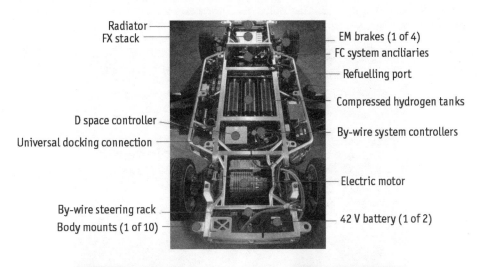

Radiator
FX stack
EM brakes (1 of 4)
FC system anciliaries
Refuelling port
Compressed hydrogen tanks
D space controller
Universal docking connection
By-wire system controllers
Electric motor
By-wire steering rack
Body mounts (1 of 10)
42 V battery (1 of 2)

FIGURE 16.3 GM Hy-wire chassis

© General Motors 2002; reprinted with permission

used on the HydroGen 3 even though the long-term AUTOnomy vision is to use four independent wheel motors for the reasons stated earlier. Unlike fuel-cell vehicles (FCVs) based on a conventional ICEV architecture, Hy-wire's novel skateboard architecture allows the hydrogen tanks to be mounted longitudinally in a central section of the chassis which has the potential (realised in Sequel) to enable longer tanks and, therefore, more hydrogen storage.

Hy-wire also incorporated by-wire chassis hardware (drive, brake and steer-by-wire) systems that run on 42 volts, created from stepping down the higher fuel-cell voltage in addition to a redundant battery for additional safety. The Hy-wire chassis contains all the running gear and is shown in Figure 16.3. This architecture allows the body to have glass front and rear ends (to help communicate with the skateboard) and, in combination with by-wire chassis technology which eliminates mechanical links between the chassis and body, the architecture facilitates ease of body interchangeability.

The interior design freedom inherent with by-wire chassis systems in the AUTOnomy concept was demonstrated with hand-operated controls, left- and right-hand drive operation, and abundant rear legroom. Different views of the exterior and interior for the GM Hy-wire are shown in Figure 16.4.

FIGURE 16.4 Exterior and interior images of GM Hy-wire

GM Sequel: world's first credible fuel-cell vehicle

The GM Sequel was introduced in January 2005 at the North American International Auto Show and is the third phase of the reinvention of the automobile around the two emerging technologies of hydrogen fuel-cell propulsion and by-wire chassis control. The key to Sequel's unprecedented performance is its unique marriage of a purpose-built architecture and state-of-the-art technologies. This combination gives it the opportunity to demonstrate, even with the limitations inherent in today's technology, that a fundamentally superior vehicle can be created around fuel-cell technology than is possible with an ICE.

Comparing Sequel to a conventional ICEV of similar size and market positioning (i.e. a crossover utility vehicle) the hydrogen fuel-cell propulsion system provides the following benefits:

● Lower fuel consumption and zero tailpipe emissions

● Quieter interior (less noise and vibration from the powertrain)

● Faster acceleration, particularly from launch (low-end torque)

Adding by-wire chassis technologies imparts the following advantages to Sequel:

● Shorter stopping distance

● Greater manoeuvrability and more precise ride and handling

● Enhanced and personalised drive comfort (speed-sensitive steering, brake feel)

In addition to these two technology enablers, Sequel's fuel cell-enabled skateboard architecture creates extra vehicle benefits and solves some of the challenges associated with integrating hydrogen fuel-cell propulsion systems into an ICEV:

● A low centre of gravity for enhanced stability

● Ideal 50:50 front to rear weight distribution

● Front compartment design to improve crash safety and thermal management

● Space for a heating, ventilation and air conditioning (HVAC) system (to create storage space in the instrument panel)

● Space for sufficient hydrogen storage to provide credible vehicle range

Each of Sequel's major vehicle systems will be described below.

Hydrogen storage system

Sequel has been designed around the hydrogen storage system. This is because a key requirement for credibility and appeal is to have a minimum of 300 miles range, based on an adjusted Federal Test Procedure (FTP) cycle (and, ideally, with an adequate fuel tank reserve). The other two major considerations for designing a credible hydrogen storage system are to meet Federal Motor Vehicle Safety Standards (FMVSS) and to have minimal impact on interior design. In conventional FCVs, based on ICEV architecture, it has not been possible, so far, to satisfy these three requirements simultaneously.

In designing the Sequel's architecture, the first factor to be considered was providing adequate space to store 8 kg of hydrogen (the initial assumption of what would be sufficient to provide 300 miles range since 1 kg of hydrogen contains approximately the same amount of energy as one US gallon of gasoline and the fuel-cell propulsion system is approximately twice as efficient as a conventional ICE).

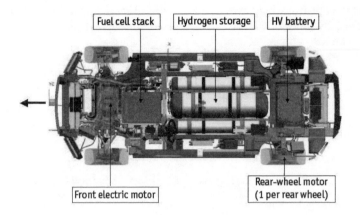

| Fuel cell stack | Hydrogen storage | HV battery |

Front electric motor

Rear-wheel motor
(1 per rear wheel)

FIGURE 16.5 Chassis package in GM Sequel

© General Motors 2005; reprinted with permission

Figure 16.5 illustrates the complete Sequel chassis with propulsion system components identified. This shows the chosen approach to hydrogen storage, chosen after rejecting many alternatives because they produced unacceptable trade-offs in occupant packaging, vehicle proportions, underbody structure integrity, crash performance or inadequate hydrogen mass storage. Hydrogen storage clearly dominates the package.

Sequel has 8 kg of hydrogen stored on-board versus 2 kg in the Hy-wire. Although the carbon fibre tanks in Sequel hold twice the pressure of those in Hy-wire, this is responsible only for approximately a 40% increase in capacity. In other words, if Hy-wire had 10,000 psi tanks there would be around 2.8 kg of hydrogen storage. The fact that Sequel has 8 kg is due to the almost threefold increase in volume, which has been accomplished by lengthening the side tanks and by lengthening and widening the middle tank.

Any FCV will have increased range from improving hydrogen storage (energy density), but Sequel's architecture will be able to exploit this breakthrough even more than a conventional architecture. This is because the skateboard essentially offers one continuous underbody bay so that if the hydrogen storage system shrinks it can allow the adjacent fuel-cell stack envelope to grow in size, thus providing the vehicle with enhanced power and performance. Moreover, Sequel has a high-performing cooling system (see section on thermal management, below) that would allow the vehicle to exploit a higher-power fuel cell. In contrast, hydrogen storage and the fuel cell are decoupled in a conventional ICEV architecture (they are at opposite ends of the vehicle) since the fuel cell is packaged inside the engine compartment and is already at its maximum size. Any increase in fuel-cell power in a conventional vehicle will have to be accomplished by increasing the power density of the stack, rather than by increasing the envelope, and this may be difficult to exploit due to thermal management limitations.

The relatively low energy density of cylindrical 10,000 psi (690 bar) hydrogen tanks dictates the length of wheelbase and height of the sandwich floor. A completely flat floor, initially preferred, does enable identical diameter tanks (producing cost savings both during development and in production) and a more flexible interior design, but it forces a higher and wider floor that will dictate an unacceptably high step-in for entry/egress and will increase width, height, frontal area and aerodynamic drag. It will also make for awkward design proportions. The design ultimately chosen does create a floor with an acceptable tunnel in the rear-seating area and is the best compromise in accommodating a reasonable floor height, attractive vehicle proportions and a 300-mile range.

Fuel-cell propulsion

To meet or exceed the performance of a typical mid-size sports utility vehicle (SUV), Sequel will accelerate from 0–60 mph in about 10 seconds (and the higher low-end torque of electric drives will help to make it launch and feel much faster than a conventional ICEV's 10 seconds 0–60 mph time). This makes it significantly faster than existing FCVs which typically accelerate from 0–60 mph in between 13 and 15 seconds (although most media reports have been satisfied with this because the launch feels faster). Sequel's acceleration time is achieved because the fuel-cell system is augmented with a HV (high-voltage) lithium–ion battery that is capable of providing more than 65 kW. The fuel cell will generate enough power for continuous road loads whereas the HV battery will provide power boost for peak loads. The battery is recharged by excess power generated by the fuel cell during light road load operation and by capturing regenerative braking energy. It is noteworthy that this power augmentation of the fuel cell in Sequel is also beneficial in providing additional (redundant) power backup for the drive-by-wire systems.

To capitalise on the extra power available, the front motor also needs to be supplemented with an additional traction system. Two 25 kW rear-wheel motors, shown in Figure 16.6, were chosen to provide this additional torque, and, as a benefit, will also

FIGURE 16.6 Wheel motor used on GM Sequel (maths data and Chevrolet S-10 pickup truck test vehicle)

provide AWD (all-wheel drive) capability (a logical feature given that Sequel is designed to be a crossover vehicle).

From Figure 16.5 it can be seen that wheel motors are also key for packaging since they create space inside the chassis to position the HV battery. The commonly expressed concern with wheel motors is the additional unsprung mass, but this is not as critical an issue for the rear wheels and should fall within the engineering bandwidth associated with differing wheel/tyre and drive axle options and suspension tuning.

Thermal management

In addition to providing credible range and exciting acceleration, a ground-up FCV offers an opportunity to address high ambient temperature operation. This is typically another challenging area for conventional FCVs because in such a vehicle the fuel cell performance is normally reduced on a hot day for three reasons:

- Inadequate grille surface area for inlet cooling air

- Inadequate airflow behind the radiator inside the engine compartment

- Reduced temperature differential created by simultaneously operating the HVAC because the inlet air temperature into the radiator is raised by operating the HVAC condenser

Sequel's thermal management system, shown in Figure 16.7, addresses each of these three challenges because an absence of an engine creates front-end flexibility between the skateboard and hood panel surfaces. This space is used not only for relocating the HVAC condenser parallel to and under the hood surface, but also for increasing the airflow behind the radiators and for designing new, larger grille apertures (these can even become a design element). Although Sequel's cooling system is complex, because of the multiple electric machines that propel the vehicle, it does provide credible perfor-

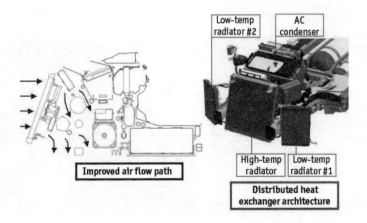

FIGURE 16.7 Front-end thermal management on the GM Sequel

mance, for the first time, in a FCV. Sequel's front-end thermal management, shown in Figure 16.7, provides credible cooling of the fuel cell, front electric motor, power electronics and HVAC. The result is that Sequel will be capable of using the full capability of the fuel cell even with the HVAC on and when the ambient temperature exceeds 38°C (100°F). This is considerably higher than can be obtained with a fuel cell in a conventional ICEV architecture.

The highly efficient, hermetically sealed HVAC unit complements the environmental theme of the vehicle since it eliminates refrigerant leaks associated with flexible and detachable lines and connections. It resembles a window air conditioning unit that just needs to be plugged in to operate. This modularity complements that of the wheel motors and chassis by-wire systems and emphasises that the electrification shift promises to not only provide technical and design benefits for the vehicle but will also simplify manufacturing assembly.

By-wire chassis system

Sequel begins with some strong fundamentals, such as a 50:50 front to rear weight distribution and a low centre of gravity. In addition, by-wire chassis systems allow the chassis to follow the driver's control input rigorously. With the actuators for steering, brakes and suspension, a co-ordinated chassis controls approach will permit an integrated chassis response to the driver's command. The brake by-wire system offers greater front compartment packaging flexibility (elimination of brake master cylinder, booster and hydraulic lines to corners) and also increases interior design freedom because it can eliminate the park brake. In Sequel, a brake pedal is retained in line with the vehicle's mission to be credible today. From a manufacturing perspective, brake by-wire will simplify the assembly of corner modules and eliminate the evacuation/fill station at the assembly plant as well as reducing assembly time for the brake subsystem.

The third series of benefits relate to performance improvements. For example, when the brake pedal is pressed, the response is immediate. Other benefits include the ability to tune brake pedal feel and to integrate with throttle, suspension and steer by-wire systems to enhance stability and active safety.

Steer by-wire offers similar types of benefits as brake by-wire (design, manufacturing and performance). For example, by eliminating the intermediate shaft it offers greater front compartment packaging flexibility. Assembly is simplified between the body and chassis because there is no I-shaft. Stability and handling are improved because the wheels can be steered independently of each other and of the steering wheel. Steering by-wire is more adaptable than conventional steering so that in a car park it can be highly manoeuvrable, whereas on the highway it will be more stable (i.e. speed-sensitive). In addition, noise and vibrations are reduced due to isolation of the steering wheel by intelligent filtering of road feedback.

Electrical and controls system

Sequel's control architecture is designed to provide the vehicle with improvements in safety (fault tolerance), range (energy management) and various aspects of performance (torque co-ordination, dynamic brake proportioning, ride and handling, stability control and tuneable response through software). It has a complex, distributed system using FlexRay communication for safety-critical systems (by-wire) with attention to redundancy and failure-accommodation strategies to ensure safe and reliable operation, including providing authority to distributed controllers in the event of failures. Redundant controllers have separate power supplies, communication channels and software.

Vehicle structure

Sequel's 300 miles operating range places a premium on lightweight construction. These conditions led to Sequel having a lower dominant aluminium space-frame structure. The lower and the upper structures are welded together to save mass, improve entry/egress and to ensure the rigidity of a fully integrated body. The body has an integral sandwich floor structure and an integral sheet dash, rear compartment, quarter inner and roof panels. The chassis, or lower part, has a ladder structure that is lacking the middle cross-structure (to accommodate sufficient hydrogen storage to provide 300 miles range). The aluminium frame has an integral shear panel deck, carriers and environmental shields that replace the functions of many cross-sills in a conventional frame.

Exterior and interior design

Figure 16.8 shows how the proportions of Sequel are being driven by three independent requirements:

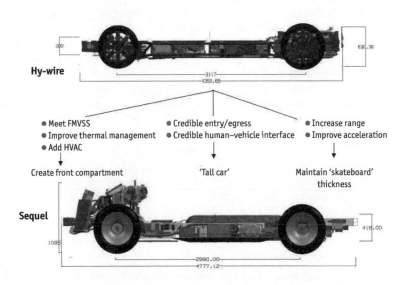

FIGURE 16.8 Evolution of proportions from the GM Hy-wire to GM Sequel

- Functional performance improvements (such as range, acceleration, hardware packaging)

- Ergonomics (entry/egress, human–vehicle interface)

- Crash safety designed to meet FMVSS

In consequence, the proportions are somewhat like a conventional crossover. Given the limitations in existing technology, the decision was made to relocate the HVAC system into the underhood region so that interior space could be created and additional storage space could be freed up inside the instrument panel.

Although the exterior proportions are somewhat familiar, the exterior appearance is differentiated because of the functional need to maximise heat rejection in order for the fuel cell to provide maximum power at elevated ambient temperatures with the HVAC in use. This requirement necessitated larger and additional apertures in the front of the vehicle, as shown in Figure 16.9.

FIGURE 16.9 Exterior images of the GM Sequel

© General Motors 2005; reprinted with permission

Ram air is used to cool front-end components whereas cooling for the wheel motors and HV battery is accomplished using rear inlets (see far-left image in Figure 16.9). These are preferred to side inlets on both an aesthetic and functional basis (less noise, less passenger compartment intrusion and less snow build-up). Although the rear inlets are in a lower pressure zone than more conventional side inlets, it is still possible to provide adequate cooling, albeit with slightly higher electric fan power consumption.

In a conventional ICEV, the HVAC system takes up considerable space inside the instrument panel, but in Sequel the HVAC system was moved out of this space and into the vacant front (engine) compartment, and inlet air for the HVAC condenser enters through a grille in the hood. Moving the HVAC module out of the instrument panel creates more space for useful storage, such as for handbag and laptop computer storage. It also reduces interior noise since the blower fans are farther away from the cabin. Figure 16.10 shows images of Sequel's interior.

Another noteworthy feature of the interior is the addition of an Onstar (telematics) function. For emergent hydrogen FCVs, this service can provide numerous reassuring advantages to the driver. For example, it can help to identify the most appropriate hydrogen refuelling station to use, based on predicted vehicle range, and it can provide remote diagnostics servicing of a new, complex propulsion technology.

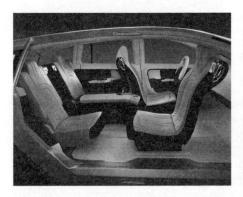 

FIGURE 16.10 Interior images of the GM Sequel

© General Motors 2005; reprinted with permission

Summary

Dramatic improvements in range, acceleration, safety, interior comfort, ride and handling make Sequel not only the world's best-performing fuel-cell vehicle but also a match for the best that conventional ICEVs can offer. This has been achieved using available technology, despite its limitations. As technologies continue to improve at a rapid pace, a Sequel with even better performance and design flexibility will be possible. For example, as by-wire chassis system reliability is proven out by Sequel under real-world conditions it should be possible to simplify the electrical architecture and reduce mass and package space. This will allow performance and range to be further improved and may also allow a reduction in the size of the tunnel.

Sequel is a real car. It has an attractive yet distinctive design that comprehends the unique range and heat rejection requirements of fuel-cell systems. It has inherent stability and unprecedented vehicle dynamics. It reinvents the three basic driving modes by launching faster, stopping sooner and steering more responsively. It is the first practical vehicle with a credible zero tailpipe emissions range and has been designed to meet safety standards. It offers an interior that is quiet and spacious and has abundant storage space. The driving controls are reassuringly familiar even though they operate by-wire chassis systems.

A real vehicle that meets and exceeds customer expectations is a prerequisite for mass production. However, it must also be affordable. GM's target remains to design and validate a fuel-cell propulsion system that competes with current ICE powertrain systems on performance and durability, and can ultimately be built in high-volume affordably. An affordable and compelling Sequel-type vehicle is what is needed to create the mass acceptance of hydrogen FCVs. This is essential because hydrogen fuel-cell technology will not benefit society until it realises its high-volume potential.

17

Conclusions

WHERE NEXT AND WHEN CAN WE BUY ONE?

Paul Nieuwenhuis and Peter Wells

ESRC Centre for Business Relationships, Accountability, Sustainability and Society, Cardiff University, UK

Philip J. Vergragt

Tellus Institute, Boston, USA

This book is an interesting amalgam of near-term and long-term sustainability thinking; of theory and practice, and of the academic and the industry practitioner. It is encouraging to see proposals for change coming from Finland to India, to see the forward thinking in business and industry of all sizes and to see attempts made by academia of many disciplines worldwide to build the bridge to a more sustainable model, both from a conceptual, social science, to a practical engineering and industrial design point of view. We hope and expect, therefore, that this book will become a major contribution to this exchange of ideas on the route to a sustainable yet mobile global society.

Powering the future

Truly sustainable future mobility implies much less material per transport or person-kilometre, and totally sustainable sources for all energy use. We are clearly a very long way from achieving this aim. First, it implies much smaller means of transport, more sharing of car use, more public transit and transit services, and more use of human power.

In addition to energy used for propulsion, it also includes the energy used for manufacturing vehicles and the necessary infrastructure, as well as the lives of all the people involved. This was explored in San Francisco in 2003 at one of the Greening of Industry Network (GIN) workshops. The starting point of this workshop was 'fuels'. Based on the suggestions from the brainstorming session, the following list of primary sources was arrived at: solar; wind; nuclear fusion; bio-fuels; fossil fuels; and geothermal. Hydrogen was also discussed as a possible storage medium in addition to the electricity generated using the fuel options in the list—it could be used to power fuel cells. Another alternative discussed was to increase the use of human power. It was also felt there was still considerable scope for improved internal combustion engines (ICEs). Nuclear fission was discussed, but in view of its legacy of waste was not considered sustainable despite its advantages in terms of lack of carbon dioxide emissions. Two scenarios emerged from this discussion, as outlined below.

Possible scenarios

Under the first scenario, nuclear fusion is made practical. This is then used to generate electricity. All other energy use is derived from that electricity. Some could, for example, be stored as hydrogen and transported in this form. This would probably imply very centralised electricity generation.

Under a second scenario, nuclear fusion is not made practical within a realistic timeframe. The team felt this would lead to a situation where a range of energy sources would be used. On the one hand various technical improvements would lead to fossil fuels being used significantly more cleanly (especially liquefied natural gas [LNG]), while on the other there would be a range of localised, decentralised, diverse sources, including geothermal, wind, solar, (micro)hydro and bio-fuels, depending on local circumstances. Hydrogen could still play a role as a secondary fuel, where appropriate, while electricity would cover the gaps elsewhere. Bio-fuels and LNG could also be distributed beyond their production locations. Propulsion would use a mix of fuel cells, battery-electric, human power, bio-fuels and clean fossil fuel. This would be combined with a dramatic reduction in the use of energy in mobility generally. Energy would be used primarily to move people rather than vehicles, thus creating a need for safe lightweight vehicles.

Linked with the second scenario would be a system of distributed production comprising smaller-scale localised production facilities which are flexible and close to the consumer market. In addition, there would be a gradual bringing-together of consumption and production, with a suggestion that the two could be combined in some way. The team felt this relocalisation could also be accompanied by more localised government, although it was also felt that some global taxation might be needed in order to deal with the global commons. This would be used, for example, to tax airline and shipping fuels.

In order to bring about the transition to the new scenario, several initiatives were suggested by the group, such as:

- **Local initiatives and social experiments to trial new solutions:** there needs to be a lot of new public–private–civic partnerships, and high-level learning by all stakeholders is part of this process

- **Government-led incentives and full-cost pricing of energy:** this would internalise the environmental and social externalities

- **A very considerable amount of additional R&D would be required:** this would involve a fair degree of public-sector involvement, possibly paid for by a fossil fuel tax

And in the real world?

So what is happening in the real world? How soon can we expect real change? There are some interesting and successful experiments in public transportation under way in places such as Curitíba (Brazil), Bogotá (Colombia) and Portland, Oregon, USA. Car-sharing initiatives are flourishing, at least in many niche markets. New bicycle designs and designs for improved rickshaw-type vehicles, as well as small electric vehicles such as electric or electrically assisted bicycles, scooters (and even motorcycles) and small city cars, are developed and close to entering the market. Hybrid cars, mainly Japanese, are unexpectedly successful. High oil prices, more appealing alternative products and changing fashions are making the US public rethink their love affair with light trucks. Sales of these stagnated from early 2005, and car giants such as General Motors and Ford face difficult financial problems. It is questionable if these old 'dinosaurs' will survive the upcoming switch to sustainable transportation.

In spite of these somewhat hopeful developments, it is clear that under current scenarios we will enjoy ICEs as the dominant powertrain offering for at least another 20 years or so. However, we can already see more and more hybrid-electric internal combustion systems creeping into the market. Equally, the pure battery electric vehicle (BEV) concept is by no means moribund, with new products and designs still being brought forward (Wells 2005a). At the same time, vehicle manufacturers are easing more automated transmission systems into their products which feature increasing degrees of electronic intervention. These are important stepping stones towards all-electric drive systems in cars and the goal of weaning consumers off conventional ICEs linked to a fixed-ratio transmission via a friction clutch and onto the smooth all-electric powertrain. This combination of incremental technology innovation and consumer education is an important prerequisite for any move to a fuel-cell future.

So, what of the fuel cell? How soon can we expect this technology, widely regarded as the most environmentally optimised by many observers today? Fuel-cell applications have been relatively limited to date—all we have seen so far are a few prototypes and some buses here and there. Indeed, the industry has been talking of a three-stage model to commercialisation for some years now, but appears to be stuck on stage one where demonstration and prototype vehicles are shown (Wells 2005b). The achievements of the fuel-cell industry, and Ballard in particular, have been impressive; the ratio of kW/$ has improved dramatically over the past 15 years or so. This has been combined with dramatic reductions in weight and size. In fact, in some respects, the fuel-cell car is competitive with the ICE car even today. So where are the problems? These appear to be in three areas: vehicle integration, manufacturability and infrastructure.

Fuel-cell vehicles have come a long way. Not too many years ago, a panel van was the smallest possible fuel cell vehicle, as the system took up so much room. During the 1990s we saw a rapid reduction in size and today's experimental fuel-cell vehicles look, in terms of packaging and presentation, uncannily like conventional internal combustion-powered vehicles. Toyota's Highlander-based fuel-cell vehicle (FCV) is a good example. There remains room for considerable progress here, particularly with respect to the hydrogen storage question.

One other issue that has been flagged up as an outstanding problem is the fuel cell's need for platinum. This precious metal is also used in catalytic converters, so the car industry is no stranger to tracking its value in the market. It is, unfortunately, relatively rare and reserves could even be stretched by the projected production volumes of cars if they were just petrol-powered and catalyst-equipped. However, at present, a fuel-cell system for a car needs at least twice as much of this metal. In view of this, the fuel-cell industry and its suppliers are looking at ways of reducing the fuel cell's platinum dependency. If they fail, we have a problem, as the required volumes can then not be achieved.

The fuel supply for the fuel cell is another issue to be resolved and one we have discussed in this book at various points. Most current automotive fuel cells run on pure hydrogen. This is a substance that does not occur in this form on our planet. On earth it only occurs bound with oxygen in the form of water, or bound with carbon in a range of hydrocarbons. In each case some process is needed to separate the hydrogen from these other elements and this requires energy, in some cases a lot of energy, such that the total life-cycle impact of hydrogen does not always make it the most environmentally optimal fuel.

On-board reforming, on the vehicle, of hydrogen from hydrocarbon fuels such as methanol or even petrol has also been suggested. This would obviously add weight and complexity to the vehicle and would also use energy. It would, however, remove the need for large hydrogen production facilities and for a hydrogen distribution infrastructure. More recently, thinking in the industry has centred on reformers based at fuel stations, such that the existing hydrocarbon distribution infrastructure can remain in place, but vehicles could fill up with hydrogen at fuel stations. Recent experiments with compressed hydrogen have at least shown that by using very high pressures, a sufficient amount of fuel can be carried in a car to give it an acceptable range of around 300 miles. This has also been an issue that has been causing concern over the years. It does show that the industry is achieving improvements in the move towards practical FCVs at a steady rate. If this continues, we are indeed likely to see some practical hydrogen FCVs within the next five years or so, and certainly by the much-forecast 2012–15 period.

Ballard is now in the early phase of setting up a manufacturing process for automotive fuel cells. This envisages a gradual, incremental increase in annual production to reach a peak of around 500,000 a year by about 2012–15 in a single factory. So, if all goes according to plan, Ballard will be able to produce some half a million automotive fuel-cell stacks each year. If we assume that the Japanese, led by Toyota, add a similar annual number, we have an annual production capacity of automotive fuel cells of around one million by 2015.

The total number of vehicles produced worldwide today is around 60 million. It is safe to assume that with China, India, Indonesia and others all in the fray by 2015, this number will have grown to nearer 80 million, if not more. The market share of newly registered fuel-cell vehicles by then will therefore be a maximum of 1/80 of the global market. As they have businesses to run, neither the Canadians at Ballard nor the Japanese are likely dramatically to increase fuel-cell production capacity before there is a clear sign of demand. Once this is apparent (and if, indeed, it materialises) the lead-time for another half million capacity facility will be at least a year, if not more (Nieuwenhuis 2004).

Let us assume, therefore, that by 2020 we will have a global automotive fuel-cell production capacity of four million stacks. If we keep to our global vehicle production figure of 80 million by then we find that 5% of vehicles made can be fitted with a fuel cell (1 in 20). At this rate it would obviously take a few decades to have the majority running on fuel cells. In practice, these FCVs would probably not be equally distributed among world markets. Instead, there are likely to be pockets of higher FCV densities. One can imagine areas such as the state of California, Iceland and the Canadian province of British Columbia (home of Ballard) enjoying a significantly higher density than Texas, Bahrain or Romania, for example.

Much has also been made of the need to replace or replicate the existing fuel supply infrastructure with a hydrogen version. The building of a dedicated infrastructure is very expensive—it has been estimated at US$5,000 per car by Keith and Ferrell (2003). There is also a chicken-and-egg situation in that few FCVs would be sold in the absence of a fuelling infrastructure, while no commercial organisation would build an infrastructure without some guarantee of demand. A range of automotive fuels is currently offered in various markets around the world. Petrol or gasoline is almost universally available, closely followed by diesel, used by heavy goods vehicles worldwide and by cars in Europe as well. In addition, many individual markets offer liquefied petroleum gas (LPG), compressed natural gas (CNG), bio-diesel, ethanol and ethanol-based E85, methanol and methanol-based M85, and other fuels.

Adding hydrogen as an additional fuel is often difficult on a crowded forecourt with a fixed number of storage tanks. With only 5% of new car sales being hydrogen-powered, this is indeed difficult to justify. However, in British Columbia and California there have been proposals for 'hydrogen highways'—corridors where hydrogen availability would be guaranteed at regular intervals (Wells 2004). In Wales, the Hydrogen Valley cluster initiative has similar long-term ambitions (Nieuwenhuis 2005). Clearly, some government support would be required to encourage such a development and in California the governor has been a keen supporter of this concept.

Hydrogen supply infrastructures are currently very rare indeed, with only the Europort area of Rotterdam in The Netherlands and the M4 corridor of South Wales in the UK as examples (Nieuwenhuis 2005). However, as mentioned above, it has also been suggested that hydrogen itself does not actually need to be distributed in the way petrol or diesel are today. In fact, rather than on-board reforming outlined earlier, some are now suggesting that this reforming (extracting hydrogen from a feedstock) can be done by larger units set up alongside fuel stations and linked to one or more pumps on the forecourt for the supply of pure hydrogen to FCVs. In this way, no significant change in the fuel distribution system would be needed.

Obstacles to the introduction of hydrogen FCVs are one by one being dismantled by technological and conceptual solutions. If this trend continues, we could have commercial FCVs appearing on the roads in at least some parts of the world in the next decade. To that extent, Ogden, Williams and Larson (2001) could be correct. They forecast an 'optimistic scenario' whereby 10,000 fuel-cell cars would be produced between 2005 and 2008 and, by 2010, this figure would be up to 300,000. One million a year would be reached before 2020, by which stage the technology would be cost-competitive with conventional cars. Beyond 2020 ten new factories would be built each year. However, it is also quite clear that, with the possible exception of Iceland, much of this hydrogen would be derived from conventional fossil fuels. Though not perhaps the most efficient use of hydrocarbon fuels, it would allow the kick-starting of a hydrogen system in preparation for more sustainable hydrogen production.

At the same time, oil-derived fuels are likely to increase in cost. Supply of oil is now estimated to peak at the latest around 2010–15, while demand from newly motorising nations such as China, India, Indonesia and Russia will continue to increase. Oil is mostly found in politically unstable areas, which makes it susceptible to rapid price fluctuations. This cost increase in conventional fuels could increase the demand for alternative fuels such as bio-fuels, and of alternative powertrain technologies such as the hydrogen fuel cell. Alternatively, the car industry may decide, in a bid to preserve the tried and trusted ICE, to go for petrol- or diesel-hybrid solutions instead. Their fuels can also be derived from natural gas, coal or biomass even when oil itself becomes too costly. This perpetuation of internal combustion technology could well be used to postpone the inevitable moment when the technology itself will no longer be viable. In that case, the hydrogen fuel cell could well continue to be the best future powertrain solution for several more decades.

China: the next major innovator?

GIN 2004 was held in the Hong Kong Special Administrative Region of the People's Republic of China. Although there was no overt mobility stream at the conference, there were a number of relevant papers and this is appropriate as China is, together with India, Indonesia, Mexico and other emerging economies, where the issues discussed in the chapters of this book will come to a head. China alone has the theoretical potential to absorb as many cars annually as Japan, the EU and US combined. From an environmental viewpoint this is a frightening thought. How will we cope? How will China cope? How will the global climate cope?

In the world of inventions, some concepts are autonomous, self-standing, while others need a supporting infrastructure in order to work. With the invention of the steam locomotive, for example, the creation of a supporting railway infrastructure was needed in order for the invention to make sense. Inventions of this nature, ones that need an infrastructure in order to work, face rather more barriers to entry to the market than those that do not need this. One of the secrets to the success of UK inventor

Trevor Bayliss's wind-up radio was this very independence, the fact that it did not even need a regular supply of batteries. The steam train was invented at a time of great technological expansion in the UK, a time when building new infrastructures was not necessarily regarded as a major obstacle to progress. At this time, canals were being constructed, factories and mines were being built, road networks and towns were subject to rapid expansion. Building a rail network fitted in well with the spirit of the age.

By the late 19th century, the industrial age in Britain and other Northern European countries had begun to reach maturity and, at this point, building a major new infrastructure in addition to the legacy of the infrastructures already built, faced stronger opposition. Thus, when Joseph Swan invented the light bulb, selling the idea of an electric infrastructure to go with it was not so easy. Instead, this aspect moved the next, implementation phase to a country that was now in a rapid expansionary phase, a country that was building new infrastructure at a rapid rate—the US. It is not surprising, therefore, that it was Scottish-born but US resident Thomas A. Edison who was able to capitalise on the new invention.

Similarly with the motor car. Although the Germans, in the persons of Daimler and Benz invented the car and the French were the first to industrialise it, the considerable infrastructure needed to move it onto the next level fell to the US, a country building new infrastructure at a prodigious rate in the late 19th and early 20th centuries. Thus Ford, using Taylor's ideas, and Budd created the mass production of cars. Only once they had proven it and created critical mass and credibility for the new systems could it return to its spiritual home; by adopting US technologies from Ford and Budd, French car-maker André Citroën became Europe's first mass producer of cars.

So what of the next revolutionary phase? There are a number of automotive technologies in the pipeline that require significant investments in infrastructure in order to work. Most significant of these is, probably, the hydrogen fuel cell. This requires a new hydrogen supply or conversion infrastructure which does not currently exist on anything approaching the required scale. However, the established car markets, the triad markets of Europe, the US and Japan, have existing infrastructures wedded to the existing automotive fuel paradigm. Change here is unlikely and scepticism is rife.

If the pattern we have just outlined is to be repeated, we should look for a location with a rapidly expanding infrastructure, with frantic construction activity and a dynamic economic drive—what has been described as a 'can do' attitude pervading the whole population. There is only one significant economy that currently fits this bill and this is China. Should we therefore conclude that China will drive the next automotive revolution, or is there more to it than this? The signs are promising. Some parts of China are already moving directly to mobile phone technology bypassing the costly intermediate phase of a landline infrastructure. This is a typical example of the pattern just outlined. But it also needs the right people factors.

Note that Swan did not move to the US, but passed the torch on to a local player in the US, albeit one of European origin. Similarly, the European inventors of the automobile had to defer to local talent to develop its mass production in the US. It seems reasonable, therefore, to assume that for the Chinese to lead the next automotive revolution they will have to rely on local talent and expertise to drive the innovation, even if it is based on Western technology and intellectual capital. It is most probable that local Chinese talent will work hand in hand with American and European expertise and business models, probably in joint ventures. There is nothing to stop China from using existing expertise in Europe, the US or Japan to build on, but some key elements will have to be home-grown, reviving the age-old tradition of Chinese innovation and inventiveness. The search is on therefore for the Chinese Henry Ford, Edward Budd or Thomas Edison to change the world. Of course, such innovations may also come from India, Indonesia, Malaysia, Korea, Philippines or Thailand, but they will, almost certainly, come from Asia.

Again, we should not rely solely on hydrogen to save us. Apart from the prospect of traffic jams of hydrogen-powered cars, we need action rather sooner than the hydrogen timetable will allow. We need to start today to reduce the impact of road transport and to move our mobility onto a genuinely sustainable footing. The promise of a hydrogen economy in the future can all too easily be used as an excuse for inaction today. In this context, the EU's policy on carbon dioxide reduction is rather more realistic and a greater contribution to this process than any speculation about a hydrogen economy, however appealing it may appear.

Prends le bon chemin	[Take the right road]
Ne marches pas dans l'ombre	[Don't walk in the shade]
Suis ton instinct	[Follow your instincts]
et n'aies peur de rien	[and fear nothing]
Plus jamais de chagrin	[Even less regret anything]
Regardes au lointain	[Look far ahead]
Imagines toi demain	[Imagine yourself tomorrow][1]

References

Keith, D., and A. Ferrell (2003) 'Rethinking hydrogen cars', *Science* 301 (18 July 2003): 315-16.

Ogden, J., R. Williams and E. Larson (2001) *Toward a Hydrogen-Based Transportation System* (Princeton, NJ: Princeton University Press).

Nieuwenhuis, P. (2004) '2003: fuel cell year zero', *Automotive Environment Analyst* 105: 36-37.

—— (2005) 'Wales launches Hydrogen Valley', *Automotive Environment Analyst* 118: 2.

Wells, P. (2004) 'Is Vancouver the new Detroit?', *Automotive Environment Analyst* 104: 22-23.

—— (2005a) 'The electric Blue Car', *Automotive Powertrain Analyst* 31: 22-23.

—— (2005b) 'Are there really three steps to (hydrogen) heaven?', *Automotive Environment Analyst* 116: 14-15.

1   Extract from 'Peur de rien', from *Pleine Lune*, by Breton folk-rock group *Merzhin* 2000.

18
Epilogue
A DAY IN A LIFE IN 2049

Boelie Elzen
Centre for Science, Technology and Society, University of Twente, The Netherlands

Wim Hafkamp
Erasmus University Rotterdam, The Netherlands

In this final chapter, the authors tell a story to bring to life some fictional aspects of mobility in The Netherlands in 2049. The Dutch setting is appropriate; as Europe's most densely populated country, many environmental issues hit here first. In addition, the fact that a significant part of the country is below sea level creates considerable interest in the issue of rising seawater levels as a result of global warming. This epilogue presents a more imaginative context within which to place the issues described and analysed in the other chapters.

Lucy in the sky with diamonds

'Wake up Luce, rise and shine!'

As I open my eyes, I see Ben's side of the bed, empty. In a split second I realise he's done it again, the moron. He's set the video system to wake me up and fool me. I hate that. I tell him I hate that every time he does it, which is always when he is away on a trip.

The voice recording continues: 'Happy birthday, Luce!' I hate that too, the way he says *Luce*, in his mistaken Italian, *Lewtsji*. It must be all those Italian movies he's been watching lately. I am not the light, certainly not on a dark December morning at 6.45 am. And he's put on a happy birthday flower display on the video screen. I am not the light and I hate video spam. He knows that too. I clear my throat, getting ready to deactivate the video system, when it buzzes. It's him. I make sure the outgoing video is off. My morning wrinkles are gorges and ashen in mid-winter. I stare at his face. His morning wrinkles seem petrified and chiselled. He certainly fits his postmodern *dirndl* hotel room in Karlsruhe.

'You moron, where's your *lederhosen*?' I ask him.

He must have had a *schnapps* too many with his inspection crew last night. He acts like he doesn't hear me.

'Congratulations honey, mwahmwah, on your forty-sixth birthday!'

Why does he have to specify the number? Why does he drive that nail in deeper? We talk a bit. We always talk a bit, and agree to meet at home at 1 pm for an afternoon walk in the sand dunes near Zandvoort. Be good for us, some fresh air, salt and chill.

I get out of bed, open the curtain a bit, and look out over the water, over the dark historic centre of Amsterdam; the lights. It's wet outside, dreary as far as I can see. Then again, I can't see that far. But hey, who said that laser treatment for eyesight was completely reliable nowadays, 'cos it's not. I take a shower, get dressed, put on my sunshine face, in spite of it all, and take the elevator. And take the same elevator back up again, to check that the door is really locked—I keep hearing those burglary stories lately—and take the same elevator down again. I am just tired.

At the ground floor I enter Hankspresso, the common space for the 120 or so residents of our building. A few years ago, one of the residents had proposed to turn the old, sterile common room into a space that was more conducive to casual encounters, talks and meetings between residents. Everyone loved the idea. I worked out the plan, donated some fabrics and carpets. Jerzy, from the rear side of the seventh floor, offered and installed a huge, ancient espresso machine. He's in catering and snatched it up in a restaurant bankruptcy. This particular model was called Hankspresso. Soon everyone started using it. The common room has lockers for snail-mail and packages. It also has depots for dry-cleaning and other goods to be picked up. Delivery people have electronic entry codes.

I grab a quick coffee to prepare for the day. Fortunately, there's nobody in Hankspresso to congratulate me. I don't feel like seeing any cheery faces right now. Well, OK, maybe it's not that bad after all. Let's go to work and just make the best of it.

I fetch my gear and when I enter the elevator to go down to the mobility cellar I see a man I never saw in our building before. He answers my uninterested nod with a cheery 'Hi'. Without looking at him I can feel he's examining me with his eyes; hate it, but feel flattered too.

'Taking the metro as well?' he asks.

I don't feel like talking but hear myself saying 'No, I hate public transport.'

'Why?' he replies, clearly astonished. 'It's so convenient.'

Well, maybe he's right. But I hate it. All those people. Too much stuff to carry for my work: samples, sketches, documentation, e-gear; whatever. I was so happy when I got the promotion and could afford the luxury of a private car. Using these things costs a fortune in fuel, parking, road fees and what have you. But then you've really got something. You just say or punch in where you want to go and the navigation system smoothly guides you to your destination.

'I need to carry too many things for my work,' I answer.

'Yeah, I can see that. I had the same problem in my earlier job. But now I'm happy I don't need the car anymore. The public system is usually a lot swifter and a hell of a lot cheaper.'

'Lucky you.' I hear the sarcastic tone in my voice.

The elevator comes to a smooth halt.

'I need to get off here,' he says. 'Take the metro. See you around.'

'Bye,' I reply mechanically.

One floor lower I take my car, punch in my standard trip to work and follow the instructions from the navigation system until I get to the main road. While I switch to automatic vehicle guidance I hear the muffled roar of my engine. I am on fuel still, a synthetic one—they say it is zero pollution with carbon compensation. I just don't trust that hydrogen story they keep trying peddle.

While the car takes care of the trip I make a call to the specialty bakery store in Weesp to order pastries to celebrate my birthday at work. I read some documents to prepare for a meeting with a client this morning.

'We take a southern route around Weesp,' the navigation system says, 'since there's been an accident on our usual route.'

I'm a bit startled; hope it works out alright. Two weeks ago the car also had me make a detour, and then it messed up my destination. I ended up in a completely alien location, 30 kilometres east of Almere when I had to meet a client at Mobilia. Fortunately, there was a flexoffice at a nearby mobility centre where I could teleconference with my client.

Today, all works well, fortunately, and just before 9 am I enter my office at Mobilia. I am glad I have the afternoon off. A couple of years ago, during the '44–46 recession, the government wanted to abolish employees' right to half a free day on their birthday, but the unions stood firm on the issue.

Lena, my secretary, comes in to tell me that the pastries have arrived by tube as well as some packages with samples of Fabrina fabrics that I ordered from the car. There are a few things missing which I ask Lena about. These were too bulky for the tube, Fabrina explained, but would arrive later today via FedEx. Shit, I need these for the client I'm seeing this morning.

My door opens. 'Happy birthday to you, happy birthday to you, happy birthday dear Lucy, happy birthday to you.' My colleagues come in, Khaled loudest of all, completely out of tune. They all give me a kiss. 'You look terrific,' says Peter. 'I wouldn't give you forty-six.'

Ouch, not again! I don't want to know.

Lena brings coffee and the pastries which everybody seems to enjoy. They have a lot of fun but I'm no part of it. It's not their fault; they're a nice bunch, but I'm just not in the mood. I'm glad when Lena comes in to tell me my client has arrived.

The client is in her late thirties, by the name of Mbele. She works for the city of Amsterdam and is responsible for the interior decoration and furnishing of the renovated offices of their public works department. I take her to the conference room and switch on the teleconference system so that the Fabrina people can also take part. Sooner than expected we come to a broad agreement on furnishing. Discussing curtains and carpets her eyes widen as I show her the samples. She touches and smells them extensively.

'I feel we're living in a world that's becoming more and more chilly,' she says. 'Everything goes via screens and telesystems. I miss the warmth of real things.' I feel my heart jump.

'I agree completely,' I answer in full honesty. 'Everything is so well organised and you can get whatever information you want. But I always love the stories from my father, who was raised in Kurdistan, when he talks about how they had almost no material things, knew little about what went on in the world, but enjoyed life far more intensely than we do now.'

Thinking about Dad I feel a sudden sadness coming over me. It apparently shows because Mbele asks me if I'm OK. I say I am. I don't want to talk about it.

Although I like her, I am glad when she leaves and I can go back to my office to be on my own. At noon I get back into my car and push the button for the ride home.

'We'll stop at the next fuel station to take fuel. I'll take regular biogas unless you instruct otherwise,' says the control system. Of course regular biogas. It's the only appropriate fuel. I never understood why they make this optional.

While the automatic system fuels the car the phone rings. 'Hi Luce, it's me. I just landed in Amsterdam North. I'll grab a bike to ride home.'

'A roofed electric bike?' I assume.

'No, an unroofed pedal bike.'

'Unroofed? Are you crazy or what? It's freezing cold.'

'No, Luce, you cold-blooded creature, it's at least five degrees.'

Cold-blooded? Me? He's the one who's cold-blooded. Always the intellectual, never showing his feelings.

'Besides, I like to freshen my head after three days in meetings and only artificial environments.'

'Well, OK. It's your choice. I should be home in a few minutes. I'll probably see you in about half an hour?'

'Yeah, more or less. See you then.'

Fifteen minutes after my return home Ben comes in. With a big smile he walks towards me, wraps his arms around me and starts kissing me like he hasn't done in 15 years.

'Happy birthday, Luce.'

We exchange a few trifles. And then go off for our afternoon in Zandvoort. I had imagined we'd take the underground connection, via the old Schiphol terminal, but Ben proposes to walk to CMC—the Amsterdam central mobility centre—and then take the old train via Haarlem.

'That's real history, Luce. It was the first train in the country, over 200 years old. It should be romantic with these 19th-century carriages.'

Fortunately, they adapted the passenger seating to current standards and I agree. We leave our building and head for the narrow bridge. It's for pedestrians and cyclists only. As we cross it a teenager on a speedboard heads our way. Ben curses and pushes him off. We continue on our way, to the old docklands, just east of CMC. It's an area that used to have shipyards and rope factories and sail repair shops. All for the Dutch East Indies Company, sometime in the 17th century. It became more or less derelict in the 19th century, while later it became the homeland of the postal services, heroin-addicted prostitutes and the first floating Chinese mega-restaurant in Europe seating over 2,000, more even than the legendary Frank Giuffreda's Hill Top Stake House just outside Boston in the US.

We take the underground entrance, and walk into CMC. Ben is well prepared and we continue straight for the platform to get on the train. Who says these trains are always messed up? We find our seats and within minutes the train slowly heads west. I feel sad while we stare into the cityscape. It rains; how can it be so dark at one in the afternoon? Come on, snap out of it.

The train tries to capture the experience of travelling in the old days. The speed is some 60 km/hour. Over the loudspeakers comes a 'dagge-dang, dagge-dang, dagge-dang' sound. The seats can be set to random rocking mode to mimic the bumpy movement of old train rides. The window view is nothing like the landscape of ancient times, everything is developed now, but you can switch the window into screen mode showing an artificial moving landscape with cows and all.

I hate all this virtual emotion-fooling. Nonetheless I must admit that I am starting to feel less tense than I did earlier today.

'Quite a difference from the trains I've been working on over the past few days,' says Ben.

'Yes, tell me about it. How was your meeting?'

Ben goes on to expand on his meeting in Karlsruhe on the German–Turkish Maglev scandal. In the first half of the 2040s a Maglev train connection was built between Amsterdam and Ankara in the middle of Turkey. Two years ago information surfaced of all kinds of bribes, crooked deals and general corruption that had influenced the decision-making process on whether or not to build the connection and to make the main construction concession go to a German–Turkish consortium. The European Commission has set up an international group of specialists, including accountants like Ben, to investigate the matter.

Ben says he's not allowed to go into details but that it's evident that some serious fraud had been going on. Assessments concluding that the connection would never be economically viable had been conveniently ignored. There had also been studies showing that the project would not help to reduce air travel, which had been one of the big arguments in its favour, but that it would just lead to more mobility. This information never entered the debate either. And now, five years after completion, these critical reports seem to be uncannily prescient.

'It all reminds me of the Betuwelijn case about half a century ago, a textbook case while I was in university,' says Ben. The decision to build a high-volume freight train connection between the Rotterdam harbour and the German Ruhrgebiet was also taken on the basis of selective information. The project turned out to be a financial catastrophe while it failed to solve any mobility problems.

I get a bit bored with all this techno-political babble, but I listen because I know it's Ben's passion. He does all the talking and I throw in an occasional word or two.

'Am I boring you?' asks Ben after a while, with an unexpected flash of empathy.

I feel suddenly caught. 'Well, eh, maybe, a bit. You know, it's just that this political stuff is not my main interest.'

'OK. Let's talk about something else. It's your birthday.'

We're silent for a while; I don't feel like saying much.

'Have you heard from your parents recently?' he asks after some time.

He hits the nail right on the head. I feel a shiver going through my body, a sudden pressure on my eyes.

Ben notices. 'Is it that bad?'

I feel tears welling up. 'I called Mom yesterday. I could tell from the main screen that she wasn't well. She looked pale, tired. They are going to stay in Kurdistan.'

Thick tears start rolling down my cheeks. Ben puts his arm around me and with his other hand gently presses my head to his shoulder.

'Oh, my love. I'm so sorry for you.'

My tears keep rolling while he gently strokes my head. It eases me. I lift up my head and with a deep sigh look him in the eyes.

'This stupid world!'

Winking both eyelids he shows he understands.

'Keep talking,' he says after a while.

I repeat the story we both know so well. How Dad's parents moved from Kurdistan late in the last century to flee oppression by the Turks and escape the continuous killing in the ensuing rebellion. How Dad became a successful building contractor in the Netherlands but grew increasingly ambivalent about how the country's over-development, missing the space and peace of his childhood. Ever more land was sacrificed to the never-ending hunger for houses, offices and roads. When even the status of a national park no longer created immunity from bulldozers he retired.

'This country destroys everything that's valuable,' he often says. 'And why? Because of a techno-economic rat-race that has become an unquestionable religion but which I don't see making anybody any happier.'

So he went looking for space to breathe and live. When they made the Maglev connection between Amsterdam and Groningen, my parents moved to the edge of Groningen city. The high-speed connection took them to my place within the hour. They often visited, which I really appreciated. We're a very close family.

But the Maglev backfired. In the early part of the century, there was a lot of open space in the rectangle between the cities of Amsterdam, The Hague, Utrecht and Rotterdam. They called it the Green Heart. But it gradually filled up. We now have one big Delta Metropolis with a few city parks. 'The Green Heart became a few green blood drops,' Dad used to say. And then the Maglev came. Within fifteen years over a million of people moved to Friesland and Groningen, many of them still working in the Delta Metropolis. Economic prosperity—one of the main justifications for the Maglev—never took off. So Groningen became an economic backwater. Dad now calls it 'the best place to do your internship for being dead'. He is good at snide remarks like that.

Two years ago he flagged the idea of moving back to Kurdistan, which scared us all, including Mom and himself. They both realised how much they would miss us, and that we would miss them. But Mom was finding the Netherlands more and more artificial and unliveable in, and so this autumn they decided to go to Kurdistan for a trial period. It quickly became clear that in terms of living environment they felt really at home there. And yesterday Mom called to say they had decided to make the trial move permanent.

'Well, we all saw it coming,' says Ben.

'Yeah, but it really upsets me. Of course they should live where they feel at home, but it's so unfair. It's because of this political-economic idiocy that it's bad for people if they don't continuously reshape the world.'

We arrive at Zandvoort station and take a roofed electric bike to a bicycle park in the sand dunes. It's a pleasant surprise that Ben doesn't propose taking a pedal bike. He's always been the sporty type, but sometimes I feel he does it just to tease me.

The bicycle park is almost empty, only three other bikes. I like that. I agree with Dad, there are too many people and I like to escape whenever I can. I cling on to Ben's arm as we cross the sand dunes to the beach. It's cold but not too windy. There's a spray in the air, a mix of drizzle and salt. Walking is difficult, but at least I have my long boots on, the ones with the fur lining. I notice Ben forgot to change his old-fashioned business brogues for something more appropriate. I hope the sea salt will eat them. But not too quickly.

'And Ahmed isn't here either. We haven't heard from him in months,' I continue our conversation about my family.

'Yeah, he could show a bit more compassion for his parents,' Ben replies. 'I just don't know what he's up to, in this nomad colony in Vancouver. All I know is that nomads are supposed to be on the move, constantly, and he just sits there, in this former zoo they squatted after the G10 meeting in '47.'

'But last year at least he sent me a present, with that wonderful poem,' I continue. It feels like a splinter shot under my finger nail, splintering families, opening raw nerves. If the world has become so much smaller, then why are Mom, Dad, Ahmed and I so far apart?

My eyes trace a line some 500 metres offshore. It's a huge dyke running parallel to the coastline, from south of Den Helder to just south of The Hague, over 100 kilometres long. Its construction started in the late 2030s, but the whole thing was finished only in recent years. Called the Stevin Dyke, after the famous geohydrologist, it is primarily a defence against rising sea levels and extreme weather events, but it also created the longest salt-water recreation lake in the world. It more than doubled our beach area with sand on both sides of the lake. People come from all over Europe in the summer for wind surfing and beach fun. On sunny days it is a true body bakery and a never-ending cacophony. I really hate it. Now, fortunately, it's very quiet. It strikes me that I actually only hear the sea in the distance. No more waves rolling in here. It's not just quiet, it's spooky too. And then, behind the dyke, there's the control tower and the panorama tower of Flyland, the artificial island below sea level on which the new Amsterdam International Airport is sited. With their fluorescent colours and their bright lights the towers stand there like two sisters, watching us.

'I have a surprise for you,' says Ben while pointing at the Flyland panorama tower. 'That's where we'll have dinner tonight.'

For a few seconds I'm stupefied, gazing at him. I can hardly believe it. I snap myself back into birthday mode. The Flyland Panorama Restaurant is the most popular restaurant in the country. The view is magnificent. Sitting 200 metres above the sea, the landscape slowly unfolds before your eyes while the restaurant rotates. Half the time you look at the land, the other half across the water.

'Are you serious? You need to book that a year in advance!'

'Tell me about it,' says Ben, beaming. 'I tried to book a year and a half ago for your forty-fifth, but it was full. So I made a reservation for this year.'

'Ben! That's terrific! I'm thrilled!'

'I hoped you would be.' He wraps his arms around me.

I give him a huge kiss. He proposes we go there now so we can enjoy the view while it's still light.

We take the old train back from Zandvoort to Haarlem station. Going down one floor we make a two-century leap in transportation technology, from the ancient carriages to the modern tubetrain. They say it's the system of the future which Eurorail is now trying out on the Haarlem–Flyland track. It's a Maglev version that moves in low-pressure tubes. It's the first time I've been in this thing. It feels a bit like a plane with its circular shaped cabin. You also need to wear seatbelts. I don't like it very much; too enclosed, no windows. It may be fast, but it's not very pleasant. Ben tells me that on a research track it reached over 850 kilometres per hour. On this small 15-kilometre stretch it doesn't go that fast, but it still takes less than five minutes to get to Flyland. I'm glad when we can get off.

When we enter the restaurant through the elevator in the centre, it's about to get dark. Our table fortunately starts with a view of the land. Hovering 200 metres above Flyland Island I think I recognise St Bavo Cathedral in Haarlem, close to where we boarded the tubetrain. Slowly, the scenery revolves while it gets darker. It's dusk when we're above the Stevin Dyke and I see an endless line of car lights disappearing into nothing. It's an amazing sight. Fifteen minutes later our view is seawards. It's almost dark now and I see a couple of lights from big ships.

Over drinks, we talk a bit more about Mom and Dad's move, but I feel guilty. Ben has given me this wonderful birthday surprise and I am just sitting here feeling depressed. I should apologise to him.

'I'm sorry Ben. I really appreciate this surprise. But I feel so sad that Mom and Dad are leaving. You know, it's the first time ever that Mom isn't here on my birthday.'

'I know Luce. I know how this must make you sad.'

There's something in his tone I don't like. I see a small grin at the corners of his mouth. He doesn't seem to be taking my feelings seriously. He occasionally checks his watch, as if he wants to know how much longer he needs to put up with me. We talk further about trivia. When I suggest we ask for the menu Ben wants to wait a bit longer.

'While we're here Luce, let's try to stay as long as possible. Look at that magnificent view.'

Looking outside, I see beautiful patterns of light on the dark land. There's the dark strip of Stevin Lake and the line of car lights on the dyke. In the distance, the replica of the IJmuiden lighthouse flashes its message over the dark sea. But the view hardly cheers me up.

I look at Ben, my forehead wrinkling. He reaches out his hand over the table to take mine.

'C'mon, Luce, I know you're sad, but we have to make the best of this together.'

Well, of course he's right.

'OK, I'll try.' I need to pull myself together. It's not fair on him.

Ben recounts some funny incidents from his trip. He even makes me laugh.

'Why don't you call the waiter for the menu?' he says after a while. 'With those girlish charms of yours, you're more likely to catch his attention than I am.'

I look towards the centre of the restaurant where the bar is. Then, suddenly . . . no . . . it can't be true. Mom? Is it really Mom? She throws a big smile at me. Yes, it's Mom, and Dad behind her. I look at Ben who beams from ear to ear.

'Ben! You knew about this!' I shout as I jump up from the table and dash towards Mom. I throw my arms around her and feel a shiver going up my spine.

'Easy, easy,' says Mom, 'you're choking me.'

I let go and look into her beaming eyes while the tears run down my face.

'Oh Mom, I'm so happy you are here!'

'What about me?' Dad asks, feigning indignation.

I give him a warm welcome as well and see that Ben has joined us and hugs Mom. When we walk back to the table I feel so much lighter than just a few minutes ago, almost like I'm floating.

Mom and Dad order drinks and we have a lively conversation. They had anticipated being here before us but had had a delay because of a strike at Berlin airport. Fortunately, they could take a Maglev from there and still be here reasonably on time.

Time flies and before I know it dessert is being served. We have a view of the land and pointing towards it Dad says: 'You see the sea of light? From here it looks terrific but down there the density of development gives me the creeps. You know, the Bible says that after creation God looked at the world and saw it was good. Well, I think he was fooled because he looked from a great distance.'

I smile at him. I love him for pointed remarks like this. He continues riding his hobby horse, blaming politics for how this country goes down the drain. But this time I enjoy listening to him.

'How could they ever be so stupid?' he continues. 'Already at the beginning of the century this was one of the most crowded countries on earth. But with an ageing society looming what did the stupid government do? Encourage people to have more kids. And what do we have now? Twenty million people and virtually no more space to breathe. Large numbers of them are in their thirties and forties, so what will we have thirty years? More elderly people than the politicians at the beginning of the century dreamt of in their worst nightmares. But they'll all be dead by then so they won't have to face the consequences. And neither will I. I'm going back to Kurdistan, one of the few places on the planet where there is still room to breathe and move, and silence.'

He suddenly stops. Nobody says a word. He looks around the table and I think he now realises that there's also a downside to leaving. He shrugs his shoulders.

Mom puts her hand on his arm. 'Easy, Jalal. Let's celebrate that we're together now. It's Lucy's birthday.'

The conversation continues on a lighter tone. Around midnight we leave. Mom and Dad will stay in a hotel in Amsterdam and we take the fast subway to Amsterdam CMC together. At Flyland station, the metal detector gate leading to the platform sounds the alarm when a passenger in front of me passes through. She is immediately taken to one side by the railway police.

'I never understood this,' says Dad. 'You have all kinds of plastic weaponry that's just as effective. It just gives people a false sense of safety.'

In the train, Dad sits opposite and looks at me, murmuring something that sounds like singing.

'What are you singing Dad?'

'The girl with kaleidoscope eyes,' he sings out loud.

'Who's the girl with kaleidoscope eyes?' I ask.

'My mother,' he replies, 'your grandmother. It's a song from a pop group from the 1960s called the Beatles. My father was a big fan and he sometimes sang this song for my mother. After all these years it just jumped into my head and I now realise it fits you much better. Because, in the song, the girl is called Lucy.'

'I like that,' I respond. 'A song with my name that grandad sang for grandma.'

'The full title is "Lucy in the sky with diamonds",' he says.

'Lucy in the sky with diamonds? Well, I do see a connection with today. I was in the sky the whole evening. And the diamonds, that's you lot, of course. To me, you are the most precious things I can imagine.'

They all smile at me; it makes me feel good.

Reflecting on it further, it does strike me as a weird title and I ask Dad about it.

'I'm not sure,' he answers. 'My father once told me there was a hidden message signified by the first letters of Lucy, Sky and Diamonds—LSD. It was a popular drug at the time.'

'I thought drugs were forbidden in those days.'

'Oh, sure, they still were in the 2010s. But that doesn't mean they weren't used. On the contrary. Drugs were a far larger problem than they are now.'

'How come?'

'Well, there was a high demand for drugs. There always has been. Because they were illegal while in high demand, a profitable worldwide crime scene developed to produce and distribute them. There was also crime at the other end. Many drug addicts could not function well enough to hold down a regular job and became petty thieves to finance their expensive needs. Many addicted girls went into prostitution to earn their keep. They were called heroin hookers.'

'Sounds horrible. How could they ever have been so stupid as to ban drugs?'

'I'm not sure. I think it was solely based on ancient moral standpoints on how people should behave. We had a wave of liberalisation in the 2010s in which some of these old rudiments went overboard. It became more accepted that people could do pretty much whatever they pleased as long as they didn't harm others. As a result, society became more relaxed and some old problems virtually disappeared. Fifty years ago, drug abuse and drug crime were enormous problems. Now I think drug abuse is a problem comparable to alcohol abuse. And all the crime has disappeared since it's a regular business.'

We sit silent for a while. I agree with Dad and Mbele who I talked to earlier today that some of the warmth in the world seems to have disappeared. But Dad's story on drugs and drug crime shows it has also become more humane. There's crime enough already. I suddenly wonder if we locked the door properly before we left. No . . . I'm sure Ben did. He's always very careful.

We arrive at Amsterdam CMC and take the elevator up to the central hall where we part. Mom and Dad will drop by tomorrow morning to spend the day with us. I'm looking forward to it. After the kisses they take the electric road shuttle to their hotel. It takes a bit longer than the underground, but Dad prefers it.

'I hate travelling underground!' he says. 'I'm not a mole.'

Ben and I take the underground people mover to our building. We walk through the mobility cellar towards the elevator for our apartment. We take one nightcap before we go to bed.

In bed, Ben looks at me with his eyebrows slightly pulled up. This is the way I love him the best. It shows his softer side, that he's insecure about something.

'Do you feel OK, Lucy?' he asks after a while.

Wow! He calls me by my real name, not even this stupid Luce! I heave a deep sigh, shake my head slightly and respond: 'C'mon, boy! Let me show you how OK I feel.'

Abbreviations

ACEA	Association des Constructeurs Europeens d'Automobiles
ADB	Asian Development Bank
AFV	alternative-fuel vehicle
AWD	all-wheel drive
BAT	best available techniques
BAU	business as usual
BEAG	Bombay Environmental Action Group
BEST	Bombay Electricity and Suburban Transport
BEV	battery electric vehicle
BG	British Gas
BIS	Bureau of Indian Standards
BISS	business models for inherently sustainable systems
BSTE	bounded sociotechnical experiments
BTA	Bombay Taximen's Association
CARB	California Air Resources Board
CH_4	methane
CNC	computer numerically controlled
CNG	compressed natural gas
CO_2	carbon dioxide
CUTE	Clean Urban Transport for Europe (EU)
DfR	design for recycling
DOE	Department of Energy (USA)
DTC	Delhi Transport Corporation
EIA	Energy Information Administration (USA)
ELV	end-of-life vehicle
EMAS	Eco-Management and Audit Scheme (EU)
EMS	environmental management system
EPA	Environmental Protection Agency
EPACT	Energy Policy Act (USA)
EPCA	Environmental Protection and Control Association (India)

ESRC	Economic and Social Research Council (Cardiff University, UK)
EU	European Union
EV	electric vehicle
EZB	Easybike
FC	fuel cell
FCV	fuel-cell vehicle
FMVSS	Federal Motor Vehicle Safety Standards (USA)
FTP	Federal Test Procedure (USA)
GAIL	Gas Authority of India Ltd
GAPC	Global Alternative Propulsion Centre (General Motors)
GDP	gross domestic product
GHG	greenhouse gas
GIN	Greening of Industry Network
GM	General Motors
GMSA	General Motors South Africa
GPS	global positioning system
GRI	Global Reporting Initiative
GSM	global system for mobile communication
HEV	hybrid electric vehicle
HV	high voltage
HVAC	heating, ventilation and air conditioning
ICE	internal combustion engine
ICEV	internal combustion engine vehicle
ICT	information and communications technologies
IGL	Indraprastha Gas Ltd (India)
INEM	International Network for Environmental Management
IPPC	Integrated Pollution Prevention and Control
ISO	International Organisation for Standardisation
ITS	intelligent transport system
LCA	life-cycle assessment
LCC	life-cycle costing
LNG	liquefied natural gas
LPG	liquefied petroleum gas
MagLev	magnetic levitation
MDI	Moteur Développement Internationale
MEA	membrane electrode assembly
MFR	micro-factory retailing
MGL	Mahanagar Gas Ltd (India)
MIT	Massachusetts Institute of Technology (USA)
Mitka	Mobility Concept for Individual Short-Distance Transport (Netherlands)
MPV	multi-purpose vehicle
N_2O	nitrous oxide
NCR	National Capital Region, New Delhi (India)
NEMA	National Environmental Management Act (South Africa)
NEV	neighbourhood electric vehicle
NEVCO	Neighborhood Electric Vehicle Company (Oregon, USA)
NGO	Non-governmental organisation

NGV	natural gas vehicle
NiMH	nickel-metal-hydride
NIS	national system of innovation
NOVEM	Nederlandse Organisatie voor Energie en Milieu (Dutch Organisation for Energy and Environment)
NO_x	nitrogen oxides
OEM	original equipment manufacturer
OPEC	Organisation of Petroleum Exporting Countries
PAL	Premier Automobiles Ltd
PEM	proton exchange membrane
PM	particulate matter
PNGV	Partnership for Next Generation Vehicles (USA)
PSS	product-service system
PZEV	partial zero-emission vehicle
R&D	research and development
ROI	return on investment
RTO	Regional Transport Office (India)
SME	small or medium-sized enterprise
SNM	strategic niche management
SO_2	sulphur dioxide
SSI	sustainable system innovation
STD	Sustainable Technological Development programme (Netherlands)
SULEV	super-ultra-low-emission vehicle
SUV	sports utility vehicle
TNO	Organisation for Applied Scientific Research (Netherlands)
TOD	transit-oriented development
TQM	total quality management
VOC	volatile organic compound
WBCSD	World Business Council for Sustainable Development
WSSD	World Summit on Sustainable Development
WTO	World Trade Organisation
ZEV	zero-emission vehicle
ZEV–AT	zero-emission vehicle alternative technology

About the contributors

Dr **Chris Borroni-Bird** joined General Motors in 2000 as Director of Design and Technology Fusion to foster collaboration between design, research and engineering. He has leads GM's Reinvention of the Automobile programme which includes AUTOnomy, Hy-wire and Sequel. Before joining GM, he was in charge of fuel-cell hybrid vehicle development at DaimlerChrysler and was inducted into the Automotive Hall of Fame as a Young Leader in 2000. Borroni-Bird has a degree in Natural Sciences from Cambridge University, a PhD in Surface Science from Liverpool University (completed at Cambridge University) and performed post-doctoral research at Tokyo University Institute of Solid State Physics.

christopher.borroni-bird@gm.com

Halina Szejnwald Brown is Professor of Environmental Health and Policy at Clark University, Worcester, Massachusetts. She currently works in the areas of environmental policy, sociotechnical innovation for sustainability, sustainability reporting by the corporate sector and pollution management. She has written two books on environmental policy and management in developing countries (*Corporate Environmentalism in a Global Economy*; Quorum, 1993) and in Poland (*Effective Environmental Regulation*; Praeger, 2000). Before joining Clark University in 1980 she was a chief toxicologist for the Massachusetts Department of Environmental Protection. Halina is a Fellow of the International Society for Risk Analysis and American Association for the Advancement of Science.

hbrown@clarku.edu

Catherine Carbone received her master's degree in environmental science and policy from Clark University, Worcester, Massachusetts, in 2003. She is currently an environmental consultant in New York State.

cassiecarbone@yahoo.com

Gordon Dower MD, FACC is the founder and president of The Ridek Corporation, established to promote and develop the Ridek electric vehicle concept. His background and much of his professional life is associated with medicine, but his interests have ranged widely over the years. More recently he has become intrigued by the quest for sustainable mobility and, as a lone maverick, has been able to arrive at an innovative solution not conceived by the leading vehicle manufacturers or others in the field. Gordon subsequently became involved in the Greening of Industry Network event in San Francisco in 2003, and has also been active in the US electric vehicle scene. He is a keen pilot, and flies his own R-44 helicopter.

dower@whidbey.com

Boelie Elzen is Senior Researcher at the Centre for Science, Technology and Society, University of Twente, Enschede, The Netherlands. His general research interest is in understanding the dynamics of sociotechnical change and using the insights gained to develop solutions to societal problems related to these change processes. Over the past decade he has focused these efforts on passenger mobility, worked on EU research projects in the area and provided consultancy advice to various institutions in The Netherlands as well as abroad.

B.Elzen@bbt.utwente.nl

Prof. Dr **Wim A. Hafkamp** is Professor of Environmental Studies at the Erasmus University in Rotterdam. He became an environmental economist in the late 1970s having studied econometrics at the Tilburg University. He took his doctor's degree, on the modelling of the interactions between economic and environmental systems, at the Free University of Amsterdam. Wim is a member of the Dutch Advisory Council on Housing, Spatial Planning and Environment (VROM-raad) and the Dutch Advisory Council for Transport and Infrastructure (V&W-raad). He is President of the European Association of Environmental Management Education and, until 2001, was Chairman of the Programme Commission of the Environment and Economics Strategic Research Programme.

hafkamp@fsw.eur.nl

Dr **Marko Hekkert** received his master's degree in chemistry at Utrecht University in 1995. He wrote his PhD thesis on the subject of more efficient material management to reduce greenhouse gas emissions. Currently, Marko is working as Associate Professor in the Department of Innovation and Environmental Sciences at Utrecht University. He co-ordinates research and education in the field of sustainable technology development and innovation, supervising a team of PhD and post-doctoral students on topics related to the transition to a sustainable energy system, hydrogen as fuel, uncertainties in energy transitions and energy innovation systems.

m.hekkert@geo.uu.nl

Tine Herreborg Jørgensen is Associate Professor at the Department of Development and Planning, Aalborg University, Denmark. Her fields of research are environmental management systems, occupational health and safety management systems and integrated management systems.

tine@plan.aau.dk

Merih Kunur is a designer and researcher based in London. His work focuses on intelligent urban transport concepts, as well as sustainability and vehicle recycling. He studied industrial design at the Faculty of Architecture, Mimar Sinan University, Istanbul, Turkey, receiving his degree in 1987. As a student he worked at Koc Holding Research and Development Centre on vehicle design projects, travelling to Zurich, Frankfurt and London to liaise with transport experts. Before joining the Royal College of Art in London as a researcher in 2001, he worked for various textile, fashion, product and architectural design companies. He completed his MPhil thesis on mobility and transport in city centres in 2003. In 2003 he became a Research Associate for the Helen Hamlyn Research Programme, based at the Royal College of Art. He is currently concentrating on PhD research on end-of-life vehicles while developing a design research project on future urban personal transport.

Merih.kunur@rca.ac.uk

Dr **Lassi Linnanen** is Professor of Environmental Technology, Economics and Management at Lappeenranta University of Technology, Finland. His main research interests include corporate responsibility strategies and system innovations for sustainable development.

lassi.linnanen@lut.fi

Adeline Maijala was a researcher in the Department of Industrial Engineering and Management at the Helsinki University of Technology when EcoTra was developed. She has worked in the sustainability services team of the consulting firm KPMG and has experience in the fields of corporate responsibility, life-cycle assessment and packaging waste management. As a PhD candidate she aims to understand the collaborative processes implied in the implementation of corporate responsibility strategies in supply chains. Today she consults companies on extended producer responsibility at Proventia Solutions.

adeline.maijala@iki.fi

Eskild Holm Nielsen is Head of Technology, Environment and Society and Associate Professor at the Department of Development and Planning, Aalborg University, Denmark. He has carried out research on the appropriation of companies, but his particular interest has been environmental regulation and self-regulation by companies.

ehn@plan.aau.dk

Dr **Paul Nieuwenhuis** studied in Australia, Belgium, Spain and Scotland and is Assistant Director of the Centre for Automotive Industry Research (CAIR) at Cardiff University which he joined in 1990. CAIR studies economic and strategic aspects of the world motor industry. Paul is a founder member of the ESRC Centre for Business Relationships, Accountability, Sustainability and Society. Paul has written a number of articles and books, including *The Green Car Guide* (Greenprint, 1992), *The Death of Motoring?* (John Wiley, 1997) and *The Automotive Industry and the Environment* (Woodhead, 2003), and is a contributor to the *Beaulieu Encyclopaedia of the Automobile* which won a Cugnot Award from the Society of Automotive Historians in 2000.

Nieuwenhuis@Cardiff.ac.uk

Dr **Renato J. Orsato** is a Senior Research Fellow at the Insead Business in Society (IBiS), INSEAD, Fontainebleau, France; and Visiting Professor at the School of Management, University of Technology, Sydney (UTS), and the Australian Center for Science, Innovation and Society (ACSIS), University of Melbourne, Australia.

Renato.orsato@insead.edu

Mahesh Patankar is a PhD candidate at the Shailesh J. Mehta School of Management, Indian Institute of Technology, Bombay. He is currently working in the area of energy efficiency as Senior Project Manager at the International Institute for Energy Conservation, an international not-for-profit non-governmental organisation. Mahesh has a degree in chemical engineering from Tatyasaheb Kore Institute of Engineering Technology, Warananagar, India and a master's in financial management from Jamnalal Bajaj Institute of Management Studies, Bombay. Mahesh works in the area of environment and energy planning, and efficiency improvement, as well as on the broader issues of market transformation processes involved in the diffusion of environmentally sound and energy efficient technologies in the transport, buildings and other end-use segments. He has supported technology assessment and market transformation processes for municipal councils and electrical utilities.

mahesh@bom2.vsnl.net.in

Anand Patwardhan is Executive Director of the Technology Information Forecasting and Assessment Council, an autonomous organisation in the Ministry of Science and Technology, Government of India. Prior to this, he was Professor and Head of the Shailesh J. Mehta School of Management at the Indian Institute of Technology (IIT), Bombay. Anand has a degree in electrical engineering from IIT, a master's in environmental science and engineering, and a PhD in engineering and public policy, both from Carnegie Mellon University. He has post-doctoral experience as a Fellow in marine policy and ocean management at the Woods Hole Oceanographic Institution. Anand works in the broad area of climate studies, focusing on the assessment of vulnerability and adaptation to climate change, and on the diffusion and adoption of clean technologies. He has been a member of the Indian delegation to the 8th and 9th Conference of Parties to the UNFCCC, and is a member of a core advisory group on climate change for the Indian government. He is a member of the Scientific and Technical Advisory Panel of the Global Environment Facility; a member of the Scientific Steering Committee for the Global Carbon Project; and a co-ordinating lead author for the Fourth Assessment Report of the Intergovernmental Panel on Climate Change.

anand@cc.iitb.ac.in

Dr **Tuula Pohjola** is Professor of Environmental and Quality Management at Helsinki University of Technology, Department of Industrial Engineering and Management. Before joining the university in 2001, she was a consultant at the Finnish Employers Management Development Institute. Her main research interests include environmental business accounting and systems to develop companies' environmental reports.

tuula.pohjola@tkk.fi

Carla K. Smink is Associate Professor at the Department of Development and Planning, Aalborg University, Denmark. She has carried out research on modernisation of environmental regulations. Her PhD dissertation is on the end-of-life vehicle regulations in The Netherlands and Denmark.

carla@plan.aau.dk

Robert van den Hoed completed his PhD thesis at the Faculty of Industrial Design Engineering, Delft University of Technology, The Netherlands, in May 2004. His thesis was an historical examination of the growing popularity of fuel-cell technology in the automotive industry, with a focus on the roles of stringent regulation, competition between automotive companies and competition between technologies. The central research question revolved around how certain technologies become institutionalised while others do not. Robert is now working at Ecofys, a sustainable energy consultancy in Utrecht, with special responsibility for hydrogen, fuel cells and sustainable transport.

R.vandenHoed@ecofys.nl

Tom van der Horst worked for 15 years at the Organisation for Applied Scientific Research (TNO), The Netherlands on sustainable innovation. He is currently manager of the business unit Innovation and Environment of TNO. Tom is a founder of the Knowledge Centre of Sustainable System Innovation and Transitions (TNO/Erasmus University Rotterdam), and is founder and former chair of O2 The Netherlands. He is involved in many different research projects at both national and EU level: for example, the Knowledge network for System Innovation (KSI) and EMUDE (Emerging User Demands for Sustainable Solutions).

Tom.vanderhorst@tno.nl

Prof. Dr **Philip J. Vergragt** is currently a Visiting Scholar at MIT, Centre for Technology, Policy and Industrial Development, Massachusetts, a Visiting Senior Fellow at Tellus Institute, Boston, and a Visiting Professorial Fellow at the Manchester Business School, University of Manchester, UK. He is Emeritus Professor of Technology at Delft University of Technology, The Netherlands. His current research interests are visioning and backcasting, social learning through bounded sociotechnical experiments, institutional change, transitions to sustainable cities, transitions towards the hydrogen economy, sustainable transportation and sustainable consumption. Philip holds a PhD in chemistry from Leiden University, taught chemistry and society at Groningen University and was a Deputy Director of the Dutch Government's Programme on Sustainable Technology Development in the 1990s. He is a founding member of the Advisory Board of the Greening of Industry Network.

pvergragt@tellus.org

Dr **Peter Wells**, after a varied background in geography and then urban planning during which he gained his BA, MSc and PhD, joined Cardiff Business School and became a founder member of the Centre for Automotive Industry Research in 1991. He then became a founder member of the ESRC Centre for Business Relationships, Accountability, Sustainability and Society, also at Cardiff University. Peter is a leading expert and commentator on the automotive industry, particularly in relation to environmental matters and materials choice. He is currently exploring the scope of industrial ecology to inform a redesign of the industry. Of particular interest is the need and scope for innovative business models in the automotive industry to accommodate the many economic, social and environmental pressures the industry faces.

WellsPE@Cardiff.ac.uk

Chad White is a doctoral candidate in the Energy and Resources Group at the University of California in Berkeley. In collaboration with the late Vicki Norberg-Bohm and as part of a Fellowship at the Kennedy School of Government at Harvard University, he conducted this research on government–industry technology partnership. His other academic and publication experience includes research on end-of-life recovery of electronic products and a dissertation on the effect of corporate environmental performance measurement and communication on organisational structures and learning. He has recently been a Fellow at the University of California's Centre for Information Technology Research in the Interest of Society (CITRIS) and a Fellow in the University of California's Toxic Substances Research and Training Programme.

cdwhite@berkeley.edu

Andrew Williams is a research associate at the ESRC Centre for Business Relationships, Accountability, Sustainability and Society at Cardiff University. His main research interests include sustainability in the automotive and electronics industries, sustainable supply chain management, and the role of product service systems and other business models in achieving system-level innovation.

WilliamsAM1@Cardiff.ac.uk

Index